THE HELL OF WAR COMES HOME

THE HELL OF WAR COMES HOME

IMAGINATIVE TEXTS
FROM THE CONFLICTS IN
AFGHANISTAN AND IRAQ

OWEN W. GILMAN JR.

UNIVERSITY PRESS OF MISSISSIPPI JACKSON

www.upress.state.ms.us

Designed by Peter D. Halverson

The University Press of Mississippi is a member of the Association of American University Presses.

First printing 2018
∞

Library of Congress Cataloging-in-Publication Data

Names: Gilman, Owen W. author.
Title: The hell of war comes home: imaginative texts from the conflicts in
    Afghanistan and Iraq / Owen W. Gilman Jr.
Description: Jackson: University Press of Mississippi, 2018. | Includes
    bibliographical references and index. |
Identifiers: LCCN 2017035685 (print) | LCCN 2017057568 (ebook) | ISBN
    9781496815774 (epub single) | ISBN 9781496815781 (epub institutional) |
    ISBN 9781496815798 (pdf single) | ISBN 9781496815804 (pdf institutional)
    | ISBN 9781496815767 (cloth: alk. paper)
Subjects: LCSH: American literature—21st century—History and criticism. |
    Afghan War, 2001-—Literature and the war. | Afghan War, 2001-—Motion
    pictures and the war. | Iraq War, 2003-2011—Literature and the war. |
    Iraq War, 2003-2011—Motion pictures and the war. | War films—United
    States—History and criticism. | War stories, American—History and
    criticism.
Classification: LCC PS231.A34 (ebook) | LCC PS231.A34 G55 2018 (print) | DDC
    810.9/3587393—dc23
LC record available at https://lccn.loc.gov/2017035685

British Library Cataloging-in-Publication Data available

THIS STUDY IS DEDICATED TO ALL PEOPLE WHO HAVE SUFFERED IN ANY WAY FROM WAR AND TO THOSE WHO HAVE USED THE POWERS OF IMAGINATION TO INCREASE OUR COLLECTIVE UNDERSTANDING OF WAR.

CONTENTS

PART III:
VETERANS LOST AS DISTRACTIONS RULE IN FANTASYLAND AMERICA

ACKNOWLEDGMENTS

Many people have made generous and insightful contributions to this study as it evolved over the past several years. I deeply appreciate all of the help that has been provided to me in so many different ways. At the University Press of Mississippi, I have benefited enormously from the steady and wise editorial guidance of Vijay Shah, and as the project moved to completion, Lisa McMurtray and Kristi Ezernack were immensely helpful in overseeing the production side of the whole editorial process. Lisa Williams provided keen copyediting work as the manuscript was made ready for printing and Christine A. Retz was most efficient and helpful in developing the index. The outside reviewers engaged by the press all offered useful insights and suggestions with regard to revisions that would make the final result more satisfying.

At Saint Joseph's University, where I have been teaching for nearly forty years, I am always grateful for the lively wit and warm support of my colleagues in English as we talk about our various endeavors in scholarship, including *The Hell of War Comes Home.* They could always be counted on for good suggestions regarding the broad scope of the study and also about specific details that are addressed. Outside of English, two wonderful colleagues—Paul Aspan, Associate Provost for Academic and Faculty Support, and Terry Furin, Coordinator of International Education Programs—both kindly read through the whole manuscript and added their insights on the themes and the style of the project. Saint Joseph's University granted me a year of sabbatical leave (2012–2013), which was enormously important in providing time for the major research effort needed for this study, and for that support, I am naturally thankful.

My wife and two sons contributed invaluable professional expertise as the project moved through its final stage of development. Mary's editorial experience helped make the title and the chapter descriptions much clearer and more effective; Andrew offered fine editing input on the whole manuscript as it went through final revision; and John brought his graphic design talents to bear in development of the cover. My debt to them is particularly great—for this endeavor and for so much else.

Finally, behind all the words of this study are the imaginative texts crafted with abiding care by creative people who have provided us with the best keys available as we try to understand war in all of its implications. I applaud them for everything that guided my own search for understanding in this study.

PART I

THE LONG ARC OF WAR EXPERIENCE FOR AMERICANS

A Brief Introduction

Veterans Face the Challenge of American Fantasyland at War

America is a nation born of war. From the beginning centuries ago, it was with us—war against indigenous tribes, against rival colonial empires, and finally in North America, the great war of Independence, with British rule replaced by self-governance. Only by war could this have happened, and as a consequence, the stamp of war is indelible upon America. The loudest and most boisterous secular holiday in America is the Fourth of July; every year on that date Americans are called to remember how they came to be independent, in charge of their destiny—entirely because a group of very brave and determined men put their lives on the line, acquiescing in the necessity of war, to secure liberty and justice for themselves and for posterity. War was with Americans in the beginning.

War remains with Americans. In 2012, during the initial stage of this study, the war in Iraq seemed to have reached a clear endpoint with the withdrawal of American combat forces, an action dictated by the *Status of Forces Agreement* signed by President George W. Bush on 14 Dec. 2008; at the same time, the war in Afghanistan had a projected timetable for American withdrawal. Thus, there would be a return to peace, to a time without war. However, as years moved along, the Afghanistan conclusion date kept getting pushed further into the future—eventually to enter into a thoroughly indefinite time frame.[1]

While the war situation in Afghanistan persisted, the forces of ISIS (Islamic State of Iraq and Syria—a movement that President Obama typically called ISIL, Islamic State of Iraq and the Levant, thereby denoting a significantly broader region of concern) took over much of northern and western Iraq (Fallujah fell early in 2014, with Mosul being captured in June of 2014), all of which constituted a devastating development for American veterans who had suffered so much in fierce battles in those areas in the first decade of the century. This setback for Iraq necessitated introduction of American military support with both air power and on-the-ground advisors.[2] The fight to regain control of Mosul, Iraq's second-largest city, took place in the summer/ fall of 2016 and winter of 2017, thirteen years after the American-led invasion to topple Saddam Hussein, and in the aftermath of fighting, deep concerns persist as to the ability of the Iraqi government to provide safety for the residents of Mosul, as well as other areas of the country.

Furthermore, elite American special forces wound up being committed to areas in Syria to bolster the fight against ISIS/ISIL. The president, as commander-in-chief, holds clear responsibility for all of the combat action and initiatives that have been deemed necessary because Americans want to be safe at home. As the second decade of the twenty-first century moved along, the standard operating procedure called for enemy forces to be engaged and defeated wherever they might be operating—Iraq, Afghanistan, Pakistan, Syria—in order to protect American domestic security. Thus, the war on terror— a worldwide phenomenon—staggers on, year by year, with no end in sight all around the planet. There are a great many locations where suicide desperados can be trained, and it is impossible to scare down people who are willing to strap explosives on their bodies and blow themselves up in attacks against innocent souls who just happen to be in the wrong place at the wrong time.

Every incident of domestic terrorism linked to ISIS/ISIL spikes anxiety. The West Coast was shocked by the November 2015 shooting in San Bernardino, and then the East Coast received a similar jolt in the Orlando nightclub attack in June 2016. When the horror of war comes home in such staggering events, around-the-clock media attention is inevitable—for a short while at least. However, when regarding war action at a distance, with combat engagements in far-off locations, Americans are generally inattentive to what their military forces are doing. There are just too many distractions. In *The Shallows: What the Internet Is Doing to Our Brains* (2010), Nicholas Carr has argued that the compulsive way we use the Internet today, repeated quick dashes to it for the need of a moment (addictive behavior that now begins in infancy and in short order will follow us to the end of our days), is making it steadily more difficult to concentrate our attention on matters that are presented to us in complex forms—the stuff of book-length narratives or even tautly inscribed and challenging poems. In the years following publication of Carr's anxious analysis of American culture, more and more of national decision making is relegated to less and less in terms of sustained attention.

Our age, early in the twenty-first century, is increasingly defined by Twitter—a form that requires just a split second of brain processing, and then we crave another hit of this digitized drug. Bouncing along, tweet to tweet, we have a pronounced tendency to shun anything that takes longer to process. The experience of war is colossal; it is profound. Veterans acquire massive memory moments that become indelible. The stories and other imaginative reflections of daunting experiences of war take great effort and persistence to engage in the degree that is warranted; consequently, these traumatic experiences and the imaginative responses to them should merit long and determined attention from those left behind on the home front. Yet instead of providing attention that would lead to depth of learning and understanding, citizens at home offer the most superficial of responses—a great vat of know-nothingness—and then turn quickly to something distracting, some facet of fantasyland, virtually anything that provides entertainment, distracts attention from reality, and demands no effort. The ultimate manifestation of this pattern is represented in the huge appeal of the actual Fantasyland at Disney theme parks, a phenomenon scrutinized in chapter 6.

Whenever possible, Americans are happy to venture off to fantasyland, through whatever means it may be realized, and this tendency has presented daunting challenges for veterans, a matter of concern that is often reflected in the imaginative texts from the conflicts in Afghanistan and Iraq. The examination of war texts here finds a serious fault line in American culture, something that is highlighted often in the memoirs, novels, poems, and films that have taken up America's most recent war experience: veterans are shown to be frequently upset in witnessing the inattentiveness of their fellow citizens with regard to these recent wars and their consequences. As Sebastian Junger has powerfully illuminated in his latest book, *Tribe: On Homecoming and Belonging* (2016), the problem for contemporary veterans transcends the effects of post-traumatic stress disorder (PTSD). The solace needed for healing is regrettably not provided by American culture in the twenty-first century.

This situation stands in stark relief to one of the first gestures toward establishing the highest bar of possible achievement for Americans, long before the development of an independent American nation. In 1630 John Winthrop delivered his "Modell of Christian Charity" sermon aboard the *Arabella*, shortly before his group of Puritans reached shore to found the Massachusetts Bay Colony. We regularly are reminded of his words by politicians striving to claim a high place for America in the world. Toward the end of his sermon, Winthrop uttered the now-famous "Citty vpon a Hill"

(32) description for the greatness that might come to distinguish this new enterprise. However, Winthrop's carefully stipulated background for these words is invariably lost in modern references; Winthrop had built his sermon on a biblical grounding that called for all members of the group, even though they represented considerable diversity, to be closely knit with the others, none to be excluded, a snug community of intensely interdependent souls. Only in the steadiness of this bound-together community could there be hope for God's approval. Should things fall apart, and the community splinter, there would be hell to pay, a stern point driven home vigorously in Winthrop's conclusion. If Winthrop could catch a glimpse of twenty-first-century America, a nation broken open, shattered, bitterly divided, spiraling downward in libertarian self-centeredness, it is certain there could be no "Citty vpon a Hill" commendation or accolade to follow.

Diverse signs in our time have appeared to suggest Americans manifest considerable animosity toward one another; a nation of virulent individuals packed with divisive impulses and equipped with technology that allows instant expression of frustration and fury produces a toxic mix of distress that is barely held together—except by war as a unifying force, *us* against *them*. However, now the unrelenting wars have produced another schism, with the war vet (a small group) set off against the non-vet (a large group); the current-day veteran is not judged negatively as soldiers returning from Vietnam often were but, rather, suffers by being lost in the deep tide of distractions so present in the activities of contemporary American culture. Without a strong tribal feeling to hold everything together, a solution longed for by Sebastian Junger as he reflects on contemporary America (and demanded ages ago by John Winthrop for the community of his day), the veteran faces a staggering sense of separateness.

Again and again, in one way or another, the imaginative texts explored in this study converge in representing feelings of anger, abandonment, and alienation by veterans as they face figurative burial beneath all the mindless distractions operating in American culture. Horrific pain that made ironic sense in the tumult of combat becomes utterly devoid of meaning against the backdrop of the superficial interests that dominate the American scene.

This study is centered on the experience of war for Americans in the twenty-first century as revealed through a wide range of imaginative texts that work hard to bring the wars in Iraq and Afghanistan home so that all can intimately know and truly comprehend the hellish nature of war in any time, including ours. The most startling revelation from these most recent American experiences with war as represented in diverse imaginative texts involves the way the hell of war becomes the hell of home: this conclusion could not have been possible without all the evidence gathered from a wide range of imaginative responses to recent war experience, stretching across all the genres. Not every text explored here arrives at this key point, but a great many bring it to the surface for concern.

This striking new development is best understood against a brief history of war as Americans have known it, albeit with much inherited from earlier cultures, even as far back as Homer's time. Wars are downright difficult to avoid, especially for nation-states that seek to influence large areas of the world. All of the efforts at civilization in the vicinity of the Mediterranean Sea—the Egyptians, the Mesopotamians, the Greeks, the Romans—involved confronting the war challenge often. Asian civilizations regularly struggled with war as well. With the rise of modern Europe and the age of colonial expansion, war was everywhere, a pattern running through Napoleon and on to culmination in two World Wars and a long cold war. War experience from the historical record is pointedly acknowledged at the outset of this study, for the past bears significantly on war as it has been known and represented by Americans.

The first chapter serves two purposes: 1) to account quickly for key patterns that have shadowed war over the centuries, including those conflicts joined by Americans since the Revolutionary War, and 2) to delineate historical, psychological, and political forces that combine to make it easier than ever before for Americans to be sent into combat somewhere. American readiness for war in the twenty-first century has much to do with the wars of our past. Going into war is increasingly easy for America; getting out of war is increasingly problematical.

Wherever and whenever there is war, there will be imaginative responses to it, and such has been the case with the wars in Afghanistan and Iraq. American soldiers were dispatched to these foreign places; they engaged enemies both expected and unexpected; and they experienced the full range of possible outcomes—from survival to death. The experience of Americans at war in our time has been rendered honestly and fully in a wide range of texts—creative nonfiction and journalism, memoir, film, poetry, and fiction. These responses, individually and in the aggregate, have packed a lot of power, fully measuring up to great war literature and film from the past. The middle portion of this study works to closely analyze salient features of the imaginative representations of war that have emerged since the trauma of 9/11, a day as loaded with infamy for Americans as December 7, 1941.

But going to war and then representing the experience of war constitute only two elements of a three-part sequence. The final consideration explores the way circumstances in American culture currently bedevil veterans, making their home a kind of hell. As long as average Americans are preoccupied with superficial nonsense, veterans will feel marginalized to the point of nonexistence (the current suicide rate for veterans—to be addressed in detail later—is provocative evidence of this problem), and this whole pattern serves at the same time to prevent literature and film of war from having deep or significant impact. In the final part of the study, a summary case is made to show that the inclinations of Americans to distract themselves in one form or another with fantasyland products and experiences significantly limit learning or growth from the stringent responses to war that have been proffered to reading and viewing audiences in the past decade. It should be noted, however, that even though book and film reviewers—potent cultural gatekeepers—have devoted appropriate attention to these imaginative responses to war, such acknowledgement by reviewers stands in stark contrast to the limits of general American public awareness about war texts of the twenty-first century, as well as about war more broadly.

Returning veterans of war often are deeply burdened as they face reentry into their cultures of origin. Haunting memories pursue them. The soldier-to-soldier bonds that supported them in war are dissolved. Their experience isolates them, setting them apart. Meanwhile, their stay-at-home compatriots make shallow gestures of appreciation: the "Support the Troops" bumper stickers, the invitations for veterans to stand for a moment of thankful applause at political rallies, the murmurings of "Thanks for your defense of our Freedom" offered to veterans at happenstance encounters. These forms of gratitude are not inherently wrong, but as balm goes, they barely touch the surface, while the hurt lies deep inside. Meanwhile, American culture hurtles along riding waves of consumption, frantically calling all to pursue their happiness as stipulated in the Declaration of Independence. In full hustle mode, hell-bent for whatever scrap of happiness can be grasped, people have almost no time to feel the pain of war.

Most Americans these days are caught up in the fight to not fall behind. This challenge is daunting, and relief is sought in distractions that serve to dull anxiety. Given that imaginative responses to the conflicts in Iraq and Afghanistan are packed with genuinely rough stuff, it is not surprising that many might opt instead for mindless distractions. Even veterans can get caught up in this escapist impulse, sometimes ironically bingeing on war video games, but for them, the respite is never long. Their pain persists; war releases its hold with agonizing slowness. In a powerful and deeply moving article early in 2017, "The Fighter," C. J. Chivers details the experience of Sam Siatta in going to fight in Afghanistan and then being beset by disabling demons throughout a long and torturous effort to return to normalcy back at home. The title subhead captures the brutal irony involved, a point to be highlighted in various ways throughout this study: "The Marine Corps Taught Sam Siatta How to Shoot. The War in Afghanistan Taught Him How to Kill. Nobody Taught Him How to Come Home." Despite some exceptions, Americans with no war experience are typically inattentive, loath to venture deep in understanding the real consequences of war as borne out in the lives of veterans and as reflected in the broad array of creative renderings of war experience. The old axiom "Ignorance is bliss" holds true on the home front, and it can be hell for veterans to face.

This inattentiveness has two equally unfortunate consequences: 1) it contributes to the alienation of veterans, and 2) it increases the likelihood that America will soon again venture into war, thus repeating the whole pattern. By the end of the study, it will be evident that our approach to war is front-loaded with fantasy, and when a war draws to a close, our approach is back-loaded with fantasy; in the middle, where there should be some clarity and depth of knowledge drawn from imaginative treatments of war experience, all we have is a muddle of long-lasting misunderstanding and anguish to be endured by veterans who ventured to war fueled by fantasy and returned betrayed by the implications of fantasy as played out in American culture at large.

The film adaptation of Ben Fountain's novel *Billy Lynn's Long Halftime Walk,* which reached just two theaters on Veterans Day in November of 2016 (and then went into nationwide release a week later), can serve handily to illustrate the essential problem that recent war literature highlights. With astute direction from Ang Lee, the film does an excellent job of showing the hellish experience of war veterans—eight surviving members of Bravo squad—as they encounter diverse home-bound fellow Americans. Following the novel quite closely, the film tracks the effort to elevate these soldiers to hero status by featuring them and their war experience as part of the halftime show at an NFL game in Texas. Against the backdrop of the usual pyrotechnic extravaganza features of halftime performances, including booty-shaking stars of the America music industry, there is hyperventilated talk of a movie deal. It's all a twenty-first-century variation on the adulation heaped on Audie Murphy (who is explicitly mentioned by the rah-rah owner of the football stadium, Norm Oglesby, played by Steve Martin) when Murphy came back from World War II with a chest full of medals and Hollywood eager to capitalize on his war exploits.

When Murphy wrote his memoir, *To Hell and Back* (1949), and then starred in the movie version a few years later, it seemed to all that the hell part was just the war. However, by the 1960s, Murphy was suffering from PTSD, clear evidence that he had brought hell back home with him. He suffered alone, however, for in the eyes of the public, there was no allowance for the hard reality of his actual experience; the American public was blissfully unaware of this development in his life.

For the soldiers brought home from Iraq in *Billy Lynn's Long Halftime Walk*, they too had experienced a version of hell in the horrific fight that attracted so much attention to them, and then they are snatched up briefly to become central figures in a public relations "Victory Tour" spectacle, before being returned to Iraq to continue their tour of duty. As it turns out, none of the survivors is a poster-boy hero type; they all have dark clouds in their life stories, most recently involving the shared loss of Sergeant Breem (nicknamed "Shroom"), a deeply liked leader who was killed in the devastating battle for which they are being celebrated. The sharp juxtaposition between the actual reality of their gruesome experiences and the pure fantasy of this victory tour—in search of a movie by way of a halftime show for a professional football game in Dallas, Texas, on Thanksgiving—constitutes another form of hell.

Reality and truth are shunted aside in favor of glitz and absurd hyperbole. To make the right impact during the halftime show, Billy's squad members have to change from the Class A Greens they wore to the stadium into their camouflage uniforms, with the change being mandated by a PR staff person at the stadium. When Billy is questioned about his war experience, his feelings, he realizes he's telling everyone what they want to hear. Please the audience! The movie deal keeps retrenching toward nonexistence throughout the football event, and when Oglesby eventually tries to command ownership of the film project, he has a sharp wake-up message for Billy: "Your story, Billy, no longer belongs to you. It's America's story now." With the power of money and the sheer force of blustery swagger seeming to trump everything else, Oglesby is used to having things go his way. However, Billy and his squad mates refuse to be bought, and in the shabby context of trivial nonsense on massive display, their integrity is refreshing.

After being onstage for a few minutes with Destiny's Child, while fireworks go off and the whole stage becomes surrounded by pyrotechnics, the squad must then get out of the way quickly so the second half of the football game can begin on time. War veterans have had their moment; it does not matter that the shock of the explosives has blasted them one degree further toward PTSD, for now the fans want football. The field crew gets into a knock-down struggle with the squad several times, first in trying to clear the stage and then later as Billy and his fellow soldiers are exiting the stadium—thus bringing war straight to Texas. The show, the whole fantasy of a football production, is everything. Reality is nothing. If Hollywood was looking to make a caustic comment on Donald Trump's 2015–2016 bellicose, bombastic, sound-and-fury-filled campaign for the presidency, *Billy Lynn's Long Halftime Walk* would certainly fill the bill. Truth is long gone in this long walk, and America is woefully lost in superficial fantasy stuff.

Because Fountain's novel (analyzed in detail in the fiction chapter) focuses in part on the idea of a film to be made from the war experience of Billy and his squad mates, Ang Lee's film adaptation brings the movie concept to completion, a brilliant metafictional move, though ironic to the core. The medium of film is spectacularly right for representing explosions of light and sound, phenomenological features that are also key elements in the experience of war in the twenty-first century. The halftime show at a professional football game, especially one staged at night, cues on extravagant display of sounds (always music but often punctuated by explosions such as one expects in fireworks displays), sounds then synchronized with bursts of light. With these details in mind, it is worth remembering the opening gesture of the game, a singing of America's national anthem, "The Star-Spangled Banner," which fixes everyone's attention on the "rockets' red glare" and "bombs bursting in air," thereby putting the essential sensory images of combat front and center for everyone to salute. At every football game, war is summoned for all to experience at least vicariously and, it must be added, very superficially! The halftime show just adds redundancy to the sensory excess of war.

Not surprisingly, though, the film generated only a modest box office (in the November 18–20 opening weekend, at 1,176 theaters nationwide, the estimated ticket sales barely cleared $900,000, a strong sign that the film would never get close to its estimated cost of $40 million; and, in fact, the *Box Office Mojo* domestic total in ticket sales stands at $1,738,477). Because of its "R" rating (for "language throughout, some war violence, sexual content, and brief drug use"), *Billy Lynn's Long Halftime Walk* was destined to be seen only by adults, but the box office results show that Americans of all stripes were in no mood to be chastised for superficiality by a film. Rather, in mid-November of 2016, half of America was deep in election shock registering at near 10 on the Richter scale and hence looking desperately anywhere for signs of peace and hope—not to be found in this film; the remaining half of America would be disgusted at the critique of football obsessiveness and pathetic, hypocritical patriotism foregrounded in the film, so they too stayed away.

As a consequence, as battles in Iraq and Afghanistan continued to involve American military forces, most Americans went in different directions for movies to watch late in 2016 (sci-fi, thrillers, comic-book derivatives—with the Ron Howard/Tom Hanks treatment of Dan Brown's *Inferno* in the rearview mirror, *Dr. Strange* pushing toward $200 million in domestic ticket sales in its first three weeks out, and tickets for *Rogue One: A Star Wars Story* already on sale in November for late-December release). Timing for the film's content was vexed beyond election results, for November is also part of high season in football, whether at the high school, collegiate, or professional level. A film exposing the shallowness of American culture to a people unable or unwilling to confront reality in any meaningful way was predictably not destined to be seen by large audiences. In sum, football is wanted straight, with no complications. At one point, Shroom tells Billy, "We're a nation of children, who go somewhere else to grow up." For those who stay home, who do not venture to war and grow up, the game is all, and it must be kept simple. Americans in 2016, as always, watched much football over the Thanksgiving weekend.

For veterans, the film highlights their plight. They have served. They have suffered. The reality they have known by hard experience is casually marginalized, misunderstood, and manipulated into strange configurations that only add to their separation from mainstream culture. The halftime show at a professional football game is pure fluff, before a return to the serious stuff of passes and runs and tackles and relentless head-banging that years later will evolve into devastating brain deterioration. Football "soldiers" in their colorful uniforms are quickly dispatched into action, in hand-to-hand combat, fighting back and forth over the hundred yards of this battlefield, relentlessly struggling to taste the sweetness of victory. Touchdowns will be scored; field goals will be kicked and recorded. Meanwhile, Billy Lynn and his fellow soldiers are bound to return to their Iraq tour, an experience that makes strikingly clear, by way of contrast, the absurd silliness of football. For those seared by the hard truths of war, America in fantasyland mode can be pure hell.

CHAPTER ONE

On Going to War the American Way

Initial Lessons from the Past

If America is born of war, then understanding our experience requires a look at our parentage. However, before excavating reasons behind a remarkable pattern that has put America at war with remarkable frequency throughout the history of the country, it would be sensible to view the full context of history and admit that war has steadily visited all corners of planet Earth for as long as humans have been around: Americans are, in this, far from alone. In *The Lessons of History* (1968), Will Durant and Ariel Durant include an observation that of the past 3,421 years, there have been only 268 free of war (81). War is mighty hard to avoid, and in the United States, the war attraction is potent in generation after generation, a steadily evolving development that might be of deep concern if not for the massive weight of cultural distractions that keep attention focused elsewhere.

Even as reverberations from the Iraq War persist and put an ominous shadow over Iraq's future, the literary and film explorations of that vexing conflict continue to build substantially. Less imaginative material linked exclusively to Afghanistan has emerged, a pattern that lines up predictably with the need to see American troops back home before fully ramping up creative treatments of the experience; nevertheless, the war in Afghanistan has already spawned some creative nonfiction, as well as powerful documentary film work (*Restrepo*, 2010) and two major film projects, *Lone Survivor* (2013) and *Whiskey, Tango, Foxtrot* (2016).

In the main, the conflict in Afghanistan, while long in duration, has seldom been sufficiently explosive in terms of combat casualties and action to attract daily attention from American mass media or the public at large, and as a consequence, it has moved to occupy a strange black hole of very dense obscurity, mostly forgotten by average Americans who have struggled to make ends meet through a recession, and steadily ignored by almost all of our political leaders, who seem completely preoccupied with concerns about devising a balanced budget but are driven at the same time by unrelenting worry that any hint of budget cutting in the broad area of national defense would lead to certain political death. Readiness for war is paramount.

It is against such a backdrop of cultural and historical parameters and circumstances that the present study examines the literature and film from our most recent war experience. To help put this new material into deeper perspective, some touchstone war texts from the Vietnam War (and, more selectively, from earlier conflicts) will be analyzed periodically as well. In contrast to a few of the big Vietnam books and films, this new war material has, for the most part, been read and watched by rather small audiences and has not generated broad discussion, despite appropriate and generally appreciative reviews in major newspapers and the most reputable cultural magazines; given the gravity and import that we might assume a war would have for the people making it, the literary and film treatments (including some strong cable TV productions) have passed by without extensive or enduring attention being paid to them, a problematical phenomenon that is broached in early chapters and then assessed in detail near the conclusion of the study, for an inclination to be easily distracted seems to permeate American life. Frequently, in diverse texts that are examined in this study, veterans and others returning home from war zones note, with distinct dismay, how little attention is being paid to the consequences of war, how fully most Americans seem to be caught up in ridiculously superficial details of their culture. Attention flits from one tweet to the next, an appalling consequence of the Age of Twitter.

As it turns out, Americans show a strong inclination to be preoccupied with fantasy, whether it manifests on big screens (e.g., *Lord of the Rings, Pirates of the Caribbean*) or in vacation destinations (Fantasyland at the Magic Kingdom). The grim reality of war pales in the bright lights of fantasy on steroids. It is the nature of American popular culture early in the twenty-first century. Fantasy demands virtually nothing; it carries no oppressive weight with it; it masks grim reality with remarkable ease—and to an astounding extent.

Most of the fiction, creative nonfiction, poetry, and film to be explored here fits sensibly with virtually everything comparable that has come to us from wars spread over the past 2,500 years. In *The March of Folly: From Troy to Vietnam* (1984), the historian Barbara Tuchman drew attention to a distinct and troublesome pattern etched across a very long stretch of time, and it would be a simple matter to extend her thesis about the foolishness of a great many wars to include the American wars in Afghanistan and Iraq. What is new—and is revealed in this study—mostly pertains to very specific matters in the settling of political scores on the contemporary world stage, to the physical conditions encountered on twenty-first-century battlefields, and to the evolving technology available for killing at this point in time. The immediate and the long-lasting trauma of war has been known from the time of Homer, a perspective to be explored shortly, and as the contemporary texts to be analyzed will show, the trauma wrought by war is as complex and as vexing now as ever.

Of course, there are a few surprises and novel twists with the most recent wars, matters of an essential sort that somehow were previously mostly marginalized, such as a recurrent close focus in observing and reporting the ways in which soldiers empty their bowels during combat.[1] Naturally, everything new and different will be scrutinized here (the new technology, the particular physical environments for combat, the evolution of equality in the makeup of America's military), but to begin to understand the experience of war for Americans from the era of Vietnam through to the era of Afghanistan and Iraq and even on into an indefinite future, as counterintuitive or retrograde as it may seem, there's good reason to reach far back and refresh our understanding of Homer's *The Iliad* and *The Odyssey*. Exploring these age-old texts from Homer in an effort to plumb the depths of nightmarish war experience in our own day is not original to this study. Others have pointed in this direction to gain purchase on understanding war and its effects.

In *War Is a Force That Gives Us Meaning* (2002), Chris Hedges sets his own extensive experience with war within the context of insights delivered by Homer in *The Iliad* (about power and force and warrior code, including heroic death [12]) and in *The Odyssey* (finally managing to contain the hero's pride in order to return to peace, a long process in which those around Odysseus suffer greatly [12]). The title alone strikes deep into the heart of the matter, but later in this chapter, as we consider the possibility that war has become a habit for Americans in trying to define our role in the world, the points offered by Hedges will be addressed further.

Back in the mid-1990s and early in this century, Jonathan Shay, a physician who for a time was an assistant professor at the Harvard Medical School, brought out two provocative and well-received studies that looked at Homer's texts for clues about how to deal with the trauma of war. Dr.

Shay focused on *The Iliad* in *Achilles in Vietnam: Combat Trauma and the Undoing of Character* (1995), and then, in *Odysseus in America: Combat Trauma and the Trials of Homecoming* (2003), he examined the lingering effect of war trauma as it is revealed in the challenge Odysseus faces in trying to get home. This pioneering work—with extraordinarily rich and nuanced readings of Homer's story for us to ponder as soldiers go off to war, experience terrible things, and suffer long-term consequences as survivors—underscores my own reading of these gifts from the deep past. My concern, however, extends beyond seeing the potent linkages between Homer's narratives and the stories carried in the souls of American veterans returning from Vietnam, from Iraq, and from Afghanistan.

We need to understand why these texts—consistently, inevitably—fail to move us beyond square one. We know we have to go to war; that much repeatedly becomes clear through the record of history, and shortly, the peculiarly American inclination toward war will be examined in detail. At the same time, we seldom see the full consequences of our decisions as they are borne out by veterans. What keeps us from seeing how it all fits together? We need better vision—for both looking back and looking ahead.

Dr. Shay went on to work as an Army physician during the Iraq War, seeking ways to prevent as much devastating effect from combat as possible by having units bond as fully as possible, and with strong and capable leadership at every turn in order to inspire soldierly cohesion and mission confidence. There is no doubt that the stress of combat can be alleviated for a time by the spirit of blood brotherhood, soldiers holding steady by linking themselves tightly to their fellow warriors, just staying in the moment of mutual protection and reinforcement; my study will certainly touch on that point from time to time, but there is a deeper matter that I hope to bring into the light concerning the way war texts have been processed in American culture over time. The cutting edge here involves a search for reasons why Americans have been, and continue to be, loath to respond very deeply to stories about war trauma. The ugly stuff of war and the brutal effects it can have on veterans tend to be shunted into the background. This pattern has been with us for a long time, and it persists, with no signs of abating or changing as we look ahead to the possibilities of future wars that involve American soldiers.

In the process of revisiting the Homeric texts as Dr. Shay did, we will have an opportunity to consider the meaning embedded in them, relative to the effects of war as those effects have slowly seeped into our awareness in the past five decades. Post-traumatic stress disorder (PTSD) became formally recognized only in 1980, when it was added to the third edition of the American Psychiatric Association's manual of mental disorders, but as the reading of Homer's *The Odyssey* will show later in this chapter, even though the devastating effects of horrific battle experience have been known to writers for a long time, American readers have typically been insufficiently mindful of them. This pattern has plenty of history, and by the end of this study, the case will be made that an overarching "fantasyland" pattern guarantees that sobering war texts will continue to be relatively inconsequential when future Americans consider war.

As we scrutinize these ancient texts in current context, we will receive the full benefit of the way these age-old narratives illuminate warfare; at the same time, we will be afforded an opportunity to confront the pesky, recurrent blockages that have rendered the literature of war so utterly useless in preventing war. From the beginning of time to the present, our engagement with war literature has turned aside our ability to grasp fully and accurately the long-term effects of war on its participants. Scrutinizing reception of Homer's epic tales reveals how easy it is to fail to appreciate the effect of war on veterans. The stories are packed with adventure and excitement and intrigue, and while a residue of caution might be detected, a certain kind of innocence has lurked in the way stories from battlefields are processed by American readers. In no way have they served as a deterrent to war—by any culture, America included.

In an American frame of reference, this pattern virtually guarantees a war for every generation from the time of the American Revolution to the newly emerging generations of the twenty-first century and far beyond. Furthermore, as will be argued in the next section, a particular set of conditions that attended the first American experience in war (the Revolutionary War) added great weight to the enduring readiness of Americans for war. Being created as a consequence of war significantly ups the ante for subsequent generations whenever conflict arises. The Founding Fathers felt compelled to go to war. How dare Americans of the present time not do the same? To avoid war is a dastardly betrayal of our basic heritage. To war we must go. This dominant pattern is virtually in the DNA of our bones and spread across the broad range of American skin tones. The divisiveness of the Vietnam War is mostly an anomaly. Sex still divides. Religion divides. Race divides. Money divides. War unites. In going off to war, the American tribe breathes briefly as one.

A Quick Look at the Classics and the Founding of America in War

As the foundation for America was being constructed in the late eighteenth century, builders of the American republic gave considerable attention to ideas about democracy and self-governance derived from Greek civiliza-tion—an experiment that had long since passed into history but was about to be given new life in a part of the world still boasting about the designa-tion of "*new.*" Many documents from that much earlier time had survived, and as Bernard Bailyn noted in *The Ideological Origins of the American Revolution*, texts from long ago were all part of the cultural baggage that ar-rived in Philadelphia with the delegates to the Constitutional Convention:

> Most conspicuous in the writings of the Revolutionary period was the heritage of classical antiquity. Knowledge of classical authors was uni-versal among colonists with any degree of education and references to them and their works abound in the literature. From the grammar schools, from the colleges, and from private tutors and independent reading came a general familiarity with and the habit of reference to the ancient authors and their heroic personalities and events of the ancient world. (23–24)

Richard Gummere, in *The American Colonial Mind and the Classical Tra-dition*, found depth of classical knowledge throughout the colonies, north and south, and noted that while both Thomas Jefferson and John Adams found separate reasons to be distressed by their engagement with Plato, they both certainly had ready familiarity with his *Republic* and other texts (195). Homer is mentioned frequently as a well-known author; James Walsh, in *Education of the Founding Fathers of the Republic: Scholasticism in the Colonial Colleges*, notes a Princeton student whose graduation exams cov-ered Homer (156), a thoroughly typical occurrence. All of these texts from antiquity proved inspirational by adding significant depth and perspective to a project wherein another group of people from a very different time and place wrestled with the challenge of shaping a government that would serve well the interests and needs of those governed. However, as the founders juxtaposed various ancient texts with one another, sometimes there was disagreement or dissonance in their midst.

For example, one of those key documents from the past, Plato's *The Republic*, served to create a kind of prejudice against taking Homer's sto-ries to heart. In Book III, during a lengthy discussion about educating the "guardians," the soldier types who would defend the republic against enemies, Socrates explicitly makes the point about the need to keep the guardians sheltered from stories that would show heroes afraid of death. Heroes were never to fear death or to prefer slavery to freedom.

To keep the republic—the state—strong, you needed to keep the guardians strong, and that meant shielding them from stories that could weaken their resolve. As *The Republic* makes clear (insofar as anything in Plato can be clear), one key danger zone involved poetry—particularly stories that veered too hard toward grim reality—and for Socrates (representing Plato's concerns), this threat loomed large in Homer's work, hence warranting severe editing of poetry in order to make it serve the needs of the state and its guardians. Reviewing some examples of narrative details that could harm the proper education of guardians, Socrates shares his concern with Adeimantus:

> And we must beg Homer and the other poets not to be angry if we strike out these and similar passages, not because they are unpoetical, or unattractive to the popular ear, but because the greater the poetical charm of them, the less they are meet for the ears of boys and men who are meant to be free, and who should fear slavery more than death. (*Republic,* Book III, 387ff)

Potential guardians would have plenty of unsettling details to consider in *The Iliad,* although extreme violence does not show up immediately. You have to read through several books in *The Iliad* to set the stage for gore. In today's world that sort of delay would try the patience of readers—or of viewers, in the case of film. When *Saving Private Ryan* premiered in 1998, there was little delay before audiences were subjected to a bracing cinematic treatment of the D-Day landings of 6 June 1944. Nobody knows film history better or reveres it more than Steven Spielberg, and Spielberg's films show an uncanny sense of how to catch an audience and get a visceral reaction from action on the screen. The blood comes early, and it runs deep very quickly in *Saving Private Ryan*; audiences have no time to steel themselves for what they will see as the landing craft start to discharge troops into the surf. The sea at the Normandy beaches turned crimson, both in 1944 and in 1998, with no slow build-up to bloodshed.

Of course, at the time when those extremely difficult beach landings actually took place—and for quite a few decades to follow—the film camera operated with strict, explicit limits on the representation of violence (as mandated in the Hollywood Motion Picture Production Code). *The Sands of Iwo Jima*, which hit movie theaters four years after the end of WWII, showed the muting effect of the code, which was in effect from the early 1930s through the mid-1960s, and the landings of Sergeant Stryker's Marines on two island beaches (the last being at Iwo Jima) present the realities of war discreetly. Soldiers, including Stryker himself as the ascent on Mt. Suribachi draws closer and closer to the iconic moment of raising the American flag, simply topple over after being hit by bullets or shrapnel; bunkers are filled with flame from flame throwers and then blown up; the action is clearly wild and chaotic, with casualties mounting.

Still, the presentation of all this mayhem is not unsettling. Stryker's own fatal wound is represented by a quarter-sized dark stain on his fatigue shirt in the middle of his back. Special effects did not have to produce quarts of pig's blood to prove Stryker's death. Sure, all of this tasteful discretion could be strangely tedious after a while, especially as years passed and movie directors eventually grew more and more devoted to showcasing violence and blood, but any viewer, of any age, could sit through *The Sands of Iwo Jima*, a film treatment (with significant assistance from the Navy) of a battle that claimed 26,000 casualties—6,800 dead—without feeling any emotional discomfort from seeing really horrible things. Thus was terror muted.

As suggested earlier, Homer delivered unmuted, seriously daunting images of war after some initial stage-setting in *The Iliad*. Just a few quick passages from this prototype war text will suffice to show that literature from its earliest days has delivered images that easily justify the observation of Gen. William Tecumseh Sherman as he reflected on the American Civil War: "War is hell." Civil wars are particularly ugly, and America has had plenty of experience in that regard—from the American Revolution, with patriots battling loyalists, to the great Civil War (where at least the opposing armies—Union and Confederate—kept the battles somewhat organized by going forward in differentiating uniforms), and finally on to Vietnam (fierce combat with the uniformed soldiers of North Vietnam—but just as harrowing opposition from non-uniformed Viet Cong—and often questionable support from the Army of the Republic of Vietnam) and then Iraq (one day in a brutal struggle with Sunni forces, the next day facing tough opposition from Shiite units). With civil war, there is no simplicity, especially when American forces served technically as outsiders trying to assist one side or steer a path down the middle in the direction of democracy.

In Homer's version of the war/hell linkage, the fundamentals of war hit readers hard. To move your agenda forward, there must be killing, and the killing is ugly. While the gods draw back to watch, the humans have at each other. Agamemnon drives his spear clean through the back of Odios, "lord of the Halizones," and "on through the chest beyond it" (Book V,1. 39–41, p. 129), dispatching an enemy while many more spears thrust and fly back and forth, each one accounting for a death. No detail is spared. Mages is the next to die, at the hand of Phyleus's son:

> Now the son of Phyleus, the spear-famed, closing upon him
> struck him with the sharp spear behind the head at the tendon,
> and straight on through the teeth and under the tongue cut the bronze
>   blade,
> and he dropped in the dust gripping in his teeth the cold bronze.
> (V,1. 73–75, p. 130)

Such is war. Here is a vivid picture, the teeth of a dying soldier gripping the "cold bronze" of a spear extruding from his mouth. Today, this sort of image is fairly standard fare in episodes of *Game of Thrones* on HBO or *Spartacus* on Starz, all of which might seem highly original and cutting edge to many viewers but which, in fact, are just contemporary versions of scenes developed by Homer thousands of years before. If the HBO or Starz material seems new, it is only because viewers are not familiar with the details of *The Iliad*.

A few lines later, Eurypylos, Euaimon's son, kills Hypsenor on the run, with a blow that detaches an arm:

> running in chase as he fled before him struck in the shoulder
> with a blow swept from the sword and cut the arm's weight from him,
> so that the arm dropped bleeding to the ground, and the red death
> and destiny the powerful took hold of both eyes. (V,1. 80–83, p. 130)

This image of combat is sufficiently potent, the combination of "red death and destiny the powerful" with an arm severed and dropped to the ground, to take "hold of both eyes." The image arrests attention; it compels notice; it must be witnessed; it must be processed through the eyes—and to the brain. Homer here gives a quick sign that readers might want to take notice as well, for readers have eyes too. But the action moves on immediately. The narrative has many miles to go before finding any rest, so there is no time to reflect on or to process any effect that this moment might have beyond taking "hold of both eyes." Furthermore, we have not really come to know who these war victims are, apart from the quick information about their being sons of someone. We have nothing that provides us a connection in any deep human sense. They are introduced to us as bit characters caught in the fury of war, to be run through by spear or chopped up by sword.

In the chapter 5 exploration of fiction from the Iraq War, we will encounter the severed arm again in Nicholas Kulish's novel *Last One In*, but the arm in his story will be all by itself, thus presenting a mystery (of sorts) as to how body and arm came to be separated; Kulish's narrative accords greater weight to the scene, for the American observer, a reporter embedded with a Marine unit on the race to Baghdad at the start of the Iraq War, broods on the implications of an arm so far apart from its original body. Very strange. How could it come to be so? It is a scene that might give rise to nightmares later—all part of the PTSD aftereffects that are well known today—a pattern of deep and lasting consequence that actually seems to be understood by Homer, as we will see when taking up *The Odyssey*.

Arrows are soon flying outside the Trojan gates, some just wounding, with spurts of blood, and some killing. A verbal exchange between humans and gods observing the slaughter provides a brief interlude, which is quickly followed by more killing as an enraged Diomedes, carrying encouragement and special guidance from Pallas Athena, eagerly sets upon the Trojans with "a strong rage . . . as of a lion. . . ." (V,1. 136, p. 131). The rage takes its toll quickly as the dead pile up. It is not quite carnage on the scale of the D-Day landings, and, unlike in that action, the combatants engage eye to eye, snarl to snarl, but Homer makes sure that any careful reader will not be unaware of the ugliness inherent in an act of killing or of the diverse effects such action has on subsequent life. Here is Diomedes on a killing spree:

> Next he killed Astynoös and Hypeiron, shepherd of the people,
> striking one with the bronze-heeled spear above the nipple,
> and cutting the other beside the shoulder through the collar-bone
> with the great sword, so that neck and back were hewn free of the
>   shoulder.
> He left these men, and went on after Polyidos and Abas,
> sons of the aged dream-interpreter, Eurydamas;
> yet for these two as they went forth the old man did not answer
> their dreams, but Diomedes the powerful slew them. Now he
> went after the two sons of Phainops, Xanthos and Thoön,
> full grown both, but Phainops was stricken in sorrowful old age

nor could breed another son to leave among his possessions.
There he killed these two and took away the dear life from them
both, leaving to their father lamentation and sorrowful
affliction, since he was not to welcome them home from the fighting
alive still; and remoter kinsmen shared his possessions.
   Next he killed two children of Dardanian Priam
who were in a single chariot, Echemmon and Chromios.
(V,1. 114–160, p. 132)

In roughly half a page of the Richard Lattimore translation of *The Iliad*, we meet eight young men, all sons of someone, and all almost instantly dead at the hand of Diomedes, who would measure up mighty well as a modern-day American Marine. The rate of killing here is almost nowhere matched in the literature and film from the Vietnam War, the Iraq War, or the Afghanistan War—although curiously it does point in the direction of the slaughter of enemy hordes in the big blockbuster fantasy films of the past ten years. In these recent wars, of course, we would not know the names of soldiers killed on one side of the action; only American soldiers had names in those conflicts. Homer's world has a peculiar intimacy to it, with everyone known to everyone else—and to readers besides.

   Furthermore, Homer makes sure in the passage above that readers see the grief suffered by parents who have lost sons in war. The familial grief pattern has been foregrounded in films like *In the Valley of Elah* and *Grace Is Gone*, as well as in Kevin Powers's novel *The Yellow Birds*, all working out the grief consequences in heightened detail in a way not possible for the grand sprawl of *The Iliad,* but Homer distinctly set the stage for this matter to be integral to narratives of war.

   Books seven and eight of *The Iliad* present huge battle scenes, comparable to the scale of colossal set-piece combat sequences in Peter Jackson's film version of *Lord of the Rings* or some other movie that pits hordes of grotesque alien figures against a mass of humans. Toward the end of book seven, the killing has to stop to allow for bodies of the dead to be gathered and burned. Here we have carnage on the order of Bull Run/Manassas, Shiloh, Fredericksburg, or Gettysburg from the American Civil War; these were battles that left acres of dead to be collected for quick burial once the armies withdrew to prepare for the next catastrophic engagement. Combat action in Vietnam, in Afghanistan, and in Iraq seldom produced that kind of mass death for American soldiers. Only in the quick push to Baghdad did Iraqi soldier deaths mount fast, although many of those soldiers, unenthusiastic about the prospect of dying for a brutal dictator, shed uniforms and beat hasty retreats in the face of overwhelming American firepower, thus saving their skins to fight again in guerilla and civil war conditions. In the middle of the century's second decade, those survivors are still brutalizing each other across the Sunni/Shia chasm, long after American troops left to return home. As civil war in Iraq raged yet again, body counts steadily rose, this time exacerbated by the onslaught of Islamic State (ISIS/ISIL) forces sweeping across huge stretches of Syria and Iraq. In these unfortunate developments, the American "victory" was severely compromised, much to the horror of veterans returned home from that war effort—all of which might have been averted if Americans had not been so full of fantasyland enchantment going into Iraq in the first place.

So . . . a close and thorough reading of Homer could enable readers to know that war is hell, but that possibility has not stopped Americans from going to some form of war almost every twenty years, all the way from 1776 to the present. Somehow we manage to shut down our engagement with the horror of war in Homer. We don't avoid Homer's stories . . . we just manage to read them without fully coming to terms with what they present to us. Our reading is thus selective and imperfect; the causes of this pattern are deeply embedded in the documentary origins of the American experiment and in the mythology that hovers over every generation of Americans.

Furthermore, for the past thirty years or so, our mass culture has presented—mostly for the consumption of our boys and young men—endless streams of comic book hero figures and, most recently, almost weekly upgrades of video games where the chief goal is killing huge numbers of enemy forces while never getting a scratch. On 8 Nov. 2011, roughly a month before the final convoy of US troops exited Iraq and entered Kuwait, the video game *Call of Duty: Modern Warfare 3* earned $400 million in immediate sales in the United States and the United Kingdom, as reported by David Thomson in *The Big Screen* (500–501). No movie has ever had such a robust opening, and the arrival of the game meant that millions of players, in the comfort of home or in quiet military barracks somewhere, could play at war for fun. Real war might be diminished, but the appetite for war action was perhaps stronger than ever. Thomson notes that there was serious competition for war game players, since *Battlefield 3* had been released just shortly before *Call of Duty*.

Intense war video games provide strange preparation for players who may then proceed to the actual experience of war (particularly for drone operators, a point emphasized by the film *Good Kill* in 2015, a film seen by a very small audience, as the dismal domestic box office of $316,471 clearly shows), and this vicarious immersion in primal war behavior can have an addictive effect for some. The game draws you in to play and play and play. One kill follows another, endlessly. But if your avatar somehow fails to win, you just start the game over and give it another go. Kill, kill, kill. There are never any consequences. Everything is virtual. Blood flows copiously, but you always move on to the next set of adversaries. In this most perfect of imaginary war scenarios, there would never be an Achilles dead and forever gone.

We all become prisoners of our own experience. Sure, it is possible to get beyond the reach of our own lives through reading and conversing with those whose lives have followed different paths than our own, but in a great many cases, when we come to a conclusion about something, it will be in accord with what we know from our experiences. Childhood and developmental-stage fantasies can easily become part of the pattern-making process. Experience has to be fitted into comprehensible patterns that we can work with and make sense of. History owns the making of patterns, and patterns of experience promulgated as history teach us like nothing else. We are never liberated by history; we are constantly bound by it. The people of a nation collectively function much in the same way individuals act. How did America begin? What was absolutely necessary for the creation of the American republic?

Our first great creative, collective document tells that story with no possible misunderstanding. The Declaration of Independence rules us all, standing in majestic form as both the cause and the means of making possible the rise of America from diverse British colonies to independent states joined together by common interests. The Declaration of Independence is a formidable work of rhetoric, and its force is very much as potent today as it was in 1776. With deductive reasoning (the opening observations about those self-evident Truths) bound tightly to copious evidence (the twenty-seven specified grievances, thus enabling the signers to make inductive proof of a point possible), a comprehensive, rock-solid case is made for action in order to establish a new form of government. With acquiescence in necessity, the action had to be war.

The document leaves no room for ambiguity. It presents the general conditions that people wish for and merit in the business of governance. It details the failures and abuses of government on the part of the British Crown and Parliament. It accounts for all of the efforts of reason and persuasion that had been attempted in order to reach a settlement short of war. And it notes the failure of all those good efforts. Then comes the kicker, the force that first impelled Americans to war and that has been recreated in every subsequent American foray into war: "We must, therefore, acquiesce in the Necessity, which denounces our Separation, and hold them, as we hold the rest of Mankind, Enemies in War, in Peace, Friends." Necessity, necessity, necessity—never was necessity summoned with greater assurance and authority. War must be. There is no other alternative.

Americans bought the argument for war in 1776, and every time the flag goes up, every time we gather for parades and palaver and fireworks on the Fourth of July, we drink the elixir of war as a necessity. We are born to it, steeped in it, bound up with it, all the days of our lives, from birth to death. The wars will come. God forbid Americans should ever not be ready to live up to this responsibility as demonstrated with such potency at the outset.

In the summer of 1776, as representative delegates from the colonies gathered in Philadelphia to settle upon a way to realize their goals for just and satisfactory governance, they all knew their Homer; they knew their Plato. The ugliness of war as pictured vividly in Homer's narratives would prove to be no deterrent to these latter-day guardians of freedom. They determined to face up squarely to the horrors of war. They produced a document that would blaze the war trail for centuries to come—not only providing cause for *a* war but also at the same time inscribing the paradigmatic cause for going to *all* wars involving future Americans.

For subsequent generations of Americans, following the compelling logic of the Declaration of Independence has been rather simple. Mexico proved hostile to the area known as Texas; war was necessary. Fort Sumter was attacked in Charleston Harbor; war was necessary. Native Americans proved hostile or were in a place needed by other Americans; war was necessary (often). Spain was dangerous in the Western (American) hemisphere; war was necessary. Americans on ships in the open seas were subject to attack in World War I—and the Germans had designs on alliance with Mexico; war was necessary. Pearl Harbor was attacked; war was necessary. North Korea invaded South Korea; war was necessary. Something like an attack appeared to happen to US warships in the Tonkin Gulf; war was necessary. Americans were threatened in Grenada; war was necessary (and proved mercifully brief). Iraq invaded Kuwait; war was necessary (again, blessedly brief). The World Trade Center was attacked on 9/11; war was necessary. There were allegations of weapons of mass destruction in Iraq; war was necessary (no weapons of mass destruction were found, but the war was long and treacherous).

Hence, one war led to many others over the years. Gradually, as American war literature began to accumulate (William Gilmore Simms, James Fenimore Cooper, Stephen Crane, Ernest Hemingway, Norman Mailer, Tim O'Brien, and many others in the past forty years), the emphasis fell increasingly on *The Odyssey* side of Homer's treatment of war. Odysseus needs ten years to get himself back with his wife, his son, and his father. The length of his return home, and all the challenges he must overcome along the way, represent the perilous aftermath of war for those who have experienced combat. Getting into war has the simplicity of a time-tested formula: "acquiesce in the necessity." Getting out for individuals who have gone to war has proved very complex and daunting. America loves simple—and does not deal well with complexity. Ronald Reagan's presidency represents this pattern perfectly.

Reagan's ideal America peaked before all the upheavals of the 1960s. It was before the riots of the civil rights movement; it was before the acceleration of demands for equality by women; it was before the growing civil disobedience with regard to the Vietnam War. The decade of the 1950s was much quieter, or so it seemed from Reagan's vantage point. In those years, Reagan enjoyed personal prosperity, making very good money helping to sell goods produced by American enterprise, a pattern to be scrutinized later. In this comprehensive vision, everyone knew his or her place and was content in it. A popular general/president ("I Like Ike" Eisenhower) kept things on an even keel. Laws were sensible, and people obeyed them. It was a good time, but by the time of Reagan's election to the presidency, America had been rent asunder, in large part, from within. It was Reagan's task to bring back the simple good times, and his two large electoral victories showed that America was right in step with his formula for salvation.

In the final debate before the election of 1984, Reagan had the last word. The debate format allowed him a couple of minutes at the very end to put his vision for the future of America, under his leadership, into place. Not surprisingly, he told a story. Eventually the story had him and his wife in a car driving down the California coast along the Pacific Ocean. The sun was setting over the ocean. It was a lovely drive. The debate moderator indicated that the president's time was almost up. The drive went on . . . and then the moderator said there was no more time. This story was halted in mid-drive; President Reagan failed to make a coherent point in traditional debate terms. While nothing like this would ever be recommended in a public speaking course—leaving the audience in the middle of nowhere, a story stopping far short of its destination—Americans voted for Reagan overwhelmingly in the election that year. His debate time expired, but he was awarded another four years in the Oval Office. Reagan's story had struck a deep chord, for it recalled a simpler time, an era where the family would pile into the station wagon for a Sunday drive, an experience that was enjoyed for the going, not for any particular destination. The family was together, happy. It was the genius of simple America.

This study will soon explore ways in which going to war has become increasingly simple, all following the deeply inscribed pattern of the Declaration of Independence. But first, the complex implications about the aftereffects of war shown in Homer's *The Odyssey* must be acknowledged. As mentioned earlier, Odysseus has a harrowing and very long return trip to Ithaca after the war in Troy. Obstacle after obstacle confronts and deters him. It is a miracle that he—alone—manages to make his way home at last, but only after falling by the wayside (or waterside) many times. Thus, Homer yields the final truth of war: getting safely home is a long and difficult process.

In preparation for delving into the grim ugliness of war as shown to us by Homer thousands of years ago, we might want to consider just one set of daunting war facts from our present day. With disturbing frequency, US veterans commit suicide. A study by the Department of Veterans Affairs in 2013 placed the veteran suicide rate at twenty-two a day between 1999 and 2010 (Haiken); a follow-up study found that the rate had dropped to twenty a day in 2014 (Goldberg); but for young veterans, under age thirty, the suicide rate increased 44 percent between 2009 and 2011 (Nicks). Certainly, many of those suicides involve factors unrelated to war experience, but in some cases these deaths, while far removed from combat engagements, nevertheless slowly but steadily escalate the human cost of brutal wars in Vietnam, in Afghanistan, and in Iraq—wars to which American soldiers were dispatched because certain "necessities" were posited and accepted. Even as the American combat presence in Afghanistan persists, the veterans still have a long and difficult journey home. Roughly every seventy minutes, the journey ends prematurely for one of them. Homer's *Iliad* and *Odyssey* still have much to teach us, if only we could be open to their lessons.

All of the digressions and divertissements that keep Odysseus away from Ithaca for so long after war's end have been enjoyed for their imaginative liveliness—indeed, their thrills of captivity and escape—by many generations of readers. Unfortunately, our pleasure in the inventiveness of all the sidetracks and impediments devised by Homer to keep us engaged with the story serve to mask the underlying problem. The dazzle of the story itself is so thrilling that we forget what came before. Odysseus, after all, had seen terrible things on the field of battle; he had been an active and skillful killer of his fellow man. Yes, he has wit and cunning. Yes, he can tell a great story. But something keeps him from getting home in a timely and comfortable way. The crucial something is a form of PTSD, inscribed eons before psychiatric practitioners got around to labeling the problem in a formal way.

Yet even after Odysseus has finally crawled ashore on familiar land, his reconnection with loved ones is problematic. His son Telemachus has worked hard to find out what happened to his father, a story line developed with a gender twist in Bobbie Ann Mason's *In Country* (1985), where a daughter is relentless in trying to find out what the Vietnam War was like for her father, who perished there before her birth. However, the reunion with wife Penelope is more complex, for it is shadowed by doubts about her fidelity. She has been surrounded by suitors eager to mate with her and supplant Odysseus in the world of Ithaca. In American literature from the Vietnam era onward, there is recurrent treatment of a "Jody" character, a man who does not go off to war and who stands ready—eager—to offer solace and/or sex to the women left behind by warriors gone to battle (the 1978 film *Coming Home*, which garnered three Academy Awards, centers on a military wife's infidelity). We will encounter this haunting figure in a number of stories from the most recent wars, and as far back as Homer's time, the "Jody" pattern was opened up as readers discover how Agamemnon's bed had been assumed by Aegisthus, Clytemnestra's lover, while Agamemnon was at war. Odysseus puts on a disguise so as to be able to snoop around and find out whether his marriage bed has been violated. With relief to Odysseus—and to any man concerned about being cuckolded—Penelope is proved to be true. But the ravages of war persist as Odysseus cannot resist settling his anger with Penelope's suitors, all of whom must be systematically slaughtered. Thus does the gore of war find its way to the homeland.

Vietnam literature and film is replete with treatments of the plight of veterans returning to face one form or another of PTSD maladjustment. Larry Heinemann's *Paco's Story* (1986 National Book Award for Fiction) focuses on a sole survivor of an attack in Vietnam that killed everyone else in his artillery battery; eventually it becomes clear that the essential story can be told only by the dead left behind, for only they can really understand Paco, who otherwise wanders hopelessly from place to place, always an alien. The lingering aftereffects of war are captured comprehensively in W. D. Ehrhart's gathering of poetry *Carrying the Darkness* (1985), which represents a broad spectrum of people who had experience with war in

Vietnam; the title speaks with metaphoric force to the presence of PTSD, something that Ehrhart himself had battled upon his return from combat duty. For Ehrhart, the therapeutic effect of writing poetry contributed to his eventual return to a successful life. Sometimes it takes decades to face up to the effects of trauma from war; such was the situation for Karl Marlantes, who seemed to fit in OK for a while after his Vietnam War experience but eventually needed sustained therapy to deal with long-buried demons, a pattern that finally brought him to write *Matterhorn* (2010), a work that lays bare concerns about potential darkness in Marine battle operations in Vietnam as soldiers at the low end of the military hierarchy were potentially sacrificed in order to secure promotions at the high end in the chain of command. The shadows cast by *Matterhorn* are dark indeed.

As early as 2006 the deep need for a way for veterans to declare and share their experiences in Iraq (as well as in Afghanistan) in preparation for their return to America was recognized in a project that resulted in a book, *Operation Homecoming: Iraq, Afghanistan, and the Home Front, in the Words of U.S. Troops and Their Families,* edited by Andrew Carroll and supported by funding from the National Endowment for the Arts (NEA) under the leadership of Dana Gioia, chairman of the NEA at that time. This whole project essentially replicates the middle portion of *The Odyssey* where Odysseus provides details of trial and error in the war and in his fateful effort to get back to Ithaca with his crew. Along the way, he went to hell and back, a frightening journey reflected in the book (and movie) that America received from Audie Murphy in the years following World War II but did not begin to fully understand until Murphy became an early advocate for helping veterans deal with PTSD (even before it had been recognized as a serious challenge to healthy and happy life). At some point, to aid and abet the return of veterans from war, stories need to be told. As this study will later show, the stories have emerged, but the audiences for them are not impressive. We crave happy . . . and shun the unhappy. Simple is good. Complex is a problem.

As final preparation for detailed analysis of the imaginative responses to our most recent wars, it will be productive to enter that territory through the lens of the Vietnam War. While the largesse of the Tonkin Gulf Resolution was soon regretted, because it offered the president much leeway in choosing military responses to apparent provocations on the part of North Vietnam (and it was later repealed, in an attachment to a bill signed by President Nixon in early 1971), as a pattern of easing around the "necessity" imperative in the Declaration of Independence, the Tonkin Gulf Resolution would constitute a kind of template for future presidents seeking sufficient authority to commit US combat forces to foreign conflicts without formal declaration of war by Congress. A pattern for the type of work-around approach to entrance into military conflict would stretch over several decades and has been brilliantly analyzed by Rachel Maddow in her 2012 book, *Drift: The Unmooring of American Military Power*, to which I will shortly turn to move our exploration of war literature and film from Vietnam to the battle zones in Afghanistan and Iraq. Before considering Maddow's exposé of developments in the political/military/industrial complex from the Vietnam War to the present, I'll quickly outline some lessons that emerged from the Vietnam War, in very broad strokes.

First and most obviously, the Vietnam War did not end well for America; American combat forces were pulled out in the spring of 1973, and then just two years later, the world watched as the North Vietnamese executed a very fast and successful attack on the South that quickly ended in the total collapse of our allies in South Vietnam. The disastrous scene in April of 1975 was a hugely bitter pill for anyone who wanted to see America—and its loudly trumpeted ideals—triumphant in all regards on the world stage. The defeat was felt most desperately by many US veterans who had given so much (the loss of limbs, the deaths of fellow soldiers, the exposure to all the ugly horrors of war) when they answered the call to military service in the 1960s and early 1970s.

Tom Bissell's 2007 book, *The Father of All Things; A Marine, His Son, and the Legacy of Vietnam*, provides an extensive and poignant rendering of the pain endured by Bissell's dad, John, when South Vietnam collapsed; all of his father's memories of his 1965 tour in Vietnam as a Marine, including wounds suffered and comrades killed, came flooding back harsher than ever in the face of transparent defeat and futility. It was a crushing blow, and it greatly contributed to John's ongoing, harrowing PTSD experience. Tom's own writing career, which has been very successful, was given a huge boost by the support of one of his father's fellow Marines, Philip Caputo, whose *Rumor of War* was one of the earliest memoirs of the Vietnam War, a provocative text analyzed later. Winning a war is not a cure-all for PTSD, as the case of Audie Murphy showed, but winning certainly helps more than losing.

Second, the Vietnam War was debated vigorously and protested violently at home throughout its duration. The war spilled over into the streets of America, and as a consequence, it was next to impossible to put the Vietnam War out of mind for even a day between 1965 and 1973. There were stand-uppers from reporters in the rice paddies or jungles of Vietnam on the evening national news most nights; the battlefield losses in killed and wounded were reckoned daily. There were militant hawks and pacifist doves wrangling in every election. There were silent vigils by Post Office buildings, protest rallies in small towns and large cities, and marches on Washington. By 1968 more than half of America had come to oppose the war in Vietnam, yet it would grind on for another five years. The American death count would push way past fifty thousand. The grim ugliness of the Vietnam War was in your face—sometimes an angry snarl, sometimes a keening howl— impossible to ignore for at least eight years of American cultural history.

Third, the soldiers who went to serve in Vietnam almost never knew much about the country where they might die in combat, and this general pattern of ignorance included their officers. The intricate history of Vietnam (especially in relationship to China) was essentially ignored; the religious and cultural patterns of the Vietnamese people were treated with derision much of the time; almost no Americans knew more than a few simple words of Vietnamese. And there was never much trust in the Army of South Vietnam (ARVN)—never a clear sense of sweeping devotion on the part of ARVN soldiers to the idealistic goals being promoted by Americans in their military involvement in Southeast Asia. The civil war dimension of conflict in Vietnam was always elusive to American understanding, always reduced to a local manifestation of large geopolitical forces, when in reality there were plenty of times when the very presence of Americans in-country seemed to be an affront to a great many Vietnamese who simply longed for the day when all outsiders would just go back home. The situation in Vietnam begged for nuanced understanding, but simple was all we took to the conflict. Simple proved to be our undoing.

Fourth, Americans generally—and US military forces particularly— proceeded with the broad belief that the world's most sophisticated and powerful armed force (supported by B-52 bombers, diverse jet fighters and combat support helicopters, massive firepower from land-based artillery and sea-based battleships) would have a relatively easy time overwhelming a minuscule Third World country, a place smaller than Montana (and combining North Vietnam and South Vietnam, just a bit larger than New Mexico). Why, a few US Marines, well fed and well equipped and full of that OOORAH "semper fi" spirit, should be able to do the job in a few days. One look at such an awesome specimen of fighting man, and the bravest of the enemy would promptly give up the ghost and go back to planting rice. It was a simplistic, goofy notion. Eight years of combat proved us wrong. But we would hate to learn a lesson, and we proved eager to trot out the same self-aggrandizing view in the soon-to-arrive new century. Just a small force would be required to topple Saddam Hussein's government and to secure freedom in Iraq.

Fifth, the presence of a draft—an operation of selective service—in America during the Vietnam War years contributed hugely to the riotous home-front reactions. The first move to mollify draft protestors and antiwar agitators involved shifting the selection process to a lottery (hence, replacing a potentially corrupt and unfair system of selection, college deferments and all) and then, as quickly as possible, moving the military to an all-volunteer force, a plan developed aggressively by General Creighton Abrams as the Vietnam War was ending for American troops. As long as soldiers were putting themselves forward for service voluntarily, it was assumed by the president and by the Pentagon that American combat troops (and their loved ones) would no longer have call to protest their going to war. By the end of the Vietnam War, the all-volunteer concept had taken deep root.

The mantra of the moment here is that Americans love simple, but simple can really come back to haunt you. Americans were aliens in Vietnam, distant on many counts. They came from away. They had no love of the land. In the main, especially as the war dragged on, they just wanted to fight and kill and be done with it—to get back home. They could not converse with their hosts. They were massively ignorant about almost everything Vietnamese, and there was much complexity even within a small country. Frances Fitzgerald's *Fire in the Lake: The Vietnamese and the Americans in Vietnam*, which provides explanations in fine detail for all of the points I have just noted quickly, did not appear until 1972, by which point the war was in large part lost, the American withdrawal under way. This final stage was also known as the "Vietnamization" of the war—a pattern almost exactly like ones that would be called for in the twenty-first-century conflicts in Iraq and Afghanistan.

There's one last feature of the Vietnam War that must be acknowledged more directly and fully now than its mention in one of the earlier points: reporters from American news outlets (television, newspapers, magazines of diverse types) roamed all over the terrain of South Vietnam. The US Military Assistance Command in Vietnam (MACV) decided early on that the American people would want to see their military getting the job done. Reporters were typically based in Saigon, but they could catch military transport (sometimes by jeep, sometimes by helicopter or plane) and go out to far-flung military units to observe some action. Typically, they would stay a brief time, then return to their hotel rooms to write the stories that would be delivered to cable operators for sending along to the mass media organizations paying the bills. The stories were sometimes mundane, sometimes riveting. On occasion, just a quick visit yielded an accurate view of the war; for example, Joseph Galloway's narrative of the November 1965 battle of the Ia Drang Valley eventually became a book (with Lt. Gen. Harold Moore: *We Were Soldiers Once . . . and Young*, 1992) and then a film (*We Were Soldiers*, 2002). However, sometimes distortions occurred in this style of reportage, a situation that was seen more than once in the chaotic upheaval during the Tet Offensive in January/February of 1968. Americans reading or watching at home (Vietnam became the "living room war," thanks to all the coverage on broadcast television nightly news) could never tell the difference between accurate and distorted. It was hopelessly complex—not good for a people seeking simple.

When the Vietnam War was finally over—except for decades of squabbling and anguishing over the ultimate definitive meaning of the whole episode—it was clear to virtually everyone that this particular pattern should never be repeated. And . . . while we have seen serious quagmires occur in our foreign relations since Vietnam, we have managed to alter a number of the key factors that bedeviled Americans back in the turbulent 1960s and 1970s. Sinister or cynical as it may sound, wars for Americans have potential to serve as a binding agent, a force of national unity that helps mitigate the impulses of people whose individualistic aspirations threaten to tear the nation into tiny pieces of incoherent and incompatible fractiousness. In this particular regard, however, the Vietnam War failed utterly, and as a result, it came to stand as a very bad example of how war could serve America.

Bad examples can teach well. In brief, here are some of the lessons taught by the Vietnam debacle, although depending on your position on the left–right political spectrum, each one could be seen as objectionable or problematic:

1) The American military must be an all-volunteer force, thus eliminating the turbulence and destabilizing effects of draft protest in the Vietnam War era;

2) No matter how far truth or reality must be stretched in the process, all justifications for war must match up closely to the "acquiesce in the necessity" language of the Declaration of Independence, and public relations campaigns for war must relentlessly stay on message to affirm the urgency and necessity of war action;

3) Reportage from the combat zone must be somehow brought under control or influence of the military leadership—in patterns safeguarding true national security but avoiding direct censorship whenever possible;

4) Given the need for quick response in foreign policy situations on the part of the president, in operational terms as much leeway as possible should be passed along from Congress to the president regarding military force commitments;

5) Americans love simple . . . and they live for risk . . . so the right kinds of war can be both very useful and effective in keeping these states (and people)*united.*

The remainder of this chapter takes us through deliberate consideration of three recent books, each one adding a unique perspective on the way war works for Americans, all necessary to provide an understanding of the literature and film from wars from Vietnam to Afghanistan and Iraq. This approach provides grounds for deep understanding of why imaginative representations of these wars have not had much of an impact in American cultural life.

Rachel Maddow's *Drift* (2012) will deal directly with most of the lessons noted above; Jonathon Haight's *The Righteous Mind: Why Good People Are Divided by Politics and Religion* (2012) fills in important background about key moral foundations for Americans and the way those foundations serve to support the cause for war; and finally, my reading of Charles Duhigg's *The Power of Habit: Why We Do What We Do in Life and Business* (2012) will underscore the concern that a habit of war was embedded in America at the outset, right there in the Declaration of Independence, and it would take a colossal effort to turn our approach to war in a different direction—thus finally validating all that Homer's *Iliad* and *Odyssey* could hope to show us about the nature of war. As it turns out, our war habit in recent times has intensified, not dimmed. We are now more primed for war than ever. With this condition settled upon us, as we look ahead, there must be war.

Politics and The Ease of Going to War: What Rachel Maddow's *Drift* Helps Us Understand

The subtitle for Rachel Maddow's *Drift* is *The Unmooring of American Military Power*, and that phrasing fits her study wonderfully well. I mentioned earlier that the delegates to the Constitutional Convention in 1787 were determined to keep a strong and aggressive executive from rushing the nation into war; the right to declare war was thus reserved for Congress, which would involve a large number of people. Only by putting many heads together could a sound and just decision to "acquiesce in the necessity" of war be reached. The model for this approach was right there in their recent past: The Declaration of Independence was itself a product of collaborative deliberation, debate, and decision. So . . . as it was in the beginning, it should ever after be.

Thus, the American military forces, under direction of the commander in chief, the president, would have to depend for their mission assignments on the will of the people as represented by Congress. The first president came from a distinguished military background, but George Washington managed to steer clear of war for eight years. Nearly two centuries later, another commander in chief with an extraordinary military background, President Eisenhower, would keep America out of war for his eight years in the White House. Eisenhower's efforts followed those of Harry Truman, whose Korean conflict involvement had proved problematic for the model established in the Constitution: war action preceded war authorization in the quick followup to the invasion of South Korea by North Korea in late June of 1950. In the world of the twentieth century, things happened a lot faster than they did in the eighteenth century. Even though Eisenhower avoided war, in his Farewell Address he voiced anxiety about the growing influence of the "military/industrial complex." Then came Vietnam, and by the end of that war, concerns about abuse of executive power resulted in congressional restraints being put on the president with regard to war powers. The main part of Maddow's book carries the story forward from the end of the Vietnam War to the present situation early in the twenty-first century.

No one should be surprised at what happened. The military/industrial complex, now including a broad span of intelligence-gathering/counterterrorism initiatives and offices, is gigantic in contrast to what it was when Eisenhower left office . . . or when Richard Nixon resigned in disgrace in 1974. The growth of military might and executive independence is not a simple story, but Maddow tells it thoroughly and thoughtfully. She has an agenda, which is presented straightforwardly: she would like to see American military activity become much more restrained, to become once again "moored." Thanks to Maddow's delineation of small but consequential moves over the past four decades, we can see how we got to our present place with regard to America and the prospect of war. However, as I will show, a number of complicating factors beyond Maddow's scope add much to the challenge of changing the course of the drift.

The first thing to note about Maddow's study is the brilliance of the title. *Drift* is a perfect word to capture the nature of developments in American governance from the 1970s through the first decade of the twenty-first century. Drifting bodies are hard to track and locate; the motion is so subtle and difficult to notice that you don't see how you're moving—and thus you arrive, surprised, in an unexpected location. It happens quietly, and with other things diverting attention in the foreground, the slow drift happens but is not immediately recognized. As I will show in the "Fantasyland" chapter at the end of the study, American popular culture generates megatons of distraction on a daily basis, so it is no wonder that our attention as a people would often stray from minding war plans and activities. A strong military exists precisely to take care of war business for us. It is not for us to wonder why, it's for them to do or die. A division of functions keeps things simple.

Maddow covers a lot of politics and history in *Drift*. Her pages are thick with details; she accounts for a host of legislative actions, presidential maneuvers, and military regrouping initiatives in the years following Vietnam. There is no one huge event here in her telling of history; one detail bleeds quietly into another as the years slip along. Enough happens that it becomes a little blurry—which is not Maddow's fault. It is our fault, for we are not good at details. We like the big picture, and as I have argued steadily, we like things to be simple.

Maddow carefully details the development of the Total Force Policy through the initiative of Gen. Creighton Abrams, chief of staff for the Army from 1972 until his death in 1974. For anyone who would like America to avoid war, Maddow's presentation of Abrams would give him hero status. Abrams had served as leader of the MACV after General Westmoreland, and he was sorely distressed at the way the war had been managed from the outset. The Army had to depend on draftees, and bringing drafted soldiers along in sufficient numbers, with adequate time for training, had presented big challenges. Additionally, the home-front forces—National Guard and Reserves—were not brought into the war in Vietnam; they provided safety zones for young men not eager to see combat. Finally, the American people, through representation in Congress, had not been sufficiently drawn into the commitment of armed forces to battle in Vietnam. As Abrams looked at this picture, he did not like it at all. Hence his push for major changes. The Total Force Policy would require depth of training and readiness on the part of the National Guard and Reserves, enough resourcing and preparation to make them ready for war—and then future war engagements would require mobilization of these back-up units. Because the home front would thus be engaged in war activity, Congress would necessarily be fully involved. At the same time, Congress reasserted its war declaration authority by passing the War Powers Resolution in 1973. By the time President Nixon exited the Oval Office in the summer of 1974, there were serious checks on any impulse to rush the US military into battle.

Getting from that point, in the mid-1970s, to President Clinton's substantial deployment of US military might in Bosnia and Kosovo in the mid-1990s (supportive of a United Nations effort) certainly involved a whole lot of drift. Even more of the same drift pattern is reflected in President Obama's commitment of US power, again within terms of a United Nations resolution—most significantly in use of ship-based missiles—to aid rebels fighting the Gadhafi government in Libya in 2011. We will get to what is represented in the wars in Afghanistan and Iraq after tracking Maddow's history from the 1970s forward.

Something must have happened in the 1980s and early 1990s to set up the Clinton and Obama actions, as well as the huge endeavors in Afghanistan after the 2001 al-Qaida attacks on the World Trade Center and the Pentagon. Veering just a little bit off the course set by Maddow's book, it might be time to revisit the "America loves simple" idea I've mentioned earlier. If anyone wants to quibble about my oft-repeated emphasis on simple as a guiding predisposition in American life, I have just one name to offer: Ronald Reagan.

President Reagan was simple personified. He was a master of presenting a strong message, vivid in language, with utmost simplicity. Tell a story, and keep it simple—that was Reagan's modus operandi. This approach, which often fed on nostalgic yearning for an earlier time, was mentioned previously in the account of President Reagan's relaxed and destination-less Pacific Coast drive in the final minutes of debate in 1984. As I will note in the next section of this chapter, which reviews key points in Jonathan Haidt's book *The Righteous Mind*, "The human mind is a story processor, not a logic processor. Everyone loves a good story; every culture bathes its children in stories" (281).

Throughout Reagan's eight years in office, he used the bully pulpit of his position vigorously and well to sell his vision of America. He always kept the story simple. America was not a land of defeat. Vietnam did not mean what many defeatists thought. America was a beacon of freedom and liberty for the world. America should take a strong and forceful role in leading the world to freedom and liberty. Americans were brave. Americans were good. Americans were generous.

With regard to "drift" developments from the 1980s in Maddox's scrupulous accounting, Reagan's forceful simplicity and speech-making in the foreground enabled much mischief and reorganizing to be done by Reagan minions in the background—whether at the high end (Ed Meese in the role of attorney general) or at the low end (Oliver North and "Bud" McFarlane scurrying about furtively to move money and arms around in ways not sanctioned or approved by Congress). In the face of a Congress still wary of replicating the mistakes of Vietnam, the Reagan operatives used extreme ingenuity (on both sides of the law) to make Reagan's vision operational in diverse locations around the globe. The invasion of Grenada (to liberate American students who might be in danger) was small-scale and rapid enough, start to finish, to slip by without too much attention or anxiety. All along, Reagan made the noise, always simple, never ambiguous.

After his leading-man acting career had sputtered to a close, and before his political career took flight, Ronald Reagan had been a public pitchman for corporations (General Electric, where Reagan had a public relations function in hosting the General Electric Theater and in giving speeches to GE gatherings of various sorts) and for products (20 Mule Team Borax, with Reagan in an advertising function helping to make the laundry of America super clean and white, as host of *Death Valley Days* in 1964–1965). Thus, from a great deal of experience, essentially unmatched in the history of the presidency, Reagan knew how to use language and style to sell things in the public arena. He was completely comfortable in this role. His soaring speeches provided cover for very shady covert stuff behind the scenes. It was an exceptionally duplicitous presidency, and if he had not been exiting office in 1988, impeachment proceedings likely would have been in the offing as more became known about illegal shenanigans devised to avoid the constraints of congressional oversight regarding budget and war-related activity.

Suffice to say here, by the time George Herbert Walker Bush was elected to the presidency in 1988, increased authority and discretion in use of military power had started to shift back toward the commander in chief in a pattern that has proven irreversible to the present day; a key part of that process involved some important developments in shifting war efforts toward the private sector, particularly in the growth of companies whose main business involved defense department contract work. Readiness for war matters and the Reagan years had contributed significantly to spreading war preparation out broadly with defense department growth.

President Bush (41) led the nation to war in 1991, in the great coalition effort to terminate the Iraqi occupation of Kuwait, and as Maddow recounts the events leading up to the 100-hour pulverizing decimation of Iraq's military forces, she acknowledges that the process of seeking and getting full Congressional approval for combat activity measured up quite well against the expectations set forth in the Constitution. Despite discouragement from Dick Cheney at the Department of Defense (and Cheney's position was always to push hard to return power to the presidency that had been stripped away in the aftermath of Vietnam), President Bush decided to seek congressional review of the war initiative being planned under the aegis of the United Nations. In early January of 1991, just a couple of weeks before the war commenced, both houses of Congress voted to support the president in leading American forces into the United Nations–sanctioned war. As Maddow concludes, this episode represented the value of the Abrams Doctrine. But much has changed since, in a quiet drift sort of way.

When President Clinton took the oath of office, it was assumed by many that a person who had voiced opposition to the Vietnam War would never want to replicate that episode in another presidency. Gulf War I (Desert Storm) had proved that America could act boldly on an international stage with astounding military success—and it could be done with the approval of Congress. Now a peacenik was in office at the White House. Everyone could breathe easy at last. Despite plenty of war activity in the past twenty years, the breathing still seems unlabored.

Maddow's *Drift*—and the history of the last two decades—shows how rather regular war action could proceed without causing undue stress. Steadily, the Department of Defense prepared to use nonmilitary resources wherever possible in future areas of conflict. It was recognized that, as in Grenada, situations could erupt suddenly, requiring almost instant response—though falling significantly short of the nuclear holocaust scenarios that kept Americans on edge through the 1950s and 1960s. Quick response military units were organized and reorganized. The aura of United Nations sanction for military action seemed to carry over through the 1990s and into the first decade of the current century. A little engineering might be needed to pull Congress along, but the pattern of having the United Nations in the foreground with sanctions or ultimatums could serve nicely to set up a presidential appeal for support to follow through with deployment of the Marines, Army, Navy, and Air Force. Sophisticated technology would enable us to go into difficult areas without danger to American lives. By the present day, drone attacks happen routinely, with very little attention paid to them. All of this is made clear by Rachel Maddow in *Drift*, and she finds most of it troubling.

The troubles piled up hugely in the long-lasting Afghanistan conflict and in the disaster that transpired in Iraq soon after the initial assault and defeat of Saddam Hussein's military. Barely three weeks into the move over the border from Kuwait, Lt. Nathaniel Fick's Marine Recon unit, moving north on the eastern side of the American push toward Baghdad, encountered fighters who had moved into Iraq from Syria in order to repel the terrible Americans and their hegemonic, demonic culture. Here was a very quick sign that the Iraq conflict would assume dimensions of complexity and difficulty completely unanticipated as the war on Saddam Hussein was planned.

But once American forces were locked in grotesque patterns of "engagement" (sometimes against devastating Improvised Explosive Devices used extensively to inflict casualties on Americans without committing fighters from an opposing side that soon would spread out to include both Sunni and Shia insurgency groups; sometimes engaged through hit-and-run ambushes, with enemy combatants slipping behind civilian cover and becoming unidentifiable to Americans on the hunt for them), much of the cost could be passed along to civilian contractors who would build bases, feed soldiers, and keep the material supplies necessary for war moving along steadily. The defense budget is colossal, and military-related spending represents a very large part of the gross domestic product (GDP). When government spending took a 15 percent dip in the last quarter of 2012, including a 22.2 percent reduction in defense outlays (the largest drop since the end of the Vietnam War), the effect showed up immediately, and the fourth-quarter GDP growth staggered in at 0.1 percent—the smallest growth in three and a half years (Brown). It could almost be said that America runs on defense.

To meet escalating force requirements in Iraq and Afghanistan, National Guard and Reserve forces were indeed mobilized, all in line with the Total Force Policy. The contracts of service neatly provided for deployment of these units overseas as deemed necessary by mission objectives. Regarding Afghanistan, the nation united quickly to avenge the attacks of September 11, and as a consequence the "acquiesce in the necessity" piece fell into place effortlessly. Congress and the president were in accord, with broad public support for war action. The Taliban was sent scurrying off in short order, but Osama bin Laden scurried away too—and then Americans found themselves mired in a land that had successfully resisted incursions from outsiders many times before.

For well more than a decade, military commanders at all levels mounted missions to engage the enemy in Afghanistan, but the whole undertaking finally drifted to a draw, and as noted in the introduction to this study, the withdrawal plan for US forces has been revised frequently. Sporadically, reports of small-scale attacks involving American soldiers emerge from Afghanistan, and almost always they are discouraging. The 2014 presidential election in Afghanistan was fraught with charges of voter fraud. Taliban forces reappear in more areas every year. Whenever America departs, Afghanistan will be mostly what it has always been. In the experience of most Americans, this conclusion will matter little. But for veterans who saw their fellow soldiers killed on patrol, who were unfortunately responsible for the deaths and suffering of unarmed civilians in the line of fire, who were devastatingly maimed when an IED destroyed their Humvee, the end of America's role in Afghanistan will be bitter indeed. Their war, a torturous odyssey, will continue for many years.

Iraq, of course, was different in quite a few respects. Maddow's *Drift* astutely addresses the finesse represented in the way President George W. Bush and his administration handled the "acquiesce in the necessity" requirement for war. Nation building does not provide grounds for necessity; freedom spreading is not by itself grounds for necessity. We have to be up against a direct and menacing threat for the process to work. Create a threat, you're set.

An extensive set of defense contractors developed depth and breadth of capability to provide immediate support of any combat initiative on the part of the US military forces; Halliburton Company and its subsidiary (until April 2007), Kellogg-Brown & Root (KBR), which became the best-known and biggest purveyor of goods and services to support American military initiatives, was always at the ready. Logistics could be handled conveniently that way; some provision was even made for contracted security if the military forces were stretched too thin to handle everything. If war should come, KBR was prepared.

Meanwhile, the United Nations had a vested stake in maintaining a close watch on Saddam Hussein's regime, particularly given the weapons and human rights violations used in the war with Iran and in suppression of Kurds and others after Gulf War I. Chemical weapons had been used in Iraq. The international community was already engaged, at least in part.

Thus, the stage was set. Some provision needed to be made to bring the American people along, with their Congress included, but a full and outright declaration of war would be problematical. The drift away from that crystal-clear kind of action had, by 2003, quite a few precedents; Gulf War I in 1991, the Kosovo intervention later in that decade, and then the 2001 war in Afghanistan all showed the way to work out commitment of American forces to combat action. The military was ready. The military is always ready. The military will go when told to go; they can make plans and devise missions wherever needed. They are professional soldiers—and proud of their professionalism.

It is important to make sure the United Nations is involved with sanctions and ultimatums. Then there has to be a grave threat. Michael Moore's documentary efforts always have large rhetorical fault lines, and his *Fahrenheit 9/11* is no exception in this regard, but it does tightly capture the heart of the "threat" generation by the Bush team. President Bush, Vice President Cheney, and top cabinet officials are shown over and over and over again in Moore's story making countless references to weapons of mass destruction. Whether the threat was said in full or referenced in short form (WMD), as long as the concept was pushed out there day after day, week after week, month after month, as a means to catch the notice of people busy at work and play, sooner or later it would become a widely held "fact" that Iraq had weapons of mass destruction—and that Iraq fully intended to use them to harm Americans. At home. No one was safe. Hence, necessity had been created by dint of repetition about the WMD threat. Say it enough, and fact it becomes, even smashing through the surfeit of distractions in American culture.

By the early spring of 2003, it was time to "acquiesce in the necessity." In the fall of 2002, the Senate had passed a resolution authorizing the president to commit military forces to action in Iraq if Saddam Hussein's government failed to comply completely and fully with United Nations requirements to give up weapons of mass destruction. In early summer of the following year, by the time the dust settled in Iraq and many Americans (plus a great many more Iraqi citizens) were dead or horribly wounded, it became clear that Iraq had no weapons of mass destruction to surrender—and that there had been some serious dissembling in the way the whole threat had been managed in order to provide warrant for war. Then the war in Iraq got seriously ugly and byzantine, packed with explosive stuff at every turn.

It was a very complex mess, yet the developments spotlighted by Maddow's *Drift* made it all possible, perhaps even inevitable, and not much has changed since. We have not yet recovered a mooring on our inclinations and abilities to go off to war whenever, wherever the spirit moves us. The war pattern is now all too easy and simple to execute. We have a deep repository of stories about Americans being ready to "acquiesce in the necessity" of war. They have been told and retold, and they are embedded deep in our culture. Do we have a moral compass that can, as a matter of balance, steer us away from war? Actually, no. Our moral compass heads us *toward* war.

On Good People Going to War: What Jonathan Haidt's *The Righteous Mind* Reveals

Rachel Maddow's approach in *Drift* presents a story of how tight control over war action on the part of the American people can be relaxed by degrees and thus be hard to notice; it simply becomes all too easy to get soldiers into conflicts far from home. We are not foolish like the folks who went off to Troy in Homer's *Iliad*, but still, we have seen a move toward relative facility and even sloppiness when we consider acts of war. It would seem we are not being sufficiently scrupulous; we are not paying close attention to what we're doing.

As we shall see later in the book, when we take up the way literary texts and films from the Afghanistan and Iraq wars have been mostly ignored by Americans, the pattern of not taking much interest in war extends way beyond the territory Maddox addresses. We are not really inclined to pay much attention to war. We will have thousands and thousands of horribly wounded and devastated war veterans in our midst for decades, but even as one of them commits suicide every seventy minutes, our culture will not take notice. We are thus quite akin to all the people through the ages who did not fully grasp the implications of war presented by Homer's narratives long ago—or by countless subsequent narratives from wars right up to the present.

This viewpoint is reinforced in a rather different way by Jonathan Haidt's fascinating study of the moral foundations that provide impetus for a wide range of public initiatives, including the business of waging war. Haidt has mostly been a liberal in his outlook on life, but in *The Righteous Mind* he takes a very nonjudgmental view of people on the right and left ends of the political spectrum. Maybe we do know, in some part of our being, that war ravages everyone who is joined to it, but something in our gut reading of the world makes all of this justifiable. Things that are repeatedly justifiable in a collective calculation are likely to be taken for granted over time. Norms are hard to change. Some things are readily deemed necessary, for good gut reasons, and Haidt shows how this process operates.

Haidt's work is carefully done, and his findings are always full of nuance, but in sum, he finds that there are essentially six strands of thinking/feeling that produce the positions we hold to be good in all realms of life. These strands are "Moral Foundations" in Haidt's analysis, and people on the conservative side warm particularly to four of the six; liberals are keen mostly on two. Four is more than two, hence the traction discernible on the conservative side in our political arena.

The six moral foundations are as follows: 1) care/harm; 2) liberty/oppression; 3) fairness/cheating; 4) loyalty/betrayal; 5) authority/subversion; 6) sanctity/degradation. If these six positions were all listed on one line, the liberal side would be on the left, with conservatives over on the right. Liberals would be most concerned about numbers 1 and 2; conservatives would be interested most in numbers 3, 4, 5, and 6, although there are ways to wrap numbers 1 and 2 in the conservative bundle, and this comprehensive approach can be seen in the way war is experienced within American culture. Liberals would be likely to see war as a threat to the participants—on all sides; the care/harm moral foundation would be engaged deeply by those on the left. However, there is also a conservative concern for care/harm, but it can be addressed simply by showing steady and strong support for soldiers. How does this work?

As an example to illustrate this point, when the battles in Iraq and Afghanistan were ongoing, a group of compassionate and dedicated patriots in West Chester, Pennsylvania, would meet on occasion in front of the Chester County courthouse at the corner of Main and Market. They proudly carried "Support the Troops" signs, and they asked drivers to beep their horns in support of the troops. This activity counts in Haidt's formulation as evidence of the care/harm moral foundation. And then there is the "care" message-on-the-move approach. If you put a "Support the Troops" bumper sticker on your SUV, you are showing that you care about soldiers and want to give them strong backing for the tough jobs they assume in going to war for everyone's benefit. Liberals are already committed by nature to moral foundation #1, so they are not going to act in ways that would harm veterans (although that was often the case back in the Vietnam era).

If war action can be presented clearly as warranted under moral foundation #2, resonating with its deep concern for the ideal of liberty (and its rejection of oppression), then both liberals and conservatives are going to be in agreement. Once the "acquiesce in the necessity" point has been reached and passed, and American forces are moving into combat, all the remaining moral foundations in Haidt's presentation are essentially lined up most forcefully on the conservative side, although depending on the war situation, the overall picture could vary. For example, in the early days in Afghanistan, the effort to topple the Taliban and capture bin Laden had most Americans lined up in support of war across the entire Moral Foundations spread; in Iraq, however, the four foundations on the right did not generate much enthusiasm from liberals, whereas conservatives took them up with vigor. For conservatives, once commitment to war is made, loyalty to authority is paramount, and the whole undertaking is accorded a kind of sanctity by virtue of American ideals about freedom and liberty. Try to go up against these forces, and you are seen as betraying America—a dangerous subversive, degrading the lofty goals of America.

Every war in American history has seen some protest activity, even World War II. We tend to ignore those who speak up against war. A fine collection from Murray Polner and Thomas Woods, *We Who Dared to Say No to War: American Antiwar Writing from 1812 to Now* (2008), sought to bring the dissenters back into our memory system. There are well-known names—Daniel Webster and Henry Clay, Jane Addams and Robert M. La Follette, George McGovern and Philip Berrigan—as well as some that would not be so readily recognized. Yet they all spoke up against war. When America is at war, it takes inordinate courage to stand up against the will of the nation. While some few consistently spoke against war, a great many found it impossible to follow those voices.

Tim O'Brien spoke directly to this problem in his Vietnam memoir, *If I Die in a Combat Zone, Box Me Up and Ship Me Home*. The early chapters of the book account for his internal debate about going to fight in Vietnam. Intellectually and morally, he saw the war as wrong, so he should not enter it. His reading convinced him he should resist serving. However, if he chose to reject the war, and to leave military service as a deserter, he would break all ties to his past, and he would face the rest of life as an exile from his country of origin. He yielded. He acquiesced. He took the path to war. And for thirty years his subsequent books all show the lasting dark effects of submitting to the force of necessity in going to war.

In time of war, the wagons are circled, and the four foundations on the right weigh especially heavy on all. To stake out an independent position means challenging the authority of government and military, betraying loyalty to country, despoiling the sanctity of American ideals regarding liberty and freedom (yes, with plenty of irony caught up in the process), and showing a selfish inclination toward cheating by not assuming the responsibility for service borne by others. This pattern puts the war protestor on the low ground, a position that often draws hostile attacks from those who have acquiesced in the necessity of war.

At this point, perhaps we should think back, for a moment, to recall Plato's concerns about the possible effect of Homer's battlefield details in order to see how they line up with the moral foundations. Most obviously and directly, Plato did not want guardians to be deterred from readiness to defend liberty—but #2 would take care of that problem, immediately positing the crucial importance of liberty, which appeals to all across the liberal/conservative spectrum. Furthermore, as Haidt summarizes the force of points on the conservative side, the patterns of the past are widely represented in the way we sort out our obligations in the present era: "Humans construct moral communities out of shared norms, institutions, and gods that, even in the twenty-first century, they fight, kill, and die to defend" (207). It seems that little changes over time. Let the narratives of suffering in war pile up over the millennia, but they are always to be outweighed by other moral foundation positions. At times, they count for naught.

Before moving on to a brief exploration of Charles Duhigg's *The Power of Habit* to see what it can add to Maddow and Haidt in helping us understand how our culture goes to war so easily—and why we pay such scant attention to the brutal human consequences of war—I think that taking a very brief look at Ronald Reagan with regard to moral foundations could be useful. As noted above, conservatives are rather keen on the four moral foundations to the right side of Haidt's paradigm, and Reagan was most at home in this territory. Again and again, Reagan told a simple story like the one involving his drive along the Pacific Coast, and America mostly followed his lead. America was great. America was special. America led the way to freedom for all people. Great Americans knew the importance of sacrifice. Good Americans were brave. Americans would be ready to fight when necessary. America was, in a word, exceptional (more about this in the next section). Ronald Reagan's simple stories and simple slogans ran vigorously and enthusiastically throughout all six of Haidt's Moral Foundations during his two terms of office, and as a consequence, throughout the years after Reagan left public office, it has been much easier to crank up support for war.

When War Becomes a Habit: What Charles Duhigg's *The Power of Habit* Confirms about America's War Pattern

It was clear from Maddow's *Drift* that a pattern has been developing over the past several decades; in that time, America has been at war a good deal, in various places, for varying reasons, but always within the guidelines of "acquiesce in the necessity" phrasing from the Declaration of Independence. America runs on words. Language is our everything. In this regard, America is unique. Language can provide amazing strength of purpose and resolve, but as we shall see, dependence on words and stories can pose grave risks. For example, stories from the past set the stage for action in the future, a pattern that can turn both positive and negative in terms of consequences. Ronald Reagan sent forth the language of American greatness in simple and easy-to-grasp phrases and stories. The wake of Reagan's presidency carried with it a strong "can-do" spirit. Defense contractors ambitiously prepared to provide instant support in the case of war. Technology has added steadily to American war readiness, always providing new tools with which to pursue missions and engage enemies. Congressional oversight with regard to war still exists, but from the 1980s onward, the whole approach has moved into a pattern whereby if there is some sort of United Nations concern, Congress will allow the president to act with military force to protect American interests. So off to war we go.

Putting all of these pieces together, what do we have? I suggest that America now has a well-defined and deeply ingrained habit of war. The collective depth of American experience with war all the way back to our origins was vigorously embraced by Reagan and then reinforced by every president since, although it was most aggressively and expansively pushed during the years of the George W. Bush presidency; this activity all points to the need to "acquiesce in the necessity" of war. President Obama did virtually nothing to constrain the war impulse, especially with the advent of drone warfare. The military—all volunteer professionals, constantly training and reinforced by Active Reserves and National Guard forces—has proved ready to act steadfastly and capably in war. Advanced weaponry, particularly the weapons available for manned aircraft or drone delivery, makes possible warlike action in many places simultaneously (in Yemen, in Pakistan, in Somalia, in Libya, in Afghanistan, in Iraq—once again in 2014 and still continuing); this part of the package operates mostly in the realm of secrecy where things happen but are supposed to remain hidden from common knowledge. Defense contractors have shown innovative ways to provide for needs driven by war, and a huge industry depends, as a consequence, on American ability to go to war.

Duhigg's book explores a wide range of situations where action is a function of habit, and habit is driven by a cycle that starts from a cue, develops into a routine, and results in a reward. The pattern is straightforward: CUE/ROUTINE/REWARD. Whether examining a personal, individual habit (going to the cafeteria at 3:30 every day to get a chocolate chip cookie) or an institutional habit (an operating room protocol at Rhode Island Hospital that privileged doctors over everyone else and put patients at risk), Duhigg always employs the cue/routine/reward paradigm to find, or to explain, a solution. Perhaps applying this paradigm to America at war could open up some useful insights.

First, we need to review the pattern of war for Americans, from the Revolutionary War right up through the war in Afghanistan. I am inclined to see the pattern as rather like the situations addressed as habits in Duhigg's book. In the 242 years between 1775 and 2017, America was involved in forty-eight wars with combat casualties over ten; a large number involved conflicts with Native Americans and were almost constant through the eighteenth and nineteenth centuries. Of late, the battle with Native Americans has taken a surprising turn, for in 2011, some 240 tribes operated 460 gambling operations, with total revenue reaching $27 billion. The losers have become huge winners.[2]

However, just considering the traditional wars involving combat deaths and in terms of pure average, America has had a war every five years. There have been only eighty-six years in which we were not at war with some enemy that involved combat casualties. Even if we narrow our focus on the large war events—Revolutionary War, War of 1812, Mexican War, Civil War, Spanish-American War (which entailed more than a decade of ugly civil war in the Philippines), World War I, World War II, Korean War, Vietnam War, Gulf War I, Afghanistan War, Iraq War (these last two are often grouped as the War on Terror)—there's still a war, on average, every twenty years. And these conflicts definitely rose to a level requiring review against the "acquiesce in the necessity" standard of the Declaration of Independence. To me, the pattern begins to look like a habit.

As we mull over the past record and ponder future implications, we need to zero in on the cue/routine/reward sequence. For war, there obviously needs to be a threat as a cue. The world is a tough place, with ferocious international competition over space, resources, and ideologies. Given the complexity of all this competitiveness, it is no wonder at all that America would face frequent challenges, often rising to direct threat levels. For example, the surprise attacks on the World Trade Center and the Pentagon in 2001 resulted from ideological conflict. The American way of life presents potent danger to harshly conservative, traditionalist societies; the idea of everyone having religious freedom (including the freedom to believe or not to believe), economic freedom, social freedom and justice, and artistic freedom is appalling in some parts of the world. The group associated with Osama bin Laden felt threatened—and struck a brutal blow.

The war cue was there, and America went through the "acquiesce in the necessity" routine to determine a response. War ensued and it was not long before the Taliban in Afghanistan (bin Laden's host) were in defeat and bin Laden was in retreat to the Pakistan/Afghanistan border mountains. The reward was partial—in seeing American force rout the Taliban; it provided confirmation of American military power. But more importantly, on a deeper level, the initial result of the battle in Afghanistan seems to show the supremacy of the American way. If we were looking for confirmation that America (and its ideals) was exceptional—superior to all challenge—the early period of the Afghanistan conflict provided heartening rewards.

The same could be said for the early results in the Iraq War in 2003. In a little over a month, American military forces (with assistance mostly from the British) pushed aggressively from Kuwait to Baghdad, the Iraqi government and its military were destroyed, and Saddam Hussein was in hiding. America had brought freedom to another part of the world, and it was heartening, for a brief period, to see the reward for American exceptionalism. Everything America is supposed to stand for, in all of our stories and at the center of our mythology, was happily presented for adoption by the people of Iraq. This sort of exhilarating liberation had been witnessed before at the end of battle—in both Germany and Japan at the conclusion to World War II.

Oh, if only the world of the twenty-first century were so simple. America loves simple, but both Afghanistan and Iraq proved to be complex. Just as in Vietnam, internecine conflicts between rival groups soon erupted, and a kind of defeat was snatched right from the jaws of victory. A bloodbath of Sunni/Shia retributions ensued, with American forces caught right in the middle of a battle that was very difficult on many fronts. The enemy was forever elusive and unclear. Americans had plenty of airpower, superb medical trauma units were never more than a few minutes away from any wounded American, and units on the ground were at length (after many deaths and horrible wounds) sufficiently equipped with the heavily armored vehicles required to diminish the effects of IED explosions. But civil wars are monstrously ugly, as has been noted previously, and plenty of civilians were caught in the crossfire; most American soldiers were thus witness to ghastly scenes of mayhem before they could rotate out. Language was a barrier. Culture was a bafflement. American commanders learned to drink tea with their Iraq or Afghanistan allies, and enormous amounts of American money was poured into reconstruction projects and efforts to bring local living conditions up to American standards. Yet even as good things were built, so were they blown up. Everything required three pictures: one to show how bad it was, one to show how great the improvement looked, and one to show the destruction after attack by insurgents. In a cycle like that, it's hard to concentrate on the reward part of the habit pattern.

However, going into battle—in Afghanistan and in Iraq—looked positive, at least through the innocent view Americans are wont to take of the world. America represents, as Lincoln declared at the end of his annual message to Congress on 1 Dec. 1862, "the last best hope of earth." Nearly a year later, at Gettysburg, Lincoln would offer mighty inspiration in the face of horrible death by noting "that this nation, under God, shall have a new birth of freedom—and that government of the people, by the people, for the people, shall not perish from the earth." Those are big words; they pack enormous power; and they summon allegiance through the ages. A nation so conceived and so tested must be extraordinary, must be exceptional— and as such, the American people bear on their shoulders every day the weight of responsibility for propelling their nation and its ideals forever forward against any foe, in any time. The reward of war is just this: a chance to show that the past is respected and that every sacrifice in history is carried forward into the future.

When would such a reward look particularly attractive? Perhaps our imaginations can help. Imagine a nation facing unbelievably complex economic circumstances, in a fiercely competitive global marketplace. Imagine steadily dwindling natural resources to heat, feed, and transport a population growing more needy and desperate every year. Imagine a nation unable to balance its wants with prudent concern for impact on the fragile atmosphere of the planet. Imagine unrelenting internal strife over the place of religion, the place of women, the place of homosexuals in American life. Imagine individual wants threatening to tear the thin fabric of community. Imagine that every year more Americans slip closer to poverty. Imagine most families needing two full incomes to have even a marginal chance of staying in the "middle" class. Imagine the cost of higher education stretching beyond the reach of most people—except through assumption of huge, crippling debt. Imagine half the nation wanting a strong, compassionate government . . . and half the nation wanting a weak, do-as-little-as-possible-and-we-must-eliminate-most-taxes government. Imagine politicians caught in endless and fruitless battles drawn on ideological lines.

Given that Americans have the most freedom in the world . . . as well as "certain unalienable Rights, that among these are Life, Liberty and the pursuit of happiness," then it would be good, once in a while, to enjoy the satisfaction of standing up for such valuable ideals—to have demonstrable proof that the American way is good . . . exceptionally good. Some distinct reward would be in order.

This line of thought is headed straight into the heart of American irony. America essentially wrote the modern Book of Irony. Here's a people prizing freedom while enslaving others. Valuing equality while preventing women from having equal rights. Protecting religious freedom while expecting all to swear allegiance "under God." Demanding individual pursuit of happiness while expecting service to the common good. The ironies go on and on and on. One of the great books I encountered early in my college education was *The Irony of American History* (1952), by Reinhold Niebuhr. The urgency behind Niebuhr's public lectures, gathered to make the book, was driven primarily by the dark threat posed by the cold war. In Vietnam in the 1960s, a trenchant irony was key to the observation "We destroyed the village to save it." Back in the nightmarish days early in the cold war, there was always the possibility of "We destroyed the world to save it," and Niebuhr's book presents a strong caution to Americans not to push ideology too far and go over the precipice of nuclear holocaust. Irony could be devastating, a terrifying killer of humankind. Niebuhr argued for humility.

However, humility may not be very satisfying for most folks. A bigger reward for the good of being American is needed. In the form of war, a great reward is in the offing, obviously attended by much irony. If you go into war, and best your enemy, the result proves the worth of your values. America wins; America is good. The proof is there for all to see, and for a while at least, the troublesome faults all along the home front can be pushed into the background. War draws attention away from internal problems—at least as long as the war can be managed in a way unlike the situation of Vietnam in the tumultuous 1960s. Of course, if the war turns out poorly, as in the case of Vietnam (largely in the case of Iraq, and almost certainly in the case of Afghanistan once American troops are completely withdrawn and the Taliban rise again), American values are given quite a bitter smack-down.

With Vietnam, it meant that sooner or later, we would need a reward that satisfied—and it would come, most demonstrably, in Gulf War I. As President Bush declared at the time, in a Saturday address to the nation early in March of 1991, the "specter of Vietnam has been buried forever in the desert sands of the Arabian Peninsula,"[3] and America rejoiced in its reward. Who could not have predicted that if we were presented with another situation in the future, drawn to fit the "acquiesce in the necessity" requirement, we would again follow the cue, move through the routine, and look for the reward?

Earlier I mentioned a book by Chris Hedges, *War Is a Force That Gives Us Meaning.* For quite a long time, Hedges was a war junkie, a journalist who tasted the effect of battle fairly early and then had to keep going back for more. In the 1970s, 1980s, and 1990s, he was hunkered down wherever bullets were flying and the chance to be dinged in the crossfire was never far away. He ran on adrenaline. Hedges notes, "The seductiveness of violence, the fascination with the grotesque—the Bible calls it 'the lust of the eye'—the god-like empowerment over other human lives and the drug of war combine, like the ecstasy of erotic love, to let our senses command our bodies" (89). Much of his writing is focused on his personal experience with war, but the intoxication that caught him as an individual might spread out to catch the spiritual inclinations of a nation looking to confirm its exceptional standing. In this light, it's essentially a self-image issue on a collective basis.

Early in his book, Hedges addresses the practical uniting and sustaining function of war:

> War makes the world understandable, a black and white tableau of them and us. It suspends thought, especially self-critical thought. All bow before the supreme effort. We are one. Most of us willingly accept war as long as we can fold it into a belief system that paints the ensuing suffering as necessary for a higher good, for human beings seek not only happiness but also meaning. And tragically war is sometimes the most powerful way in human society to achieve meaning. (10)

A bit later, in the chapter "The Plague of Nationalism," Hedges looks at the larger picture from an American standpoint in history and puts the label of "Nationalist triumphalism" upon the spirit that swept America through the Reagan years and on into our own present time. This label serves well to encapsulate the points I've been making about the need to confirm the exceptional quality of America in some demonstrable way. The way would be war. From the vantage point of 2002, Hedges concluded, "The infection of nationalism now lies unchecked and blindly accepted in the march we make as a nation towards another war, one as ill-conceived as the war we lost in southeast Asia" (61). We then indeed plunged into Iraq, completely uninformed about the complex layers of potential conflict that could burst into flame once the tyranny of the Saddam Hussein years was put to an end. We expected a great reward, but the proliferation of insurgencies and bizarrely twisted patterns of violence dulled our satisfaction year after year.

Still, even as we await the final days of the Afghanistan War, and ISIS/ ISIL adds threatening challenges that seem to line up with the "acquiesce in the necessity" stipulation, conditions within America nevertheless show steady fragmentation impulses. The Constitutional Congress of 1787 produced a Constitution miraculously achieved by serious compromises—plus a deep anxiety about the ability of a people to rule themselves. The separation of powers into three parts represents this anxiety absolutely, and over the years, the three-way teeter-totter of our government puts everything on edge; these competitive forces are clearly represented in the Philadelphia Constitution Center display on the Congress, the president, and the Supreme Court; balance is impossible to maintain for long. Mere babes can accomplish balance on a playground seesaw, but adding a third point of balance has made sustained equilibrium impossible on the American home front.

In such a perilous state of being, it may not be long before yet another war looms as a necessity. Meanwhile, a strange gulf seems to have emerged between the American military and the American people. James Fallows has addressed this ironic twist in "The Tragedy of the American Military," noting that while Americans were thoroughly involved with their military forces in World War II, in the present day nothing like that pattern of connectedness is evident; Americans admire the military—but from a great distance, without careful or deep understanding. Against such a backdrop, it is small wonder that Americans show little interest in exposing themselves to the dark complications of combat situations that are brought to light in the creative nonfiction, poetry, film, and fiction from the wars in Afghanistan and Iraq. Plato's concerns about the negative impact of Homer's war stories have long since proved to be completely groundless. In American culture, with war as a very frequent experience, we have found no deterrent force in the imaginative renderings of combat and the long-term consequences of battle experience. Instead of looking hard and deep into the morass of war, we would much rather wander off into fantasyland. Fantasyland, American style, will be explored in depth in the conclusion of this study. Before that, however, we need to get inside the experience of war in Afghanistan and Iraq, insofar as it is possible for anyone who did not go there in a combat role—and to bring these wars to vivid life, nothing can serve better than the imaginative responses that have come in memoirs and other creative nonfiction accounts, in films, in poems, in novels and short stories.

Exploration of the creative work dealing with the most recent American war efforts was wonderfully initiated by Stacey Peebles in her 2011 study *Welcome to the Suck: Narrating the American Soldier's Experience in Iraq*. Peebles develops a clear, vigorous, admirably perceptive focus on a select number of works from the Iraq conflict, and yet she also is adept at placing these representative efforts against a broader background of war literature. She astutely notes the remarkable presence of personal communications technology in combat zones—computers available in base camps, smart-phones carried into combat—even available for calls home during actual fighting as seen in the film version of *American Sniper*. Her second chapter, "Making a Military Man: Iraq, Gender, and the Failure of the Masculine Collective" is especially trenchant, a must-read for anyone looking to un-derstand the raw and ravaging inequities that underlie the contemporary American military force, with its admirable but terribly vexed mixing of genders in virtually all units sent off into combat zones. Peebles is superb in her reading of Kayla Williams's first memoir, *Love My Rifle More than You: Young and Female in the U.S. Army*, which will be examined later in the final consideration of the reception war literature and film meet in a culture obsessively concentrating on fantasyland impulses.

PART II

AMERICA'S RECENT WAR EXPERIENCE COMES HOME IN IMAGINATIVE TEXTS

The Efforts of Journalists and Writers of Creative Nonfiction to Deliver War for Readers at Home

Journalists and The First Try at Truth, Vietnam Background

In any country where truth matters and decisions about public policy depend upon it, journalists are vital elements in the process of truth discernment, and they carry a heavy burden of responsibility for the service they provide to citizens concerned with being knowledgeable and responsible in the discharge of their civic duties. Never has this obligation been more consequential than in the present time. For quite a long time now, it has been known that the managers of war—the political leaders, whether elected or thrust into power by some other means—have cause to conceal truth. This pattern of concealment creates a big challenge for those responsible for covering events, digging out the facts, and presenting the truth of a circumstance as accurately as possible in a world always complicated by human foibles. This challenge can be as daunting in a democracy as in less open and free systems of government. Good writers love challenge, and the impulse to serve democracy with lively, strong, and honest writing has propelled plenty of writers in the last half century to bring out the truth of war, no matter what the consequence.

When Emily Dickinson opened one of her great poems with the lines, "Tell all the Truth but tell it slant—Success in Circuit Lies" (248), she could have been providing spot-on direction for writers of fiction, but at the same time she was elucidating one of the most perilous challenges for journalists. Journalists are forever looking to get a story straight, to tell it without slant or deceptive circuit, and yet much of their information often comes from sources whose agenda is directed at getting the news out with a specific

bias. For reporters in time of war, this challenge becomes particularly vexing. Politicians managing the case for war on the civilian side—as well as
public information officers standing guard over on the military side of
war—know full well that the risks of spilling the truth are sometimes grave,
to be avoided at all costs. Truth winds up being caught in a crossfire of
purposes.

Just as the Vietnam War was coming to its ignominious end with the
collapse of the Republic of Vietnam in the spring of 1975, Phillip Knightley
brought out a superbly comprehensive examination of the work of journalists in service to truth from the middle of the nineteenth century right
up through the Vietnam War. Knightley's title, *The First Casualty—from
the Crimea to Vietnam: The War Correspondent as Hero, Propagandist, and
Myth Maker*, derives from a 1917 observation frequently attributed to Sen.
Hiram Johnson, of California, reflecting on the entry of the United States
into World War I: "The first casualty when war comes is truth" (epigraph,
Knightley, *The First Casualty*). One of the great values in Knightley's approach involves his presentation of the gradual evolution of the journalism profession, slowly backing away from getting caught up in either propaganda on behalf of the state or self-aggrandizement that would mostly
serve the image of the individual journalist as the centerpiece of the story.
By the time of Vietnam, the profession of journalism had matured—with
several distinguished schools of journalism well established, and concerted
efforts made to set standards to guarantee veracity in the work of reporting. Mainstream journalists, whether working in print or in broadcast media, had become mostly settled on serving the quest for truth objectively,
without bias.

However, even proceeding with such a noble goal in mind, the American
journalists in the era of Vietnam faced plenty of obstacles to finding out
exactly what was going on at any given stage of the war. Many of the dif-
ficulties involved some form of obfuscation or evasion on the part of government or military sources. A perfect case in point would be the efforts of
David Halberstam to root out truth while on assignment for the *New York
Times* in Vietnam from mid-1962 to late 1963; Halberstam went out into the
countryside and talked with plenty of sources far removed from the public
relations center in Saigon, and from these investigative excursions, he grew
increasingly certain that things were indeed not going very well. His reports
in this vein unnerved people at every level of the American military and political establishment right up to President Kennedy, who wanted the *Times*
to get Halberstam out of Vietnam. Halberstam later reviewed his struggle to

contend with a political and military bias that would have the world believe things were moving along successfully for the allies of America in Vietnam, and his comprehensive overview on the subject, *The Making of a Quagmire: America and Vietnam during the Kennedy Era*, appeared as a book in April 1965—just a few months prior to President Johnson's escalation of the war in the immediate aftermath of the Tonkin Gulf incident, which in itself was about as murky and impenetrable for journalists as an event could be.

When American forces poured into Vietnam, there was renewed hope that the tide of war would turn favorable. Over time, however, Halberstam's title gained traction and influence, first with other journalists who went out to remote firebases and operation zones to see for themselves what was actually happening in the field, and then with the American public at large, as sobering reports from the battlefields of Vietnam poured in day after day, year after year. By the end, despite the arduous efforts of military briefing officers and guarded politicians, the word that seemed to best capture the torturous experience of Vietnam for Americans was "quagmire," and for a few decades, quagmire was definitely a thing to avoid when war options unfolded.

Naturally enough, Americans generally wanted the Vietnam War to go well and end happily with a victory. Frequently, reporters did not deliver news pointing in that direction, and for quite a few Americans, this represented a failure on the part of the journalism profession. If only the reporters had written relentlessly positive stories, the result might have been quite different. From this angry perspective, it seemed that deficient journalists managed to frustrate or even possibly to deny the victory that would otherwise have been reachable. There was even some squabbling about this point in the world of journalism, and in some situations, the known circumstances could indeed have been interpreted in diverse ways.

Furthermore, it should be noted that a great many journalists who ventured with press credentials to "cover" the war in Vietnam went without any depth of knowledge about the place where they were headed. They were not schooled in the history of Southeast Asia; they knew virtually nothing about Vietnamese culture, on any level; they typically spoke only English. With very few exceptions, shallowness was the rule of the day.

Maybe they read Bernard Fall's *Hell in a Very Small Place: The Siege of Dien Bien Phu* (1966, reissued in a second edition in 1967 after Fall's death from a land mine while accompanying a unit of US Marines in Thua Thien Province), but while the French defeat at Dien Bien Phu in the early 1950s seemed ominous, it nevertheless made for shallow preparation on the part of American journalists. Still, despite the denunciations thrown against journalists for failure to hew to a patriotic line, anyone reading the last chapter of Knightley's *The First Casualty* could not honestly say the war was lost because of journalists. No indeed! The impossible circumstances of a long and very ugly civil war were primarily responsible for the ending that transpired in the mid-1970s.

Journalists covering that war sometimes managed to reflect deeper understanding of the whole context of combat in Vietnam than either military officials or politicians prosecuting the conflict, but having huge numbers of journalists present—and with open access to almost all regions of Vietnam and all units of US forces—was no certain guarantee that the truth could be known and reported well. The place was murky. The times were dark. The truth was elusive. For sure, simple was missing from the scene.

A couple of reporters proved exceptionally adept at reaching significant depth of perspective on the Vietnam War: Gloria Emerson and Michael Herr. Emerson had been in Vietnam in the mid-1950s, then returned in 1970 on assignment from the *New York Times* to develop stories about the Vietnamese—an unusual focus, to be sure, and one that would have been almost unthinkable in 1965. By 1970, as the war had moved from popular support in America to disapproval, the draft had been converted to a lottery system, and the process of creating an all-volunteer military had begun, the *Times* was ready to provide a detailed look at the people who had suffered most directly from the long war effort. In the first essay of Emerson's *Winners & Losers: Battles, Retreats, Gains, Losses and Ruins from the Vietnam War*, she acknowledges that for the longest time, American reporters had no way of understanding the ideas, feelings, and experiences of the enemy, whether the Viet Cong or the North Vietnamese army. Her approach, which actually included conversation with Viet Cong in Paris during the peace talks held there, came at the very end of the conflict. What if we had known at the outset as much as she discovered so close to the finish? If you understand only one side of a conflict, do you really understand it?

Gloria Emerson's book moves over the territory of Vietnam the way Emily Dickinson's poems circumscribe death—another deep and dark subject to plumb. The essays of *Winners & Losers* move in and out of interwoven layers of the conflict over many years, at one point focusing on American prisoners of war held captive in Hanoi, at another accounting for the night attack on a US Artillery firebase (with many American dead and wounded), and in yet another reflecting on the relationship between the Montagnards and the Green Berets. In a style steadily factual and carefully measured, her work draws in the feelings of veterans' families . . . the viewpoints of Senators McCarthy and McGovern . . . the roles of diverse academic experts across the political spectrum. Having one vantage point is absurd; a great many are required. Not much is left untouched by the time the last page is reached, and the picture of the Vietnam War provided by Gloria Emerson, taken as a whole, can only be described as intensely complex.

Much the same could be said of Michael Herr's reporting during a correspondent stint in Vietnam between 1967 and 1969 for *Esquire* magazine— material that became highly celebrated when it appeared in book form in 1977 as *Dispatches*. Herr knew Vietnam intimately; he had a great eye for detail and an incredibly fine-tuned ear for picking up revelatory argot from the full range of American types who wound up in the combat zone. Unlike Emerson's approach, where the prose is always under careful control, Herr's style runs on a turbocharged, hyperdrive energy that seems to mimic the crazy unpredictability of everything about the Vietnam experience. To feel the clashing contradictions from phrase to phrase in Herr's writing is to be in the moment, to be in Vietnam via linguistic transportation. Herr's writing was sometimes boosted by alcohol, sometimes by other systemic stimulants, but the greatest stimulant of all was Vietnam as Herr experienced it. His kinetic sentences rode the juice of the place as it ran through his body and out onto paper.

Herr's writing in *Dispatches* has been touted by many readers and reviewers as the best ever about war, and to date, he has almost no peers, at least in regard to the way a new journalist's writing style catches the flavor, the pulsing beat, the bizarro oxymoronic clashing that was spread everywhere over the Vietnam war zone. From the opening chapter, "Breathing In," to the final one, "Breathing Out," readers get to inhale all the imaginable fumes produced by napalm, terror, weed, regular shit, and regular Army bullshit. Quite a few writers of creative nonfiction accounts of war in Afghanistan and Iraq owe Herr a great credit for guidance on the need to listen closely to pick up the rhythms of hype and linguistic bravado that soldiers facing combat crank up on the way to do or die. Following the lead of Herr, our more recent writers have captured the jokes, the insults, the let's-rip-and-tear in language style, the I-don't-really-give-a-fuck attitude that builds in the tension of soldiers before the bullets start to fly. We thus get some unfiltered reality—in overdrive—but no one has consistently matched Herr's style in any war reporting since Vietnam. Some of the book blurb comments for Iraq or Afghanistan narratives mention kinship with Herr, but there is really nothing as a whole to match what he did. Herr stands alone.

Journalists were plentiful in Vietnam; they were everywhere, looking and listening and reporting. The print types filed cable dispatches; the broadcast television folks sent their tapes home for the evening news reports. The military managed to control very little of what was reported—apart from occasional circumstances like the effort to suppress any news escaping from the village of My Lai after the massacre there, or the Pentagon Papers material that was brought to light only after extensive paranoia-driven attempts by the military and political leadership to keep it suppressed behind closed doors and shuttered windows.

By the time it was evident that America had lost the war in Vietnam, it was equally clear to the American military leadership that much needed to be different in the way reporters would operate in future conflicts. And things went as planned; as we will shortly see, recent reporting protocols and circumstances of battlefield news coverage have been distinctly different from what was typical in Vietnam.

Fighters Turned Writers, in Creative Nonfiction—The Vietnam Models

Before delving into the journalistic/creative nonfiction writing from the wars in Afghanistan and Iraq, one more type of creative nonfiction must be introduced for consideration: the stories that come out when actual combatants put down weapons of death and pick up weapons of communication. By way of background, just a couple of examples from the Vietnam era will suffice to set up exploration of more recent fighters-turned-writers: Tim O'Brien and Philip Caputo. Both of these combat veterans brought out hugely powerful memoirs of the Vietnam War, and the power of their contribution to the memoir form helped propel this genre upward toward the prominent place it occupies in American letters early in the twenty-first century.

It should be noted here that the vast outpouring of texts (literary and cinematic, whether works of fiction or drawn from life experience in memoir form) that came out of the Vietnam experience began in earnest only after 1975. Particularly for veterans, it was imperative to wait until US soldiers were out of harm's way before going back in-country with either fiction or first-person narrative accounts. Very rarely did a book or movie take up the Vietnam experience until American troops had been removed from Vietnam.[1] In general, this restraint pattern has not been operative with regard to the most recent American war experiences. As the Iraq War effort staggered through years of divisive mayhem, memoirists, novelists, and even some moviemakers took up the challenge of representing this experience for the American public. Back in the Vietnam era, however, for the most part imaginative interrogation of the war had to wait for the finish.

Eventually the agony of combat in Vietnam drew to a close; American soldiers were back home, and the subject opened up to widespread exploration. Tim O'Brien is probably the most widely read and best known of the Vietnam writers, and O'Brien's career as a writer was launched by his memoir, *If I Die in a Combat Zone, Box Me Up and Ship Me Home*, in 1975, just as Vietnam slipped ignominiously into the loss column.

In the 1960s, as O'Brien finished his education at Macalester College in St. Paul, Minnesota, O'Brien's home state, the draft was still in operation, and draft boards often swooped in to pick up young men who had enjoyed years of college deferments. O'Brien was not a gung-ho patriot, although the place of his origin was certainly deeply steeped in Americana and patriotism. Baseball. Apple Pie. The Fourth of July.

But O'Brien had gone to college, read lots of books, done a good bit of independent thinking—and so when his draft notice came and he was inducted into service in the Army, he was not exactly the ideal soldier type. He was capable of being trained to do everything required by soldiers in an infantry unit, but he was also full of questions. Deep questions. He pondered the morality of the Vietnam War. If he went to a bad place, and participated in a bad war, might his soul be lost? He debated in his mind whether he should break away, leave the country. However, he knew that such a move would sunder him from his past, from his community, from his source of identity—and so he went off to Vietnam. All of this is accounted for in the early chapters of *If I Die in a Combat Zone*, and it makes good reading. The drama of a person in crisis is explosive, and O'Brien's case was replicated by many other soldiers caught up in the Vietnam mess.

All the way through his year of duty in Vietnam, O'Brien kept brooding about the implications of this experience for his life. His Americal Division unit patrolled in the vicinity of My Lai, where the massacre occurred; he knew firsthand the treacherousness of walking through that part of the country—the mines, booby traps, and ambushes that kept you on edge all the time. Searching tunnels was a nightmare. He faced the daunting ambiguity about the identity of the enemy—an enemy who could be a young kid, or an old woman. *If I Die in a Combat Zone* recounts all the details of danger and doubt spread over 365 days. The book opens with a chapter called "Days." It could be daze just as well—is meant to be so. It's hot. It's dull and boring—but then there's an explosion of uncertainty, an encounter where death is a close visitor, and thence back to the basic routine, one day after another, to reach the magic of 365. Finally, reaping the benefits of good luck, presto! You get on an airplane and cross the Pacific again. You see the flat expanses of Minnesota again. You descend to begin life after Vietnam.

The descent for Tim O'Brien would go on for roughly thirty years. After *If I Die*, he would often return to Vietnam in imagination, from *Going After Cacciato* (1978—probably his best work of fiction, and one in which he broke away from the Hemingway style of narration that served him so well in *If I Die*, allowing his mordant sense of humor to percolate along with the tunnel-searching deaths that define Vietnam for Cacciato's fellow soldiers), on through another powerful memoir (*The Things They Carried*, 1990) and finally to the bottom of bottoms, a novel called *In the Lake of the Woods* (1994), which ends in a super-cold whiteout at the northern border of Minnesota, with John Wade hurtling off toward abandoning his country, never to return, a point of departure that O'Brien himself never reached. He did not leave his country for Canada and Sweden in the 1960s; he did not succumb to death. He survived Vietnam and its long aftermath. His fighter-turned-writer stories have filled in a lot of otherwise blank space for a great many readers who have needed to know about the Vietnam War in the past four decades.

Philip Caputo was a Marine lieutenant in the mid-1960s when the American forces in Vietnam escalated and joined in the frustrating and sometimes deadly effort to root out the Viet Cong. Caputo joined a war of attrition—relentless patrols and skirmishes, plenty of booby-traps and snipers, almost never a definitive engagement that proved the power of the American military. Soldiers got wounded; soldiers died; survivors went home after a year, as Caputo did. Caputo's memoir, like O'Brien's, carries forward quite a few features of Hemingway's engagement with the subject of war in the 1920s and 1930s—as shown in the following reflection from his Pulitzer Prizewinning memoir, *Rumor of War* (1997), a passage that speaks to the nature of the "best" soldier type:

> Men with active imaginations were most prey to these fears. A man needs many things in war, but a strong imagination is not one of them. In Vietnam, the best soldiers were usually unimaginative men who did not feel afraid until there was obvious reason. But the rest of us suffered from a constant expectancy, feeling that something was about to happen, waiting for it to happen, wishing it would happen just so the tension would be relieved. (80)

Caputo obviously had an imagination—and it was caught in fascination with the experience of war. His combat tour ended in 1966, but he went back to Vietnam as a correspondent in 1975—and was one of the last Americans evacuated when the government in Saigon fell to the invasion from North Vietnam. He thus had an opportunity in a prologue and an epilogue to try to put the whole episode in perspective. The conclusion to his prologue piece will serve handily to bring to a close the Vietnam background exploration in this study, and to set up examination of the literature and film that has come from our most recent wars, a few decades after Vietnam:

> Finally, this book ought not to be regarded as a protest. Protest arises from a belief that one can change things or influence events. I am not egotistical enough to believe I can. Besides, it no longer seems necessary to register an objection to the war, because the war is over. We lost it, and no amount of objecting will resurrect the men who died, without redeeming anything, on calvaries like Hamburger Hill and the Rockpile.
>
> It might, perhaps, prevent the next generation from being crucified in the next war.
>
> But I don't think so. (xxi)

In 1977 Philip Caputo, Marine veteran of Vietnam and witness to the collapse of South Vietnam, was skeptical that his memoir would have any deterrent effect on future Americans when an "acquiesce in the necessity" moment arrived. In 2017 America is in the sixteenth year of a war in Afghanistan, with no final withdrawal projected now—and eerily distinct signs suggest that Afghanistan could sink just as South Vietnam did two years after American combat forces left. Not long ago, an eight-year war in Iraq concluded with an American pull-out, but incidents of sectarian clashes occur with jarring frequency, often in the form of bombings that kill civilians. It is not at all unthinkable that Iraq could slip into civil war at some point, although such a disaster was narrowly averted in 2014 when prime minister Nouri al-Maliki was eased out of power and replaced by Haidar al-Abadi, who looked to make the Iraqi government more inclusive of diverse sects. When fighters for the Islamic State of Iraq and Syria/Levant (ISIS/ISIL) captured large chunks of territory in Iraq in the summer of 2014, portending horrific violence to be directed at any country opposing its totalitarian operations, President Obama set about organizing a united military force to meet this challenge and protect Iraq. However, plenty of signs point toward a long-lasting conflict over the destiny of Iraq as a nation.

Each of these situations confirms Caputo's insight at the end of his prologue. The ugliness of war has been shown. The brutality of the Vietnam War was not hidden from Americans. Yet another generation has gone off to experience the devastating effects of war. And now there have been substantial additions to the work of O'Brien and Caputo and a host of other writers—not to mention filmmakers—in efforts to process and expose the raw truths of combat in Afghanistan and Iraq. But the pattern persists. The future is as clear today as it was in Caputo's vision from the last line of the passage above. The next generation of Americans will go off to war. For Americans, war is everlasting.

The Embedded Journalists—First Reports from the Wars in Afghanistan and Iraq

When the US military took stock of the Vietnam War experience, it was immediately clear that in future wars, there had to be greater control or at least influence over the way journalists covered day-by-day developments. In general, it would not work to just have regular briefings for reporters in secure rear-echelon locations—although for an extremely fast-moving assault such as the one in Gulf War I, when Iraqi military forces were driven back out of Kuwait in one hundred hours, this kind of control seemed both necessary and reasonable. For any longer-term operations, reporters and the American audience would expect more immediate and close-in coverage of action as it unfolded on the battlefield, wherever and whatever that might be.

In the initial stages of the 2001 US-led coalition attacks on the Taliban in Afghanistan, reporters were not provided with up-close observation of the assault, but as that situation soon settled into a long, drawn-out battle with the resurrected elements of anti-government forces (mostly grouped under the umbrella heading of *Taliban*), it became necessary to "embed" some reporters with American units. This process was extended to the invasion of Iraq in the spring of 2003, where a wide range of US military units accommodated reporters from diverse news organizations. The whole embedding situation has been vexed and controversial, for it carries with it potential for undue influence and pressure on journalists seeking to write the stories they want to tell, even when those stories do not line up with what the military would like to have going back to readers and viewers on the home front.

Over the course of events throughout the wars in Afghanistan and Iraq, there have been many times when journalists felt aggrieved at their lack of access to information and to scenes that could make great stories—and there have certainly been just as many times when the military has been disappointed with the stories journalists have chosen to send home to their audiences. Both sides have complained; it has been a very complex relationship. Furthermore, the stakes have been high for journalists working the dangerous territory of our recent wars; journalists in these wars have been treated as targets of opportunity—for capture or for killing. The number of journalists who have been killed in these wars is astounding.

If you were a journalist sitting in the backseat of a Humvee racing toward Baghdad, you had no special armor, no protection from enemy fire, no special shield. If you ventured out from your hotel in Baghdad to get a story with your driver/interpreter, you were a ready target, especially if you were a woman. The risks for reporters in Afghanistan and Iraq were particularly high and intense. Good stories came with life in the balance. The high rush of intense danger thus came to be part of the work of journalists in Afghanistan and Iraq, so it is no surprise that quite a few of them have suffered from PTSD; the return to normalcy after exiting the battle zone was by no means immediate. They too were subject to the pattern presented initially in Homer's *Odyssey*—but this time with the effects extending even to those who did not pull a trigger, did not see a life end at their hands.

When Philip D. Beidler brought out his groundbreaking study of Vietnam War literature in 1982, *American Literature and the Experience of Vietnam,* he did not have a specific section devoted to journalism, although Michael Herr's *Dispatches* is appropriately given a place of prominence for its estimable literary worth, particularly the invigorating style with which it addresses the subject of war in Herr's new-journalistic experience of it. Anyone interested in Vietnam War literature must read Beidler's book, for even as the book proves to be authoritative and rigorously analytical, the style moves along with a megavolt energy rarely witnessed in academic writing. There have been other rock-solid studies of Vietnam War writing, but none of them have matched Beidler's analysis for stylistic energy.

John Hellman's *American Myth and the Legacy of Vietnam* (1986), Thomas Myers's *Walking Point: American Narratives of Vietnam* (1988), and Milton Bates's *The Wars We Took to Vietnam: Cultural Conflict and Storytelling* (1996) all take the same approach adopted by Beidler, rarely if ever dealing with the world of journalism (except for the routine inclusion of Michael Herr as representative of New Journalism), concentrating instead on the contributions of fiction, memoir, poetry, and film as they seek to uncover important truths, myths, and myopias in the realm of the Vietnam War. Despite the great achievements in the study of war literature and film attributable to the books noted above, there are several reasons for taking a different approach in this study—for using the books of journalists as a starting point to lead into the realms of film and fiction and poetry.

First, the journalists provide a baseline of details about what happened in the field in both Afghanistan and Iraq. Whether occupying embedded positions or attempting independent activities by moving out of the "secure" areas of Kabul or Baghdad to find stories to send to their editors and broadcast supervisors, journalists have had good vantage points to see close-up the reality of war as it unfolded before them; they provide a kind of unfiltered or unrefracted vision of things to which filmmakers and fiction writers and poets would then bring imaginative refocusing techniques and storylines designed to show the human heart as deeply conflicted.

Second, while the journalists included in this study represent just a portion of all the reporting work done on the wars in Afghanistan and Iraq, they nevertheless provide a wealth of images that in their own right can serve to stand for the truth and the reality of those conflicts—and a few of them, particularly in the structure of the books produced, offer startling insight into the connections between war front and home front.

Third, as an extension of the war front/home front relationship issue, the journalistic (creative nonfiction) books have had no better luck than films or fictionalized stories in terms of reaching a broad audience at home. Fantasyland has proved to be a very difficult region to reach with substantive reflections of war, whether delivered straight from the journalists or reformulated through imagination in film and fiction. If there's a war going on, fantasyland would hear/see very little of it! That is to say, for the most part, Americans have employed a host of distractions to keep from attending too much to war and its consequences. The books about Iraq have been plentiful (fewer on Afghanistan), but from the American public they typically merit hardly a glance.

To get an overview of the writing that came out of the embedding experience for journalists assigned to cover our most recent wars, there is no better starting place than *Embedded: The Media at War in Iraq, an Oral History*, a collection assembled by Bill Katovsky and Timothy Carlson in 2003. Some sixty different journalistic perspectives are included, ranging across a broad spectrum of experience and circumstance: a few examples include Jim Axelrod (*CBS Evening News* correspondent), David Zucchino (*Los Angeles Times* staff writer, but earlier with the *Philadelphia Inquirer* for war coverage in Bosnia, Chechnya, Ethiopia, Libya, Angola, Mozambique, and Uganda), Matt Schofield (*Kansas City Star* staff writer—and carrying the Hemingway legacy forward into another century), Eric Westervelt (*National Public Radio* correspondent), and Evan Wright (*Rolling Stone* reporter, shortly to be scrutinized in detail). They are all strong writers—and the wars attracted many more like them, several of whom will be featured later in this chapter. They filed their immediate reports, which in the era of digital bits and bytes have no staying power unless some detail happens to kick up a few giga-notches and go viral in social media, but that did not happen to workaday reportage. Each report had its broadcast moment—or its publication date—and then faded into the ether.

This study does not attempt to sort out all the fractious problems involved in the way journalists looked to get good material for stories, nor does it hope to comprehensively cover all the fine writing that was generated by reporters covering the wars in Afghanistan and Iraq. Rather, it focuses on a representative sample of books that have come along after reporters left the world of combat and attempted to put their material into long-form stories. It seems to me that quite a few of these projects sensibly qualify as part of the literary realm. They tell gripping stories. They work with exact and explosive detail. They catch the rhythms and idioms of soldier talk. Their accounts drip with irony of various kinds. Their narrative structures are layered and nuanced. In sum, there has been plenty of imaginative book writing on the part of journalists who covered the action in Afghanistan and Iraq—more from Iraq because the territory was easier to cover, the embedding practice was widespread, and the battles produced more casualties, on a more regular basis.

The rest of this chapter and much of the following chapters on film, fiction, and poetry will skew mostly toward Iraq—but that said, we can start by looking at a book by a writer, Dexter Filkins, who seems to have been everywhere (another war junkie like Ernest Hemingway, like Chris Hedges, like Philip Caputo, all previously mentioned)—and whose title, *The Forever War*, commingles tightly with the initial subtitle of my study: "America and the Everlasting Wars." As a superb journalist, Filkins deals in painstaking accuracy with the details of what happened. I applaud him for what he does—but also look to push the implications behind his stories and into the future of America.

Filkins opens his book with an eyewitness account of the justice system imposed by the Taliban during their era of control in Afghanistan—in
1998—long before the 9/11 attack, long before the sixteen-year American effort to root out the Taliban, long before an American exit from Afghanistan
that would leave the Taliban still an active and threatening presence. The
scene is dramatic as it unfolds. The site is a soccer field, complete with loudspeakers to announce the event of the day: administration of Sharia justice.
A white Toyota Hilux drives up, with four hooded men and "a prisoner, no
hood" (13). The prisoner's hand is soon cut off and displayed to the crowd—
the traditional punishment for pickpockets. It proves to be the warm-up
act, and another Hilux arrives, maroon in color, with another prisoner, this
time blindfolded. Filkins slips in the detail here that the Hilux is a sure sign
of the Taliban—and "you could be sure something bad was going to happen" (14). This prisoner is a murderer; his case is quickly noted; his father
begs for mercy; the father of the murdered man refuses to consider anything but death, and the murdered victim's brother gets the AK-47 to do the
execution. One shot to the head—another to be sure. Revenge is complete.
Filkins has his story, and the Taliban have shown the world reached by the
New York Times how things work in Afghanistan.

This scene serves as a kind of echo to an event from the Vietnam War—
the Loan shooting during the 1968 Tet Offensive, which proved to be deeply
troubling to the American public. Here, too, is a revenge shooting. Another
prisoner falls to the ground after a shot to the head. The Loan shooting
came as a shock several years into major American involvement in Vietnam; in this instance, we register an equally shocking execution several
years *before* American involvement.

Of course, except for some reporting by Dexter Filkins and a few others,
Afghanistan was definitely not on the radar for Americans back in 1998.
Afghanistan was such an obscure place—and so far away from America, in
all respects. It was the time when the news was dominated by the Clinton
impeachment, a lurid but inconsequential sex scandal. For Republicans, the
fantasyland of that moment involved the tantalizing prospect of bringing
down President Clinton; for some others, it was just a juicy story of stains
on a dress. Interest in Afghanistan would have to wait until the attack of
September 11—and when the invasion of Afghanistan was initiated soon
afterwards, Americans were intent on getting the Taliban out of the country, for their quick and harsh justice system looked to be way out of line
with the more deliberate and decorous process employed in America to
deal with crime—the trial by peers, careful consideration of evidence, and

reflection on mitigating circumstances, all in the absence of Toyota pickup trucks and a soccer field with loudspeakers.

Yet ironically, America was quickly embarking on a revenge agenda comparable, on a larger scale, to the revenge execution that provides a starting point for *The Forever War.* The Taliban does revenge; America does revenge. And yes, the Vietnamese did revenge. Wherever you look, you see the same thing. When the scene turned to Iraq, Filkins saw a familiar pattern unfold: "Following Saddam's fall, Iraq became a theater of revenge, each murder inspiring another and then another" (77). If you look far enough back, you see plenty of revenge activity in *The Iliad* and The *Odyssey.* The surface of human life changes over the millennia, but the motives and actions vary not a whit as time passes. In every generation we manage to mire ourselves in misery.

But before Iraq became the dominant theater, Filkins had an opportunity to observe results from the American-led invasion of Afghanistan. He didn't travel with American troops. He was already there, already privy to the world of the Taliban and to their Northern Alliance enemies, who would soon have the satisfaction of victory. He really knows the players, for he has visited most of them, studied their operations, talked with them. He notes the amazing conversion of one major Taliban commander, Mullah Abdullah, who one day is commanding Talibs and the next day is rounding them up as prisoners for the Northern Alliance. A certain opportunism is clearly evident here, an ambiguity of motives and allegiances that would prove to be very daunting as Americans settled in and struggled to maintain control of the country. From one moment to the next, could you tell who was with you, who was against you?

And then, it was on to Iraq—for Americans and for Filkins. However, he was not embedded. He had his own transportation, a rented GMC Yukon, and as American forces pushed toward Baghdad, Filkins trailed along, stopping to pick up as much information from the Iraqi people as possible, looking for clues as to what might happen once the Saddam Hussein regime collapsed in full. His independence thus always provided him with a broader perspective than was possible for the reporters traveling right in the middle of US military units. He became aware, quickly enough, that the ambiguity and treacherousness in Afghanistan had its equal in Iraq, and the murkiness expanded dramatically when the tight control of Saddam's government evaporated. The following passage encapsulates the heart of the problem, and as it turned out, even Americans in Iraq clung to their own variety of fantasyland—an inability to connect with reality:

There were always two conversations in Iraq, the one the Iraqis were having with the Americans and the one they were having among themselves. The one the Iraqis were having with us—that was positive and predictable and boring, and it made the Americans happy because it made them think they were winning. And the Iraqis kept it up because it kept the money flowing, or because it bought them a little peace. The conversation they were having with each other was the one that really mattered, of course. That conversation was the chatter of a whole other world, a parallel reality, which sometimes unfolded right next to the Americans, even right in front of them. And we almost never saw it. (115)

This book has distinct literary standing, for it presents a fleshed-out, blown-up adaptation of Shakespeare's *King Lear*, with Americans in the title role—delusional, deceived, and very dangerous as a result. When any nation charges blindly into a war, tragedy is in the offing. In this regard, the Shakespeares of our day have plenty of fresh material to develop.

While Filkins could see clearly enough what was going on—and what was being missed by American officials, civilian and military alike—his knowledge did not translate into safety for him. He was, after all, an American, and he was a journalist; both identities made him a marked man. Between 1992 and 2011, some 151 journalists were killed in Iraq; several Americans are included in that number, along with quite a few Iraqis who served as interpreters for journalists. For example, in early August 2005, Steven Vincent, a freelance journalist, was abducted and shot to death in Basra—not long after filing a story with the *New York Times* alleging that the Basra police force had been infiltrated by Shiite militiamen. Jill Carroll, reporting for the *Christian Science Monitor* in Iraq, was kidnapped in Baghdad on 7 Jan. 2006; her case was covered intensely until her release from captivity on 30 March.

One day in 2005, as the murderous brutality of suicide bombing was escalating and the targeting of Americans was on the increase, Filkins had his own brush with mob violence. While bombs were going off all over Baghdad, Filkins and his team (driver, interpreter, photographers) went into Shaab, a poor Shiite neighborhood. Soon they were surrounded—with calls for their death. Filkins was grabbed , and he had a moment of panic before he was pulled away by Waleed, his driver, and they were able to escape with their lives. In Vietnam, correspondents were seen as potential helpers by the enemies of the South Vietnamese government, for they would send back stories of death and suffering . . . even of defeat; in Iraq, foreign journalists (and their Iraqi assistants) were just part of the enemy much of the time.

Filkins was undeterred by his brush with death. Soon he was off to Fallujah—this time shadowing Bravo Company, a Marine unit under the command of Captain Omohundro, in some of the ugliest street fighting in Iraq. Bravo Company would suffer heavy casualties in the Fallujah campaign, with roughly a quarter of its members dead or wounded. Enemy snipers took their toll. The uncertain conditions created fear that could cause even strong leaders to crack, but the sweep effort continued, day and night.

Of course, even on the move in a hostile environment, bodily eliminations are still necessary. Marines improvised. They carried cardboard boxes along with them to collect their shit; it was an imperfect solution. If they found toilets in the houses they searched, they filled them. Armies on the move have always faced the waste disposal problem, but in Iraq the story came into the foreground. As a footnote in the previous chapter indicated, Vonnegut's latrine scene in *Slaughterhouse-Five* had broached the issue; Bruce Weigl's poem "Burning Shit at An Khe" cleverly induces readers to understand the comprehensive meaning of the entire Vietnam experience in just one word—and anyone over five can figure out what that word is. Reporters on patrol with US soldiers in Iraq added some striking images and opened up the "War is shit" theme:

> Most days, though, traveling through the city, we just used somebody's bathroom. We'd break into their house and shit in their toilet until it overflowed and then we just used the floor. There'd be piles and piles of the stuff by the time we got going again. Shitting in the house of a person I'd never met—there were worse things that happened in Iraq every day. Still I didn't feel very good about it. (Filkins 196)

If, for all their good intentions, Americans left a certain stink in their wake as they campaigned for freedom across Iraq, Filkins provides a clear enough picture of how some part of it happened. The explicit image above has symbolic portent.

Before the Fallujah operation came to an end, leaving the city in ruins, Filkins was a close witness to a particularly gruesome death for an American soldier: Lance Corporal William Miller, from Pearland, Texas, who had pushed ahead of Filkins and his photographer, Ashley, as the unit searched a mosque for enemy snipers. Miller was shot going up the stairs to the top, his face blown open by the bullet. Miller's death weighs directly on Filkins and the photographer, for the Marine had gone in front of them to clear the way. Journalists were not above the scene; they were not safely detached. They were immersed—and they could get caught by war: "Your photographer needed a corpse for the newspaper, so you and a bunch of marines went out to get one. Then suddenly it's there, the warm liquid on your face, the death you've always avoided, smiling back at you like it knew all along. Your fault" (210).

All the way along, from Afghanistan to Iraq, Filkins continued to collect the baggage of experience in war. At a certain point, the close witness to war has so much invested that it is very difficult to move on, especially to return to an America that on so many levels was essentially disconnected from Iraq all along, another world, really:

> As much as I hated arriving, I hated leaving more. After so long I'd become part of the place, part of the despair, part of the death and the bad food and the heat and the sandy-colored brown of it. I felt I understood its complications and its paradoxes and even its humor, felt a jealous brotherhood with everyone who was trying to keep it from sinking even deeper. . . . And when the car hit the long flat stretch of airport road my stomach tightened, not from the danger of the place but from the anticipation. From the thought of leaving the world, the big, wise, only world, and moving to the next one. The two worlds. There was nothing in between, no way station, no purgatory, only this world and the other. (147)

Finally, though, Dexter Filkins had to leave for good. He confronts the indifference back home, especially notable as he connects with the families of some soldiers he had known in the war: "The soldiers and their wives and the moms and the dads: they wanted to talk. Maybe nobody else did but they did. Back in the world, there was a kind of underground conversation about Iraq and Afghanistan. Underground and underclass. The rest of the country didn't much care" (340). Filkins joined the conversation as a person from away—but a person with knowledge and interest in the effects of war. His story closes with a visit to the Miller family—whose son took a bullet that might have otherwise been his. They are glad to see him, although the family's hearty cheerfulness in the face of death is rather unsettling. He departs with some images of Billy impressed upon him by the Millers. He drives off in his car. Hence, this story of Iraq and Afghanistan comes to a muted close. No triumph. No parade. Instead, in the quietest way imaginable, there is the sense that the war will go on . . . and on . . . and on.

A more tightly focused war account resulted from Evan Wright's embedded experience with a Marine recon unit that was often in the vanguard of the push up from Kuwait to Baghdad at the outset of the war in Iraq. Wright was on assignment for *Rolling Stone* magazine, a fact that won him some quick points with the tussle-hungry, ready-for-action Marines he met in Kuwait a short while before the assault began. The title of his book, which became an HBO multipart series that put his work in front of many more people than read his book (a series of seven episodes in all, which premiered on 13 July 2008, long before American soldiers were withdrawn from Iraq), is in itself provocative and attention-grabbing: *Generation Kill: Devil Dogs, Iceman, Captain America and the New Face of American War.* The book itself was published in 2004, just a year after the action described in it took place during the first month of the war.

Wright was assigned to the First Reconnaissance Battalion (led by Lieutenant Colonel Ferrando), which was an elite element of the First Marine Division under the command of Maj. Gen. James Mattis. The combat unit with which Wright traveled was the Second Platoon of Bravo Company, led by 1st Lt. Nathaniel Fick. Fick would go on to write his own memoir, *One Bullet Away: The Making of a Marine Officer* (2006), to be discussed later in this chapter. The Humvee where Wright had a backseat view of the war was under the control of Sgt. Brad Colbert (the "Iceman" of the title).

To be in Recon is to be a super-Marine—extra training, extra-hard preparation, extra-refined combat skills, extra-extra attitude. The opening chapter of Wright's book, which introduces us to the Recon Marines, makes explicitly clear the guiding lights of these American fighting men. They are physically tough. The best of them are quick witted, as ready to tangle in word games and slogan battles as to blow up buildings and decimate their battlefield enemies. Testosterone levels are off the charts. Their verbal sparring can be deft and subtle at times, yet at the core of the Corps, everything becomes, at least before the first bullets are fired, explosively simple. To a person, they know they are there to kill, and no one wants to be left out of that action. They were not all born to kill, not exactly, but their training has burned this motive deep in their being. Wright goes right to this issue, just two pages into his account, while still in the Kuwaiti desert:

Later, when a pair of Cobra helicopter gunships thumped overhead, flying north, presumably on their way to battle, Marines pumped their fists in the air and screamed, "Yeah! Get some!"

Get some! is the unofficial Marine Corps cheer. It's shouted when a brother Marine is struggling to beat his personal best in a fitness run.

It punctuates stories told at night about getting laid in whorehouses in Thailand and Australia. It's the cry of exhilaration after firing a burst from a .50-caliber machine gun. *Get some!* expresses, in two simple words, the excitement, the fear, the feelings of power and the erotic-tinged thrill that come from confronting the extreme physical and emotional challenges posed by death, which is, of course, what war is all about. Nearly every Marine I've met is hoping this war with Iraq will be his chance to get some. (2)

It's simple. Americans love simple. Marines fight hard and they fuck hard. The prospect of killing gets them all hyped and hot. But more than a tinge of irony lurks ahead on the horizon. Right away, we meet Sgt. Colbert, the "Iceman," who is a techno-geek of the first order—a strikingly distinct individual, always the coolest one in the hottest firefight—and there he is, as Wright watches admiringly: "Colbert appears utterly calm. He leans out his window in front of me, methodically pumping grenades into nearby buildings with his rifle launcher" (3). So, simple is quickly complicated by an antitype. Here's a guy who is just extremely proficient at soldiering; he isn't getting an orgasmic charge out of the action; he merely does his job and does it consummately well.

Colbert will be at the center of quite a few scenes captured exceptionally well by Wright. Several scenes involve his bowel movements; it seems his concern for control and order extend to waste products from his body. He regularly queries his men about their eliminations—and he's careful to be as regular as possible with regard to his own. It's no easy matter to unload the bowels when driving relentlessly through hostile territory—with lots of gear and protective clothing to be unfastened before the dump can take place. Yes, it's all about taking a dump. On one occasion Sgt. Colbert just slips out of the Humvee to squat by the roadside in a momentary lull on the drive north. As accompaniment to this necessary act of nature, Corporal Person, Colbert's driver, sings Country Joe McDonald's Vietnam antiwar song, "I-Feel-Like-I'm-Fixin'-to-Die Rag." For the HBO version, Wright and others in that Humvee sing along, thus rendering everyday business extraordinarily unique. On an earlier occasion, Colbert returns to the vehicle after a particularly satisfying dump, with the remark "Shit my brains out" (81), a belated echo of Vonnegut's words from the latrine scene in *Slaughter-house-Five* where Billy Pilgrim comes upon a primitive field latrine packed with Americans who have a digestive malady that causes explosive diarrhea; Vonnegut's mordant humor goes into overdrive with the message posted on the facility: "PLEASE LEAVE THIS LATRINE AS TIDY AS YOU FOUND IT!" (125). Billy investigates further, which leads to one of the most audacious insertions ever of an author into text:

> An American near Billy wailed that he had excreted everything but his brains. Moments later he said, "There they go, there they go." He meant his brains.
>
> That was I. That was me. That was the author of this book. (125)

In terms of irony, however, almost nothing tops another roadside dump moment, just after the one by Colbert noted above. With Wright operating in full-truth-and-spare-no-details style, we have the Marines, America's finest fighting force, stopped for a brief respite on the race to topple Saddam's army and liberate the Iraqi people. The White House was making this effort into a crusade, a grand gesture to extend the freedoms of America to a nation suffering from oppression. The flags wave, patriotism swells; it's a magnificent adventure of heroic proportions. Against that background, here is the scene as observed and detailed by Wright:

> There is a cluster of mud-hut homes about thirty meters across from the platoon's position by the road. Old ladies in black robes and scarves stand in front of the homes, staring at the pale, white ass of a Marine. He's naked from the waist down, taking a dump in their front yard.
>
> A Marine on Espera's team who's helping him pick up the trash gestures toward this odd scene and says, "Can you imagine if this was reversed, and some army came into suburbia and was crapping in everyone's front lawns? It's fucking wild." (83)

In Vietnam one of the famous ironic expressions was "We destroyed the village in order to save it." And in Iraq we shit on the country to save it. It is an inglorious image, any way you look at it.

How much weight should we ascribe to these waste elimination episodes? First off, the "shit" moments of *Generation Kill* serve to set this narrative (and yes, even this war) apart from others. Gore aplenty was in *The Iliad*, but Homer didn't find occasion to zero in on routine bodily functions. Stephen Crane didn't bother to go there in *The Red Badge of Courage*. Hemingway passed on the option in all his war writing. As mentioned already, Vonnegut has his latrine scene in *Slaughterhouse-Five*, and Bruce Weigl makes sure we know that the shit scene in Vietnam was not pleasant.

But now, early in the twenty-first century, an embedded reporter is brought face to rear with a basic function in life. It could always be ignored, of course—pretend it never happened, keep the focus on other things, perhaps even more pleasant things. However, it seems clear to me that Wright intends for these particular details to make a point—and the point is ironic. America was in the Iraqi desert to attempt good, but in innumerable ways, at virtually every turn, something not very pleasant was always right there too. Before his story ends, with Recon 1 up in Baghdad, plenty more darkside ironies are presented for our consideration.

At the start, the American military goal was to engage and destroy the enemy, which was blithely assumed to be the army of Saddam Hussein's regime. However, Fick's platoon almost never finds any regular military units (large or small) to engage. Plenty of recent soldiers show up to surrender, in numbers far beyond the American resources available for dealing with prisoners of war. The dead are much easier to handle than the living. But the big surprise is quick to strike Fick's Marines. The absence of regular military forces does not mean that there's no resistance.

On the contrary, the landscape is treacherous, all the more so because it quickly becomes apparent that the real story of American military action in Iraq will involve guerilla tactics. Almost instantly there are insurgent forces in numbers sufficient to make the experience dangerous and deadly for the Marines. AK-47 bullets, mortar rounds, and rocket-propelled grenades are all soon bearing down on the unit with which Wright travels. There's no protective armor; the Humvees provide almost no safety when they are under fire. Not to worry. The "get some" Marines respond to incoming fire with a wide range of potent firepower at their disposal—which is great, especially when there's enough lubricant of the right kind to keep the turret-mounted MK-17 functioning, spewing out grenades at the rate of one per second—a very nice offensive resource to have when dashing through towns bristling with hostile elements.

As we read along, we come to know and admire the Marines who are hosting Evan Wright. His neck is as much as risk as theirs, so he has a very privileged position to capture the reality of combat in the first month of the Iraq War. The personalities of men in Fick's command are diverse, and some prove to be better under fire than others, although none close at hand proves to be incompetent. However, despite the rigorous training behind the Recon Marines in preparation for war, incompetence still manages to infiltrate the American forces. Two of Lt. Fick's fellow officers—his company commander (Capt. Craig Schwetje, derogatively called "Encino Man" by many in his command), and another platoon leader in the company (Capt. Dave McGraw, mockingly known as "Captain America" for his foolish bravado)—repeatedly commit dangerous errors that reveal how ill-suited they are for the positions of authority and responsibility they occupy. Military ineptness is not exactly a new story in the literature of war, but *Generation Kill* does not flinch in locating it within the American forces on the route to Baghdad.

The "get some" Marines prove more than able in war action. They get their kills—sometimes while racing down streets through towns along the way, sometimes in ambush at a bridge, sometimes taking down mortar spotters with deadly sniper shots. In those situations, where there is enemy fire being directed at them, with muzzle flashes and bullets pinging their Humvees, the rules of engagement are simple. Simple is good. They are trying to kill you. You try to kill them first. A chaplain, Navy Lieutenant Commander Bodley, is taken aback at the eagerness of Marines to do their main job: "'The zeal these young men have for killing surprises me,' Bodley admits. 'It instills in me a sense of disbelief and rage'" (183). To kill is good.

But here the Iraq War served up another irony. Sometimes the kill impulse wrought woeful consequences. Unfortunately, innocent civilians were all around, and inevitably they got in harm's way. The best rules of engagement (ROEs) are never good enough to safeguard noncombatants when the danger threshold is sky-high and judgments must be made in a flash. With insurgents hiding in plain sight as part of the population—then popping out to strike a quick blow before scuttling back under cover of the innocent—no amount of training or discipline can prevent civilian casualties. Bad stuff is bound to happen, and even in the first month of a war that would fester along for many years afterward, American forces met the dark downside of guerilla war—the scene when your bullets go out and find unwanted and unintended targets in women, old people, children. Wright's story details several horrible scenes involving children who are wounded or killed by American weapons. These sad encounters are the antithesis of simple.

One of the most poignant and gripping accidental shootings takes place as the Recon platoon raced to secure an airfield in the middle of the desert. Forging their way through the night, with darkness surrounding them, they expected the enemy to put up quite a fight to defend the airfield. Accordingly, the ROE changed—on orders of the battalion commander, Lt. Col. Ferrando. One company commander, Captain Peterson, decides not to pass this change along to his men—but Fick's team leaders hear the new orders, which involve treating everyone as an enemy—a target to take down. Sergeant Colbert makes it succinct: "You see anybody, shoot 'em!" (167).

Sure enough, Corporal Trombley sees activity in a village and fires his weapon in a couple of bursts. Wright sees only some camels running around like crazy. But the next day, after the airfield is secured without any enemy resistance, two women approach, one young, one old. They drag a blanket, and when they reach the Marines, a bloody body—a twelve-year-old boy—tumbles out, shot four times in the abdomen. The wounds came from Trombley's weapon, and he is devastated at the result of his war work. Fick and others hatch a plan to coerce Lieutenant Colonel Ferrando into giving the OK to medevac the boy to a field hospital. Trombley still feels the shock of horror at his action, but Sergeant Colbert insists on carrying the responsibility for what happened; he passed the order to shoot everybody. Colbert, the cool and dispassionate professional soldier, shares his thoughts with Wright:

> "I'm going to have to bring this home with me and live with it," he says. "A pilot doesn't go down and look at the civilians his bombs have hit. Artillerymen don't see the effects of what they do. But guys on the ground do. This is killing me inside." He walks off, privately inconsolable. (174)

If the "Iceman" is shaken to his core by this sort of experience, which would be repeated in many variations throughout the Iraq War, one can only imagine the long-term repercussions for less disciplined individuals. Moments like this have incredibly long lives; they haunt and taunt for years upon years. In this scene and others like it, Wright provides a clear glimpse of the future for American veterans of Iraq. For many of them, the war will go on far into the decades to come.

Filkins proved to be the consummate war junkie, for many years hooked on the adrenaline rush of being in dangerous places. As much as an American can, he came to know the inside of Afghanistan and then moved along to Iraq to inhale and ingest as much as possible from that conflict zone. He survived and, not surprisingly, in February 2013, had a piece called "After Syria" published in the *New Yorker*—a bit of reportage trying to sort out the implications of the civil war in Syria as they would play out in Lebanon. War is simply his bread and butter, his thing. He will always have a war to cover.

Wright's experience is less wide-ranging, but his account of Recon 1 on the route from Kuwait to Baghdad is packed with telling details. It's a gripping story, full of eccentric characters and loaded with enough scary moments to make for easy migration to the HBO environment. Any reader heaping Wright on top of Filkins would have plenty of insights about the war in Iraq. Is there anything more to consider?

Yes, indeed. Our experience in Iraq has produced a steady stream of book accounts. While they converge on one or two points, they diverge in points of view and also structural devices employed to deliver the stories they contain. A quick analysis of ten very different books should show the range of literature that has boiled to the surface of the cauldron in Iraq.

Fighters Turned Writers, Iraq

Nathaniel Fick's first-person account, *One Bullet Away: The Making of a Marine Officer*, will serve handily to lead off the texts being analyzed. And to understand his story, we need to know a little about the recruitment strategies of the US armed forces.

In order to maintain the all-volunteer military forces (the standard operating mode for all branches of service since the turn away from a draft as the Vietnam War drew to a close) recruiters have often met their monthly quotas by appealing to men and women far down on the socioeconomic scale. The recruiters show up at high schools often in marginal communities—always ready to offer cash incentives for joining military service. To young people living close to the poverty line, whether technically above or below it, a flash of cash has lots of appeal. It's a way out, a means to self-improvement, a chance for a better life.

This approach—looking to simultaneously address the problem of poverty and maintain the necessary level of military forces—had been tried before, with very mixed results, in "Project 100,000," which Defense Secretary Robert S. McNamara created in October 1966 to help maintain the military force levels needed to prosecute the Vietnam War. Residents of inner-city ghettos were targeted, along with young men in other known areas of hard poverty, such as Appalachia. Recruitment standards were adjusted downward as necessary to reach goals of the program. By the time the program was discontinued in 1971, it had brought roughly one-third of a million soldiers into service. Many found that the road to a better life ran through Vietnam. Studies of the program have indicated that on many counts, it was not very successful. Desertion rates were high, as recruits discerned that promises of a better life didn't measure up well to the realities of combat in Vietnam. Veterans of this program statistically wound up worse off than nonveterans from the same demographic backgrounds.

However, as the Iraq War dragged on—and despite the use of National Guard and Army Reserve units to help cover military force needs with tours abroad (something which had not been part of the situation in the Vietnam era)—recruitment goals proved a serious challenge; and, as already noted, key target areas involved locations with low incomes and high unemployment. That said, the military also continued to attract people from much higher positions in American culture. Nathaniel Fick represents this alternative service pattern well. His background was comfortably middle class, and he was drawn to military service in his years as an Ivy League student at Dartmouth. He did not have to serve to make ends meet; great promise awaited him upon graduation. But he felt the call of duty, felt the lure of testing himself against brutally tough challenges, the sort of thing that would make any college exam seem like a walk in a park, with the sun shining, flowers in bloom, just a gentle breeze moving leaves on the trees by the brick walkway. That easy!

The early part of Fick's story takes us through the rigors of Marine Corps officer training. Imagine the first part of *Full Metal Jacket* ramped up a hundredfold in terms of physical difficulty and challenges to both stamina and character. Fick would eventually opt for Recon assignment, which involved still harder training. Suffice to say, anyone passing through all the staggering physical conditioning and the equally rough mental disciplining should be a match for any challenges combat can produce. The reservoirs of confidence and skill are deep; the buy-in to the Marine Corps spirit is total. As a result, all the socioeconomic differences bleed together and become non-issues. When Fick's unit is inserted in Afghanistan and has to make an insanely long and difficult walk to a new combat location, carrying the huge weight of equipment all the way, he has a flash of insight about how all the shared training transcends demographic background:

> Now, as I had at OCS, I sensed an outpouring of grit, pride, and raw desire to live up to the traditions we'd inherited. These Marines came from places like Erie and Tuscaloosa and Bedford Falls. The most junior of them earned nine hundred dollars a month. Some had joined the Corps for adventure, others for a steady pay check or to stay out of jail. Now they all kept walking for one another. (133)

Back in the United States after his brief posting to Afghanistan, Fick experienced feelings of disorientation regarding the way folks at home wanted to engage the war only in generic, patriotic terms—not in reality. In terms of this present study, Fick met the fantasyland phenomenon and was dispirited by it:

> I saw mourning and sorrow, but also bluster, posturing. People vowed not to interrupt their daily routines, not to let "them" destroy our way of life. My time in Afghanistan hadn't been traumatic. I hadn't killed anyone, and no one had come all that close to killing me. But jingoism, however mild, rang hollow. Flag-waving, tough talk, a yellow ribbon on every bumper, I didn't see any real interest in understanding the war on the ground. No one acknowledged that the fight would be long and dirty, and that maybe the enemy had courage and ideals, too. When people learned I had just come from Afghanistan, they grew quiet and deferential. But they seemed disappointed that I didn't share in the general bloodlust. (143)

In innumerable stories, veterans meet a strange disconnect on the part of citizens who are not linked to the wars in Iraq or Afghanistan by blood relations. The veterans understand the wars one way, typically free of sweeping political or ideological points of reference, with memories loaded to the gills with scenes of action (or inaction), often grim (but not always), all of which, in retrospect, don't add up to much of anything except deeply shared experiences with other veterans. Homeland citizens grab on to grandiose patriotic slogans and concepts that are often quite at odds with the realities known to soldiers. There is very little of the outright hostility displayed toward veterans coming back from Vietnam, but there's still a colossal gulf between what the veteran carries for knowledge and the notions borne by people at home.

When Fick's unit moves to Iraq, they finally have opportunities to engage enemy forces in combat, and the same close connectedness observed above binds the men of his platoon together tightly. As long as they are on a mission in Iraq, whether dealing directly with hostile forces or just contending with the physical miseries of desert warfare, they are strong and united in their shared experience. They meld together as one.

Three quarters of the way through Fick's narrative, which concludes with his platoon settled in for patrol duty in Baghdad, the platoon is ambushed at a bridge crossing, and a firefight lasts for most of the night. An inspection of the dead insurgents the next day reveals a surprise, a twist that would link up with other twists to bedevil and confound the American presence in Iraq right through to the final withdrawal. Who were the men who had ambushed Fick's men? As it turns out, they carried Syrian passports, with visas stamped for entry to Iraq during the first week of the war, not long before they died at the hands of Fick's platoon. Because Americans were fighting in Iraq, Syrians had come to kill them. Eventually, the war would produce a wide range of enemy forces, often united solely in the desire to rid the country of Americans.

Fick's story was published in 2005, and as a relatively early firsthand account of the Iraq War, it enjoyed brisk sales upon publication; the war was, at that time, getting more bloody and complicated year by year. Civil wars are never simple. America went to Iraq looking to find simple. It was not to be. As the war dragged on, interest on the home front waned, and books that came after Fick's had a progressively more difficult time catching attention.

At the end, the veterans had each other. Fick's position is clear in his conclusion:

> I took sixty-five men to war and brought sixty-five home. I gave them everything I had. Together, we passed the test. Fear didn't beat us. I hope life improves for the people of Afghanistan and Iraq, but that's not why we did it. We fought for each other. I am proud. (369)

Fick finished his military commitment and went on to get a master's degree from the Kennedy School of Government at Harvard, with subsequent study at the Harvard Business School and a career most recently spent building a cybersecurity business. An admissions officer at the Kennedy School was a bit unnerved by the fact that an actual war veteran, one whose efforts had been chronicled at length by Evan Wright for *Rolling Stone* and who had expressed satisfaction in the opportunity to kill people, would be on campus—but without much explanation, Fick declared no intention of being another Charles Whitman shooting students from a clock tower. He was admitted, and his personal story of accomplishment continued apace. Fick succeeded in becoming a Marine. He led men successfully in combat. He has moved on after that experience, another success. His story rings true, but it stands as one story. No one story can represent the American war experience in Iraq . . . or in Afghanistan.

Nathaniel Fick's story can be deftly paired with the account provided by Donovan Campbell as a tribute to the soldiers he commanded as a platoon leader with a Marine unit engaged in heavy fighting in Ramadi in 2004. His book, *Joker One: A Marine Platoon's Story of Courage, Leadership, and Brotherhood*, appeared in 2009 but accounts for the intense battle for Ramadi five years earlier. Campbell's background matches up tightly with Fick's: another Ivy League product (this time at Princeton), another graduate of Harvard Business School, another American businessman, another quest by a man to prove himself via the Marines. Fick is a friend of Campbell and encouraged him to write his account. However, half the members of Campbell's platoon were wounded in the ugly street fighting for control of Ramadi, and he did not bring everyone home alive, thus giving particular weight to his opening reflection: "But it's so hard to tell the truth, because the telling means dragging up painful memories, opening doors that you thought you had closed, and revisiting a past you hoped you had put behind you" (8–9).

Campbell provides a steady, unflamboyant accounting for all the action his unit saw in their effort to keep Ramadi out of the control of insurgents. Right in the middle of the book, we get a full-frontal sense of the nature of the opposition facing the Americans under Campbell's command. From all of the minarets in the city came the same call: "JIHAD, JIHAD, JIHAD" (156). Obviously the message was intended to motivate and spur someone to action against the American presence in Iraq; and Campbell admits, "Unbeknownst to us, during the previous week several hundred hard-core insurgents had infiltrated the city with the intent of attacking head-on, and ultimately crumbling, the weak American Marines" (156).

Well, we know that the Marines ultimately prevailed, but the circumstances described by Campbell warrant further scrutiny. It would seemingly be easy for Iraqis to infiltrate an Iraqi city. Campbell notes that the insurgents threatened local inhabitants not to reveal their presence or turn over their arms caches to the Americans. Why would a few hundred insurgents think they could defeat the US Marines, part of the best equipped, most powerful military force on the planet? The insurgents had no attack helicopters to call in, no jet fighters, no tanks, no trauma centers a few minutes away from any battlefield to treat the wounded. Were the insurgents crazy? If not outright crazy, at the very least they were phenomenally dedicated to the idea that American forces had to be expelled from Iraq, no matter what the cost. They had to know that their mission was tantamount to suicide, but they went ahead anyway.

The insurgents were hell-bent on driving the Marines out. The Marines were hell-bent on driving the insurgents out. It was a pitched battle, and it went on for many days. Insurgents were ready to die. Marines were ready to die. Plenty of combatants on both sides were dead at the end, with many more wounded. Campbell's unit, minus the dead and wounded, rotated stateside eventually. Many of his Marines continued to believe in the bonds they had forged in adversity, and quite a few were reluctant to give up before the job was completely done in Iraq. Campbell, though, found it hard to see that point: "I couldn't in any way relate to wanting to stay in Ramadi. A good portion of the city's residents hated us just for being American, and a smaller but still sizable chunk of them actively tried to kill us every day. Why would anyone want to risk his life to help these people?" (300). The book closes soon afterward with a meditation of the meaning of love—essentially on the love Campbell's Marines had for one another, a togetherness strengthened intensely by the hardships they had endured in support of one another. Once you are in it, you are in, and the force of commitment deepens as the shared experiences grow in number.

Surely, it had to be the same for both sides, with something equally fierce driving those "hard-core insurgents" to assume the daunting task of confronting US Marines, although we never care to know the other side. America was caught in a boiling cauldron of violent antipathies—the typical brutality of civil war. We had jumped in freely, had actually set the pot to boil. It soon was scalding hot, and plenty of soldiers got burned badly in the process. When we finally got ourselves out, the pot was still very close to the boiling point, and there's no telling if internal divisions in Iraq will again heat up—or, contrarily, simmer down. In late 2014 the forces of ISIS/ISIL gouged out control over large chunks of northern and western Iraq, and for a time the area tottered on the brink of disaster.

While it is clear Americans left the political landscape in Iraq seriously altered, in narrative after narrative from those who were there to witness or to fight, the endings are almost always very muted—although the next section of this chapter will explore one notable exception (*American Sniper*) to the overarching feeling that, as potent as the American fighting machine is, we were damned lucky to get out without destroying a whole lot more lives. The military met its mission objectives as well as could be expected, but the background political situation tempered any gains on the ground in day-to-day confrontations with hostile elements within the Iraqi national community.

John Crawford's *The Last True Story I'll Ever Tell: An Accidental Soldier's Account of the War in Iraq* is governed from first page to last by the sense that we sort of blundered into something that was way more complicated than we expected. Our love for simple was frustrated to the max. Crawford was not looking to prove something by going to war; he had served in the 101st Airborne Division, then had gone to college and, to help pay the costs, joined the Florida National Guard. It was all meant to be sort of a lark—weekend duty to pay bills. Then he got blindsided; his unit was dispatched to Kuwait and on to Iraq in 2003. This surprise happened to a lot of American men and women in Guard and Reserve units. As a consequence, they got a lot of story material. Crawford puts it this way in his preface:

> This book is the story of a group of college students, American boys who wanted nothing to do with someone else's war. It is our story. The world hears war stories told by reporters and retired generals who keep extensive notebooks and journals. They carry pens as they walk, whereas I carried a machine gun. (xiii).

Stories, stories, stories—Crawford collected plenty, and he packed his short book with them. Does he think they will change the world? No. Will they solve the pain caused by traumatic war experience? No. The offering is modest, just some stories to add to the understanding of war. As he notes, "It won't assuage the suffering inside me, inside all of us. It won't bring back anyone's son or brother or wife. It will simply make people aware, if only for one glimmering moment, of what war is really like" (xiv). There is poignancy as Crawford recognizes that the essential story involves "innocence not lost but stolen, of lies and blackness—a story not of the insanity of war, but of the insanity of men" (xiv). With all that said, he confesses that his service made his dad proud. Not a simple story.

Then it's on to the first chapter, "Empty Breath," perhaps a distant and quiet echo of Herr's opening for *Dispatches*, "Breathing In," an echo with distortion. Crawford's narrative is raw and gritty. He doesn't have the literary aspirations or sense of nuance seen in the work of a Tim O'Brien, but he pours out a rich mix of stories nevertheless. He was on his honeymoon on a ship in the Caribbean when he got the news from his dad that his National Guard unit had been put on alert for mobilization. He told his wife he'd always be there with her. Three weeks later he was off to war, a liar. Of course, he survived. Some didn't. He got to tell the stories. One of them (which turns out to be a dream vision) accounts for the answer to a question lurking around the home front when veterans return—the "did you kill anyone?" inquiry.

I once invited Bill Ehrhart to one of my college composition courses where we were using his poetry collection *Carrying the Darkness*. After Ehrhart read some poems, providing useful bits of background to set them up, he opened the discussion up to questions. A freshman in the back row came right out with a bull's-eye shot: "Did you kill anyone?" Ehrhart didn't hesitate before providing details about two kills. The first brief story involved a quick reaction shot on a kid running toward his jeep while it was passing through a Vietnamese village. The kid had something in his hand. Ehrhart's M-16 round dropped him. It was a stunning classroom moment—absolutely out of synch with much of what transpires in college courses. Anyway, in the dream vision narrative, Crawford squeezes the trigger on a young Iraqi boy who has just the muzzle, not the stock, of an AK-47, a scavenged "toy" that unfortunately looks real enough to agitate a trigger finger. Powerful story, explosive, anything but simple.

Crawford's book came out in 2005. He was interviewed by Terry Gross on *Fresh Air* (3 Aug. 2005), and his accounts of scrounging for equipment in Iraq sparked plenty of interest in the interview; his yarns directly countered the usual image of the super-equipped American in uniform. His book sold quite well and got a further boost from an appearance on Jon Stewart's *Daily Show* after the *Fresh Air* program. In talking with Stewart, Crawford admitted that he wasn't closely following the ongoing war in Iraq. He had been there. He had his experience. He had written it out. And he was promoting his book. He was back in fantasyland—after a diversionary side trip to a very strange place with a bunch of other young Americans. Quite a few copies of *The Last True Story I'll Ever Tell* were sold, and the reviewers in "Goodreads" note much satisfaction in the raw energy of the book, the everyday weirdness of military operations in a war zone that tumbles out page after page as Crawford's National Guard soldiers muddle through their Iraq posting. However, as honest and good as it is, Crawford's memoir is not the one that represents the vision that fantasyland Americans want to see of American service in Iraq. No, that honor must go to the best-selling book by Chris Kyle, *American Sniper: The Autobiography of the Most Lethal Sniper in U.S. Military History*.

Fantasyland Falls Big for *American Sniper*

Chris Kyle's *American Sniper* (written with Scott McEwen and Jim DeFelice) appeared in 2012 and went right to the top of the best-seller list. It had amazing staying power, although by year's end it had slipped a little. However, Kyle was killed along with a companion, Chad Littlefield, at a shooting range in Texas in early February 2013, trying to help a fellow veteran, Eddie Ray Routh. Kyle had taken Routh to the range in an effort to help him work through PTSD. In a horrific moment of monumental irony, Routh turned his weapon on them at close range and got two kills. Shades of *Generation Kill*, alas. Kyle's funeral was huge, truly Texan in size, and the shock of his death propelled *American Sniper* back up near the top of the best-seller list.

Here's a simple book to fit the quest for simple in American fantasyland. Kyle shared much with America's fantasyland hero of World War II, Audie Murphy. Both hailed from Texas, and both got guns in their hands for hunting very early in life. Kyle's family was much more stable and middle class than Murphy's, but Kyle found ways to burnish his self-image as a rough and tough cowboy, and as a consequence, he comes off as the iconic man of the West. He's big . . . and he definitely lusted to have something very big to go up against to prove his machismo. Even while attending college—without very much enthusiasm for that learning experience—he worked as a ranch hand, his best fallback Wild West option after he broke bones and severely messed himself up physically in an accident that ended his short career riding bulls and broncos in rodeo shows.

While cowboy stuff figures quite high in American mythology, after a while it left Kyle feeling that he should challenge himself more ambitiously. He had a craving for big risk. In military service he found the challenge and risk he had to have. The army told him he'd have to serve for several years before being able to compete to enter Special Forces. The navy said he could go in for the SEALS right away—but then it seemed his wrist pins (from his bronco riding accident) would keep him out of the service. Eventually, though, the navy called him back, let him join, and sure enough, he made it through the rigors of SEAL training. Ahhhhh, the running, running, running—ohhhhhh the push-ups, push-ups, push-ups—ughhhh, the pull-ups, pull-ups, pull-ups. Psychological game playing and harassment. Days of constant movement. No sleep. Launching rubber boats through rough surf into the cold Pacific. Eventually, Kyle would prove himself worthy enough to go through sniper training.

Yes, it's Audie Murphy on steroids. But we also encounter a hard edge of uncompromising patriotism that wasn't so evident in *To Hell and Back*. Right away, in a prologue, Kyle lays out his credo:

> I was raised with, and still believe in, the Christian faith. If I had to order my priorities, they would be God, Country, Family. There might be some debate on where those last two fall—these days I've come to believing that Family may, under some circumstances, outrank Country. But it's a close race. (7–8)

By the end of his book, Kyle has been married several years, and he has a son and a daughter. Even though Kyle's devotion to Country took him four deployments deep in his Iraq War experience, the question of family priorities was eventually resolved in his leaving the SEALs in 2009 to return to civilian life—at the request of his wife, Taya, whose feelings and concerns are interspersed throughout the story as Chris moves along through his war experience. Whether the children, especially the son, would be encouraged to follow in his father's path to military service remains an open question at the end. Taya is mostly in favor of having the new generation of Kyles skip service to country. Chris's over-the-top service should suffice for quite a while.

While the family matters are one thing, the real heart of Chris Kyle's story has everything to do with what the book title announces. Kyle's main claim to fame involves the 160 confirmed kills he had as a sniper—the most ever by anyone wearing an American uniform. He accounts for his first sniper kill just three pages into the book, quite a while before he was formally given sniper training. He's in Iraq. His chief alerts him to notice a woman, in the distance, who is preparing to throw a Chinese grenade at some Marines on patrol. He takes aim and fires, killing the woman, saving the Marines. And here's how he sorts out the situation after the fact:

> It was my duty to shoot, and I don't regret it. The woman was already dead. I was just making sure she didn't take any Marines with her.
>
> It was clear that not only did she want to kill them, but she didn't care about anybody else nearby who would have been blown up by the grenade or killed in the firefight. Children on the street, people in the houses, maybe her child . . .
>
> She was too blinded by evil to consider them. She just wanted Americans dead, no matter what.

My shots saved several Americans, whose lives were clearly worth more than that woman's twisted soul. I can stand before God with a clear conscience about doing my job. But I truly, deeply hated the evil that woman possessed. I hate it to this day.

Savage, despicable evil. That's what we were fighting in Iraq. That's why a lot of people, myself included, called the enemy "savages." There really was no other way to describe what we encountered there. (3–4)

Chris Kyle really got into the killing habit. He was always eager to go out on a sniper setup, and sometimes when business was slow for sniper action, he'd get himself hooked up with other ground units to sweep neighborhoods to roust insurgents from their homes in the middle of the night. You read *American Sniper*, and you are hidebound to an American totally convinced of the rectitude of his actions, absolutely set in seeing insurgents as savages. He made his mark in life as a killer, and he wants the whole world to understand his achievement. He's totally loyal to his fellow American soldiers, quick to join fights in bars to defend the honor of somebody or something, a man who seems born to kill and who was certainly trained to be exceptionally proficient at it.

The end of Kyle's book echoes its beginning. At that point in time, he has left the SEALs and gone into business training others in his area of expertise. His closing reflections involve God and his Christian faith. He's sure that God approves of it all, all 160 confirmed kills (not to mention a whole lot more killing in a slew of village and city firefights, where the counting was never very precise): "But in that backroom or whatever it is when God confronts me with my sins, I do not believe any of the kills I had during the war will be among them. Everyone I shot was evil. I had good cause on every shot. They all deserved to die" (379).

If we think back to the discussion of Jonathan Haidt's moral imperatives in chapter 1, it is clear that Chris Kyle's point of view is perfectly in line with the fixed compass for the conservative side of the spectrum explored in *The Righteous Mind*. In terms of the loyalty/betrayal, authority/subversion, and sanctity/degradation imperatives, Kyle's position is rock-steady. America sent him to war. People in Iraq tried to kill Americans. Those people were evil. They deserved to die. It is a formula with no room for subtlety, no place for equivocation, absolutely set against any second-guessing. It is simplicity to the max. America loves simple. And *American Sniper* is very, very, very popular with American readers.

This book will surely inspire many young men to follow Kyle's example. With combat positions opening up to women, perhaps the next record for human hunting will be set by a woman. The final segment of *Full Metal Jacket* clearly indicates that a woman can be mighty lethal with a sniper rifle. Kyle's story is a perfect recruiting tool for the SEALs—really, for any branch of American military service. The great success of *American Sniper* in fantasyland is a clear indication that when the next war comes, once the torturous business in Afghanistan has drawn to a whimpering close, there will be a plentiful supply of eager killers looking to top the Kyle record.

On 25 Dec. 2014, America received a very special present—a limited opening of *American Sniper*, directed by Clint Eastwood (after Steven Spielberg dropped out of the directing role in 2013) and starring Bradley Cooper as Kyle. Even though the film does not feature all 160 sniper kills, it surely stands as the bloodiest and ghastliest Christmas film release ever. The rest of America got a chance to see the film starting in mid-January 2015. Audiences turned out in droves, and the film ignited many layers of controversy and debate. An account of the film's highly predictable success—and an exploration of how the film significantly alters the Chris Kyle story—appears in the next chapter.

Oral Stories—A Jumble of Complexity

Much of the writing surveyed in this study comes from professionals, people who make their living from words. When conditions are just right—a writer working with an exceptional style, drawing upon revelations wrought by experience and then shaped by imagination—then the results can be transcendent, and we find an achievement to last for centuries. Given the explosive and hellacious force of war in human experience, most wars have produced something in text form that can stand up over time. Of the modern and postmodern conflicts, Vietnam stands out for having produced an exceptionally large number of memorable texts, n print and on film.

Sometimes, though, it is useful to parse the words of nonprofessionals, to see how ordinary people with experience in war have spoken to capture as much as possible from what they saw, what they did, what they felt, what they thought. Trish Wood, an investigative reporter, set out to spend a couple of years interviewing veterans of the Iraq War, and in *What Was Asked of Us: An Oral History of the Iraq War by the Soldiers Who Fought It*, she presents the insights and reactions of twenty-nine soldiers, both men and women. The stories collected in the book prove absolutely that there is never *one* story that represents anything, certainly not the war in Iraq.

Bobby Muller, a paraplegic Vietnam War veteran and founder of Vietnam Veterans of America, provides a superb introduction for the collection. In his youth, having returned, wounded, to the United States while the war in Vietnam was still a long way from over, he was distressed that a lot of people weren't really paying much attention—didn't seem to be sufficiently or even modestly invested in what soldiers at war were trying to do for their country. In the Iraq War there was a similar disconnect, but one much more pronounced and sweeping, as this study looks to explore.

The veterans who talked to Woods, who bared the traumatic moments of their time on the battlefields of Iraq, all offered extraordinary truths straight from life experience. The particulars varied greatly, and as you move from one perspective to another, you come to know that this whole episode in national history is fraught with complexity and turmoil. None of the accounts tries to boil it down to right or wrong. As Muller says, it's "not an antiwar book or a prowar book" (xv). It's just an honest, unadorned, and straightforward war book. No single narrative is more profound or significant than the others. They must be taken collectively, and collectively they add up to much more than Americans are interested in knowing. Too much detail, too much complexity—informational and experiential overload. It's a tremendously worthwhile publishing endeavor, taken on by a first-rate publisher (Little, Brown), but it has no chance of competing with *American Sniper*. One shot. One kill. Simple wins many readers.

More Journalists, Men Hunting for Lasting Truth

David Finkel is a highly regarded and deeply experienced reporter for the *Washington Post*. In *The Good Soldiers* he chronicles the efforts of the 2–16 Infantry Battalion (the Rangers) during the fifteen months of chaotic engagement in the 2007–2008 surge effort in Baghdad. At the center of the narrative is the battalion commander, Lt. Col. Ralph Kauzlarich, a man who desperately tries to stay optimistic—although as his men fall to attacks from relentless insurgents and encounter one IED explosion after another, his optimism understandably wanes.

On 6 Apr. 2007, Kauzlarich loses his first soldier, PFC Jay Cajimat, age twenty, killed in an IED explosion. Finkel opens the story explosively, with a set of disturbing images from the interior lives of many soldiers, including the battalion commander, as the Cajimat death moment unfolds. On the day of Cajimat's memorial service, the battalion's tour is extended from twelve months to fifteen months. Just a year would have produced plenty of suffering.

Finkel's account spares us nothing. We are there with Maria Emery in the hospital as she tries to deal with her husband's severe head wound—and also contend, in anger, with President Bush, who has dropped by to support the troops and who fails—utterly—to understand her feelings. There are recruits who come in with criminal records, and most prove to be good soldiers. The sergeant who recruited Jay March, and was inspirational during the recruitment phase, commits suicide. Kauzlarich briefs General Petraeus on the harsh reality of the surge while President Bush boasts to the Australian prime minister, "We're kicking ass" (128). Joshua Reeves dies on the same day he learns from his wife he's a first-time father. Soldiers watch war protests in Washington during a brief lull in combat. Folks at home don't want to hear details of war from soldiers on leave. Adam Schumann's PTSD reflects the incredibly high cost of treating veterans over time.

The Penelope home-front vigil is tightly woven into Finkel's narrative, particularly with a scene captured of Kauzlarich's wife and home during a winter storm while he is off at war. On a leave, Kauzlarich takes his family to Disney World—indeed, a venture directly into the domain of fantasyland—and then he goes off to visit a severely wounded soldier, Duncan Crookston, at the Brook Army Medical Center in San Antonio. Crookston will not survive, dying soon after receiving his medals from Kauzlarich, one day before his twentieth birthday. Jay March reenlists for a bonus of $13,500. At the end, with the unit finally sent home, there is a Ranger Ball. Finkel's sense of irony is good to the last word, and if you are looking to harvest a great crop of irony, *The Good Soldiers* would certainly provision you well.

We have already encountered a great many scenes of staggering hardship—suffering and death borne by American soldiers in a wide range of assignments and locations in the Iraq War—but before turning to the perspectives brought to the war by female writers, it is necessary to focus closely on at least one of the dreadfully dark and ugly atrocities that marked the American efforts to subdue subversives over many tough years.

Jim Frederick, a *Time* contributing editor, provides a detailed story of one act of brutality committed against Iraqi citizens by American soldiers. The time was 2006, the place was Iraq's Triangle of Death, south of Baghdad, and the unit in close focus for Frederick's book *Black Hearts: One*

Platoon's Descent into Madness in Iraq's Triangle of Death, was the 502nd Infantry Regiment (the Black Heart Brigade) of the 101st Airborne Division.

The abuse of prisoners at Abu Ghraib prison became well known with disturbing pictures and weeks of media coverage, a national embarrassment. The subject of Frederick's book, an atrocity involving rape and murder committed by a few soldiers one night against Iraqis in their home, is not so well known; *Black Hearts*, published in 2010, is designed to correct that situation.

The background conditions faced by the Black Hearts were similar to those that bedeviled and eventually disabled the moral compass of Lt. William Calley's platoon as they massacred the villagers at My Lai in Vietnam. The IED attacks were incessant, and it always seemed logical to American soldiers that local residents had to be aware of the insurgent activities. They had to be colluding and so were easy to distrust, and just about as easy to hate. When your nerves are relentlessly frayed and you have only low regard for the population all around you, the chances of an ugly incident happening move in closer and closer.

Finally, the restraint snapped for a few soldiers in a squad of First Platoon, Bravo Company. They had faced death, and they had engaged the enemy. They had killed but there had been no sex. A plan is hatched to rape a girl in a family's home not far from the unit's base. Under cover of darkness, the plan is put into action. The girl is gang-raped—and she and her family are shot in cold blood. Eventually, as in the My Lai case, the story broke out, and the men were tried—and found guilty. It's an ugly story, one that attracted the notice of Brian De Palma, who would use it as the basis for his film *Redacted*, which will be examined in the next chapter.

Women in Pursuit of Truth

This chapter concludes with exploration of war in three books by women, all journalists by profession, all with experience in trying to represent the Iraq story truthfully: Martha Raddatz's *The Long Road Home: A Story of War and Family* (2007); Anne Garrels's *Naked in Baghdad: The Iraq War as Seen by NPR's Correspondent* (2003); and Jackie Spinner's *Tell Them I Didn't Cry: A Young Journalist's Story of Joy, Loss, and Survival in Iraq* (2006, in collaboration with Jenny Spinner). In various ways, all three texts emphasize the importance of connections between people in a combat zone and their loved ones back home. The home-front link will also figure prominently in a number of the fictional works examined later.

Martha Raddatz has had a long and distinguished career as a broadcast journalist, most recently serving as chief global affairs correspondent for ABC News. She has been to Afghanistan many times, and she logged twenty-one trips to Iraq to cover the war. She participated in the final withdrawal of American forces from Iraq, and on 8 June 2006, she broke the story of the US airstrike that killed Abu Musab al-Zarqawi, the al-Qaida leader in Iraq. In *The Long Road Home*, she demonstrates masterful storytelling control over the nightmarish moments stretched throughout a day-long attack on the patrol of a First Cavalry Division platoon as it tried to move through Sadr City on the northeastern side of Baghdad. The ambush of the platoon led by Lt. Shane Aguero on 4 Apr. 2004—and subsequent attacks on the US forces that came to try to extract the platoon from continuing deadly engagement—was attributed to elements of Muqtada al-Sadr's Mahdi militia. It served notice that Sadr City was now a very dangerous place, as it would be for a very long time.

Raddatz captures the dire circumstances of Aguero and his men in fine detail. None of the battle action scenes produced by men in uniform seem any more accurate or riveting than the hour-by-hour accounts as rendered by Raddatz. She understands the tactical situation; she knows the equipment nomenclature; she spares no detail in representing the physical ugliness of the location and situation (the "what-the-fuck" pools of excrement that filled ditches and roadside cavities—as well as the physical wounds and deaths suffered by American soldiers in the firefight through the late day and into the night). Eight American soldiers lost their lives in that particular engagement; Raddatz's story gives each and every reader an intense place in the battle; her prose is tough and clear. If you want to know the war in Iraq, there's no better source of insight than can be gained in *The Long Road Home*.

Sometimes, in a carefully disciplined way, she tucks in perspective on a small detail, drawing out the implications of action even as it unfolds before our eyes. A relief effort—ultimately not successful—is led by Capt. Troy Denomy. His driver, SPC Seth Wiebly, can see almost nothing through the mess of raw sewage that splashed up on the Humvee's windshield as they tried to reach the area where Aguero's men are holed up in a building. Denomy can still see out his side of his vehicle. Just a glance gives him a picture he never wanted to collect in war—in Iraq or anywhere:

Denomy caught a glimpse of something outside his window that left him momentarily frozen. A boy of about twelve, in blue pants and a multicolored T-shirt, lay dead in the street next to an AK-47. He'd fallen on his knees, his body twisted backward, his eyes closed. Denomy was a new father. The sight horrified him, a sickening image that would later remind him of all that was wrong in Iraq. (175)

The American military was initially dispatched to Iraq to defeat Saddam Hussein's standing army, men trained and equipped to defend the country. That army collapsed almost immediately, but then the real war began, and it took a painfully long time for the American side to realize it was now up against a totally different kind of enemy, fighting a radically different war. The boy in Denomy's vision represents that different war. A nation always sends its young men into battle—to die for the goals of the old men—and the boy seen by Denomy throws that dreadful reality into stark relief. Almost certainly, in the next ten to fifteen years, another war will come along, which will call Denomy's son to serve for America. Are we not all a bit too ready to sacrifice our young?

Raddatz does not equivocate in her portrait of the situation faced by the First Cavalry units as they tried to maneuver back to safety outside Sadr City. A superbly powerful American military had smashed Saddam Hussein's forces in a month, but Raddatz correctly notes, "The American forces which had so swiftly defeated Saddam Hussein's regular army were ill prepared to fight the urban, guerilla-style warfare now unfolding before their eyes" (165). Yes, indeed. Of course, a new set of tactics designed for routing out guerillas was soon developed and implemented, but it would prove to be very costly—in time, in money, and in life—for the local people always have a huge advantage over an occupying force from outside. Frequently, the main American accomplishment was to unite opposition and fuel resistance. If we have any choice regarding future war involvement by American troops, it would be wise to never again join a civil war conflict where we get to play "Monkey in the Middle."

The Raddatz book has one further feature of consequence to note. She interweaves the story of family members in the states with the hour-by-hour combat developments. While all hell is breaking loose in Sadr City, back at Ft. Hood in Texas, "largest armored training installation in the free world" (18), it's a quiet Palm Sunday. Raddatz introduces us to the families of the men who are fighting so desperately far away. It is as if Penelope's home story is right there on the flip side of Odysseus's faraway adventure story, with the sides quickly alternating. Iraq—Home: Home—Iraq. For the families, as the bullets flew and the IEDs exploded, fantasyland America provided no failsafe escape, no relief, no way to avoid the throbbing angst of war.

Not all the loved ones were at Ft. Hood, however. Allison Cason had traveled to Alabama for her grandfather's birthday in Tuscaloosa. It's an idyllic scene, and Raddatz juxtaposes it dramatically against the backdrop of bloody fighting in Iraq; at the exact moment Allison Cason's twenty-four-year-old husband took a bullet in his abdomen, she was celebrating her grandfather's eighty-first year of life at his home in Tuscaloosa, Alabama. She experienced no sudden feeling of dread, no searing sympathetic pain, no notion that her husband was fighting for breath eight thousand miles away. The young mother was enjoying her last hours of ignorant bliss.

In an appendix Raddatz provides updated information on all of the key soldiers who were caught in the ambush and rescue mission on April 4—and she also accounts for their loved ones, including Allison Cason, whose husband, Ahmed, was buried in Hoover, Alabama, the Monday after Easter, one of eight American dead from that battle. Gen. Peter Chiarelli originally suggested that Raddatz spend time with the families of his First Cav soldiers, and in the exquisite balance of her narrative as war and home are woven together, she made the most of the idea to draw Penelope close together with Odysseus as they tracked through the grotesque crucible of war.

Ann Garrels is a familiar voice to millions of listeners of National Public Radio over the past few decades. She moved to NPR in 1988 after stints working as a correspondent for ABC and then NBC. She was among a small group of journalists who were in Baghdad in March of 2003 when the American-led assault on Saddam Hussein's regime began. She was not embedded; she was on her own, in the company of a small contingent of likewise-situated foreign correspondents. It was an extraordinarily dangerous place to be—in the capital city of a nation under massive attack. Her experiences, and her reflections on those experiences as they unfolded, are all accounted for in *Naked in Baghdad*. Iraq was a strange place before the regime change; it was a strange place after the regime change. Garrels has the depth of experience to account for what the country was and what it became. Her familiarity with the world of Baghdad was exceptional; the planners of the war in America never seemed to have as clear an understanding of how things worked—and did not work—in the nation of people whose future we set out to redesign.

One of the unique features of the stories we find in *Naked in Baghdad*—and will also see in *Tell Them I Didn't Cry*—centers on the level of effort used in trying to engage Iraqi people in order to understand them. I'm convinced that this sort of empathetic approach—a deep and sincere need to know the people of a place—is most likely to happen when a woman is doing the observing and the writing. There is always much more to war than the battles , and the people of a nation at war are forced to deal with horror and hardships in ways that the men who go to war (whether for fighting or for writing) barely, if ever, register. Gloria Emerson's stories from the Vietnam War had this comprehensive, engage-the-people approach, and her lead has been matched with great power and discernment by Garrels . . . and by Spinner.

The men who go off to war, as soldiers or as correspondents, see plenty. They are not blind to irony. They behold all the ugliness and hell that war action can produce. They pay mightily in blood and in the trauma that lasts long after the last troops are withdrawn. But they have a simple, narrow focus: they assume the existence of an enemy (whether an army in uniform or insurgents who hide in the civilian population), and soon enough, their presence is met with hostile attacks. Winning the war invariably means defeating the enemy, knocking out the will to fight. Along the way, some genuine efforts are made to do constructive things that might win over the support of people caught in the war (winning hearts and minds). But the true heart of military action is simple: engage the enemy and defeat that enemy. Very simple. And it means that very little effort needs to be made to actually understand the people and the culture where the war is taking place. Instead of gaining mastery of a people through understanding, we proceed with weapons at the ready. Let them do the tough work. It is way too much trouble to learn a strange language, to sort out the differences between sects of a different kind of religious belief. Better to travel light in knowledge and empathy—and to bring on the massive firepower.

On one level, it makes perfect sense not to know much about an enemy. Knowledge tends to humanize situations, and the last thing a soldier needs is to see the enemy as a human being.

The Garrels memoir moves in another direction. Her effort was guided by a relentless desire "to understand how Iraqis see themselves, their government, and the world around them" (7). Imagine that! She depends on a driver/minder named Amer to help her gather information and put it in sensible perspective. Because of the dangers of an American woman going out into the neighborhoods of Baghdad (especially as time passed and security became more and more tenuous after the initial battles to topple Saddam), Garrels often came to depend on Amer to bring in information, and to provide leads for story ideas. Sometimes, with a good sense of where to find material to use, and by exercising cleverness, she managed to get moments alone with ordinary Iraqi people to find out their ideas and concerns. She continued to build trust (and use of an electronic code system) with Amer, always looking for a "string" (27) to thread a story together.

Throughout the book, e-mail notes from her husband (V. for Vint) are interpolated. These links from the home front serve a couple of purposes—one explicit, one implicit. Explicitly, V. provides very helpful background information about the work of Garrels the correspondent. He explains the workings of a journalist at war: the need to "string" stories, the "sucking air" moments when broadcast journalists have to fill "minutes of air time without the support of discernable facts" (58), his acceptance of his wife's need to venture to dangerous places to get important stories. Implicitly, the V. notes serve to reveal how the war goes home in intimate terms. Those venturing to the war zone live on the edge, get the adrenaline rushes when bombs and missiles hit close to a hotel room that is not a safe sanctuary, thrill in the exhilaration of getting a great story and telling it well. The correspondent, like the soldier, is at war. War is packed with explosive risk—the sort of intensity and super-incandescent moments that are scarcely present—if ever—in the routines of daily life back home. And yet, and yet, and yet, these V. missives show how the anxiety and stress of a war zone stretch to reach those back home. V. is there to offer jocular updates about the reporting coups of his "Brenda Starr"—and he is there to hear Garrels explaining her nakedness in her room as she anticipates incursions by security officials looking for her satellite uplink dish (of course, a funny story)—but most importantly, V's contribution makes clear the direct way war and home are tied together, demonstrating yet one more variation on the Penelope/Odysseus connection, but this time with Penelope off at war.

Finally, by reading *Naked in Baghdad*, we see and feel the way war was brought to Iraq. The errant bombs kill people. A "vicious civil war" (46) erupts. A knowledgeable witness to Iraq is full of doubts about the American case for weapons of mass destruction, and she is quick to grasp that "even those who don't like Saddam resent American interference" (146). She understands the firing of Peter Arnett and the disembedding of Geraldo Rivera, both for bad judgment in the reporting profession. At the end, she knows she had been hooked by her experience, sobbing in the shower in

Amman, Jordan, having "left part of me behind in Baghdad" (212). But it is time to go home, and she makes it successfully, with a kit carrying a few small mementos. Mementos are one thing, memories are another. *Naked in Baghdad* closes with one haunting memory—of a colleague, Elizabeth Neuffer, of the *Boston Globe*, killed in a car crash on the route between Tikrit and Baghdad. One last time, the war in Iraq struck home.

The structure of *Tell Them I Didn't Cry* puts the war zone/home front connection in the foreground all the way through, for it represents the uniquely tight link that twin siblings have. Jackie Spinner went off to Baghdad to cover the war for the *Washington Post*; her twin sister, Jenny Spinner, stayed in America. It is part of the twin phenomenon to share life experiences at a very deep level, sometimes via intuition. One is not one alone; always there is another. Twins have an astounding empathetic capacity for knowing each other, even when separated by oceans and huge gulfs of experience. In a note from the author, Jackie explains the twin thing in detail:

> Being a twin, I never felt loneliness. To this day, I have no idea of what that feels like. I have always had a soul mate, someone whose thoughts echo within me before they ever are birthed into words. I know instinctively how she feels, and she knows me better than anyone.
>
> When we were about eight years old, late at night, alone in our togetherness, we imagined our worst-case scenario. A man with a gun was going to shoot us both. We wondered who should die first and what would be worse: being the last one standing, grieving, or leaving the last one standing, grieving. We simply could not imagine life without each other. We debated this scenario into young adulthood without finding an answer. We debated it until speaking the unthinkable became too morbid. We replaced it with more realistic fears of cancer and car accidents—but never war.
>
> Before I left for Iraq, Jenny told me that if anything happened to me, she would never feel joy again. I tucked her voice, those words, deep within me, and off I went, on a journey of a lifetime, on a journey into life.
>
> I went alone. (xiv–xv)

Of course, in all truth, an indelible piece of Jenny went too. Periodically through the book, Jenny writes her war story—the twin physically far away but in heartfelt intense connection every day. This book thus intensifies the war/home fusion even more forcefully than Raddatz's account of family life in the middle of the ongoing firefight in Sadr City or in V.'s efforts to help provide context for the reports Garrels was developing in Iraq for NPR.

Jackie's explanation for the reasons behind her going off to war may in fact illuminate the whole American effort in Iraq—the individual/personal illustrating the general/cultural. Here's Jackie's take on her decision:

> Most of my family and friends could not understand why anyone would volunteer to go to a place where every day would be a test of survival. I went to Iraq because I am a journalist: we drive into hurricanes, not away from them. We chase the very elements of life that most people try to avoid.
>
> When I left for Iraq, I had no idea what danger really was; I knew only that I had a deep sense of responsibility for the story, and I was bored. I had been sitting in Washington writing about accounting policy and Iraq reconstruction contracts the year before I went to Iraq. I was dying a slow professional death. (3)

Early in this study I brooded a bit about the possibility that Americans have a deeply seated need to take on high risk. Our government is built on a system that maximizes risk. Capitalism depends absolutely on risk takers. The three-way balance of power in Washington is fraught with risk and tension, tipping one way or another, invariably putting one group or another on edge. And we have gone to war almost incessantly, with risk always in the offing. The Marine training accounted for in the life stories of Nathaniel Fick and Donovan Campbell involves extraordinary physical and psychological challenge, with intense risk of failure at the break of every new day. The flame of war burns brightly. We are drawn to it. Jackie Spinner felt the necessity of going to Iraq. It beat boredom and professional death in the mundane details of routine experience. Until the end of time, the history of war will always have this story in it. It rings supremely true.

Like Anne Garrels, Jackie Spinner took care to know the Iraqi people, especially all the translators and guides who served foreign correspondents in a great many ways, always at high risk to their own lives. Why is this important, a hurdle that the American military could never effectively surmount? Jackie observes that without connecting with individuals in Iraq, "everyone becomes the enemy and winning peace becomes impossible" (46). Jackie connected deeply with many Iraqis. She tells their stories—the dangerous excursions she took with them to gather stories, the crazy meals they shared, the collective misery they suffered because of the falling-apart systems in Iraq, the breakdowns of water supply and electricity.

Of all the Iraqis she came to know well—Falah, Little Naseer, Bassam, Abu Haider, Luma—Luma stood out. Jackie felt a certain kinship with Luma, another woman with a zest for life, although she had been raped by one of Saddam's sons. To provide a bit of relief and joy, Jackie arranged for Luma to join her on a short vacation trip to Amman, Jordan. They enjoyed relaxing at a Four Seasons hotel, quite a contrast to the roughness of their accommodations in Iraq. Eventually, Luma went off to try to help her mother, and Jackie never saw her again, although she learned later that Luma had become a victim of the war.

Still, the intensity of the Iraq War environment had Jackie in thrall, even after a brush with horror when she was surrounded by hostile Iraqis outside the Abu Ghraib prison and pulled away from her handlers, only to be rescued at the last moment. Incredibly intense experiences—the danger, the deprivation, the camaraderie in suffering, the satisfaction in prying out the details to make a strong story—they function like an addictive drug. Jackie was hooked good. Somehow, though, it had to end, and for the sake of twin-ness, the ending had to involve recovering Jackie alive and well. It would be a considerable challenge. Jenny's stories of trying to help bring her sister back into the fold of home are unstintingly honest and gripping. Jackie had been embedded briefly with a US Army Corps of Engineers unit in January of 2004, then had gone to Iraq for a long assignment starting in May 2004; she was there until March 2005, when she returned to the United States. She was home . . . sort of but not really. Odysseus took ten years to get back to Ithaca—and his long, long, long and complex return after the trauma of war has served as an instructive lesson for those who have waged war since Homer created his epic ages ago.

At Jackie's initial homecoming (she would be drawn back to Iraq yet again, later in the year, for a second, shorter stint to cover the trial of Saddam Hussein), Jenny was unsurprisingly eager to see her sister safe at home, twins reunited. But throughout the time they spent together in reunion activities, it was all too clear that the war had not left Jackie. Jenny and Jackie traveled to a professional conference together—and yet not together, as Jenny's account bluntly reveals:

The trip did not go well. During our evening dinners together, my sister drank too much wine, talking angrily and loudly about the morons around us. I tried to hush her, but she lashed out at me, too.

When I pointed to her shaking hands wrapped around her third glass of water in ten minutes, she pushed herself a little farther from the table, farther from me. In the hotel room we shared, she refused the bed, opting to sleep in the closet instead. I fell asleep to her tapping on the computer; emails sent to "the guys back home." Home. Iraq. (244)

When Odysseus returned to Ithaca and Penelope, it was most clear that he was *home* when he retired to the very special bed in his home, the bed he carved from a live olive tree before his departure for war. Neither of the beds in the hotel room shared by the Spinner sisters has the extraordinary symbolic force of the Penelope/Odysseus marriage bed, but the fact that Jackie could not use a bed—and had to sleep in a closet—carries its own perilous symbolic weight. She was in America—but desperately far from home.

In this contemporary war narrative, *Tell Them I Didn't Cry*, we have a Penelope/Penelope variation on the *Odyssey* original. One Penelope went to war; one Penelope stayed home. Once Jackie was back physically, she was still at a loss in fantasyland. She explodes in outrage at the astounding inattention to war on the part of her fellow Americans:

I tried to embrace America, but I resented it too, resented that so many people went about their days oblivious to the struggles in Iraq. America was at war, but so few really had to sacrifice. At a café one afternoon, I tried to block out the voice of a young woman recounting some water cooler drama on her cell phone. I willed her to shut up, but she did not. I wanted to punch her into submission, but I did not. Instead, I left my cup of tea and uneaten sandwich and walked out into the sunshine. Did anybody know? Did anybody care? Halfway across the world, people were suffering, Americans were dying, Iraqis were dying. I suddenly hated these drones who called themselves Americans, who went about their day complaining about such stupid inconveniences like traffic, just as, I acknowledged, I had once done. I could not bear to turn on the television, to the reality TV shows, the obsession with the Michael Jackson trial. Celebrities competing to lose weight? Give me a break! "Get a life," I screamed at the TV before I unplugged it. (248)

The rage in that comment was all part of PTSD, of course, the delayed release of darkly shrouded nightmarish experience, and the war would claim Jackie as a casualty for some time. Eventually, healing got the upper hand again, and life went on full of exciting new projects and happy prospects.

Jackie's recovery from war was helped inestimably by the steady support of her twin sister, whose office here at Saint Joseph's University is right next to my own. It's an unusual story of war, probably not unique, but unquestionably rare. A great many veterans come back and find themselves alone—even the ones with marriage partners and other family members close by. The ravages of war after a veteran's return to the homeland frequently tear asunder the bonds of matrimony. Parents are often at a loss, too, unable to connect with their sons and daughters. Shared experiences in life unite us. Experiences that are not shared often serve to separate us from others. Veterans have a phenomenal bond with their fellow soldiers in the life-and-death dice game of war. Back in America, in fantasyland, a cavern of emptiness often opens up. Jenny was there unwaveringly for Jackie, Penelope to Penelope, rock solid. It's a great story—even as it points to the chasms of despair that open up to swallow those for whom no twin exists.

Thus far, we have examined our recent wars via firsthand accounts: the contributions of distinguished and dedicated journalists as well as the efforts of fighters who turned writers in the mode of creative nonfiction. From this quick survey, which is meant to be representative, not all-inclusive, it is possible to draw some conclusions about the most recent American forays into war.

First, because the journalistic reporting was so strong, the writing so vivid, and the coverage so widespread, any investigation of consequential literature from the American combat activity in Afghanistan and Iraq most sensibly and naturally begins with nonfiction. Our culture currently has a strong bias toward creative nonfiction. We love our stories to be dredged directly from life experience. The firsthand accounts provide a baseline of documentable reality. While there has been no contemporary writer as yet to match Tim O'Brien (of *If I Die In a Combat Zone* and *The Things They Carried*) or Michael Herr (of *Dispatches*) in inking or keystroking the war action of Iraq and Afghanistan in memoir or reportage form, the writing in this domain is nevertheless vibrant, rich in telling details, and painstakingly honest. If writing about any subject in human experience can serve the purpose of truth and open up the dark quirks of life to at least a glimmer of understanding, the creative nonfiction and journalism from America's most recent war endeavors would seem to measure up decently well.

Second, since the advent of New Journalism roughly fifty years ago, fiction has had to struggle to hold its own in the American marketplace. The revolutionaries of the 1960s operated with the commandment, "Tell it like it is." In that era, there was a widespread distrust of deception, of subverting truth for whatever reason or purpose. Instead, everyone was directed bluntly to "let it all hang out." These slogans were mouthed incessantly by young people coming of age in the Age of Aquarius; they expected and demanded many much-needed changes in the world as it opened up to them in their struggle toward maturity. Many members of that generation compromised nearly every dream as they eventually settled into routines of life in the 1970s, 1980s, 1990s—and on into the new millennium—but perhaps the slow, steady rise of creative nonfiction to the highest place of authority and credibility in the landscape of literary arts is a surviving vestige of the truth-seeking passions of the young back when anthems of change, in simple harmony, were sung across America. This study will turn to fiction from the twenty-first-century American war experience, of course, but it takes its turn most naturally in the wake of nonfiction.

However, before the exploration of imaginative engagement with recent American wars concludes with fiction, some scrutiny of film and of poetry is warranted.

CHAPTER THREE

The Contribution of Films, from *The Hurt Locker* to *American Sniper* . . . with Many Films Ignored

The Hurt Locker: A Breakout American War Film

Unlike the pattern that held sway during the Vietnam War, where almost no film explorations of the war were presented to the American public until US forces were finally withdrawn from combat engagement in March of 1973 (a moment noisily marked by celebratory car horns honking all across the land), cinematic interrogations of the Iraq War began long before the withdrawal of American combat forces in 2011. As noted in an earlier chapter, the jarring exception to this pattern of restraint during the Vietnam era appeared in 1968, right at the height of American involvement in Vietnam and just as American opinion about the war was tipping from positive to negative; this was the film version of Robin Moore's best-selling 1965 novel, *The Green Berets*.

The Green Berets film included a choral arrangement of the inspirational and wildly popular song written by Robin Moore and SSgt. Barry Sadler, "The Ballad of the Green Berets," which Sadler sang first on the Ed Sullivan variety TV show on 30 Jan. 1966. The whole enterprise—John Wayne's starring role, the emotionally compelling song, the gung-ho spirit of American forces fighting to preserve freedom in Vietnam—was designed to be front-and-center patriotic. The film proved to be singularly exceptional in this regard, as well as in the fact that it appeared during the years of fierce combat activity. Almost all of the Vietnam War films worthy of note appeared after 1975. Finally, when South Vietnam collapsed, the film floodgates opened.

In this chapter we will survey a range of films exploring the wars in Afghanistan and Iraq, with particular emphasis on the Iraq conflict, and at the outset we will contend with the two films to break—albeit marginally and in two very different genres—into the consciousness of Americans in fantasyland: Michael Moore's provocative, incendiary *Fahrenheit 9/11* (2004) and Kathryn Bigelow's *The Hurt Locker* (2009).

Michael Moore has positioned himself as high interrogator of American misdirection for several decades, beginning with a stringent critique of the effects of moving jobs out of America, with particular emphasis on the automobile industry—featuring Roger Smith, former CEO of General Motors, as key culprit—a story worked out in Moore's first documentary effort, *Roger & Me* (1989). Thirteen years later, with *Bowling for Columbine* (2002), a lively but sometimes mish-mashed attack on gun violence in America, Moore was hailed internationally (Anniversary Prize winner at the Cannes Film Festival) and nationally (Academy Award for Documentary Feature). This background set Moore up to reach box office heights with his next effort, *Fahrenheit 9/11,* in 2004. By that time, America had sent troops into Iraq, an operation driven forward by frenetic claims by high officials in American government (including President George Bush and Vice President Richard Cheney) that Iraq possessed dangerous weapons of mass destruction and could not be trusted to avoid their use. America was at grave risk, so the claim went. By the time Moore's treatment of this whole endeavor reached its final frame, the official case for war looked incredibly wrong—twisted, contorted, contrived, and—in essence—false to the core. That's a big dose of cod liver oil to administer to a nation at war, yet the box office results (according to data at *Box Office Mojo* for 2004, the film settled at #17 that year, with a gross of $119,194,771) suggest that plenty of Americans were already looking for a way to flush the experience out, some means of eliminating the mess; it stands as the highest-grossing documentary to date (over $200 million worldwide).

Moore's *Fahrenheit 9/11* is confrontational from first scene to last; it generated great controversy, on many levels. There were fierce industry struggles over production and distribution; a fight developed over the film's rating (it wound up with an "R," which would keep a substantial segment of America's future "guardians" out of theaters). The film was not expensive to produce, coming in handily under a $6,000,000 budget; most of the stars were unpaid, with notables such as George W. Bush, Condoleezza Rice, Donald Rumsfeld, and even Osama bin Laden appearing without a paycheck (all from archival footage). It was an election year, so the film's rejection of a war being fought on false pretexts was certain to play some sort of role in the politics of that year. Conservative groups worked hard to steer people away from seeing the film; liberal groups encouraged people to attend screenings. In the end, conservative voters were surely not won over—and liberal voters were enthusiastically receptive. Status was quo in the wake of *Fahrenheit 9/11*.

However, fantasyland America was, in the main, elsewhere, as results tallied in *Box Office Mojo* clearly show. *Shrek 2* commanded the largest audience ($441,226,247—roughly four times the gross for Moore's film); *Spider-Man 2* produced $373,585,825 (more than three times the Moore total); and Mel Gibson's *The Passion of the Christ* collected $370,274,604 (again, three times the return for *Fahrenheit 9/11*). The top-grossing films were all safe, highly predictable in their storylines. Shrek made growing-at-the-waistband Americans feel OK with their girth; Spider-Man was certain to triumph over evil; and Christ would be Christ, once and always the redeemer, the one to take away all our ghastly mistakes and deliver us despite our shortcomings. That set of films could constitute a universal cure-all.

Kathryn Bigelow's *The Hurt Locker* stands somewhat apart from *Fahrenheit 9/11* in that the politics of the Iraq War are kept quietly out of the action-packed foreground. *The Hurt Locker* also separates itself from almost all the other war films from the past fourteen years in that it managed to generate fair (but way, way, way short of blockbuster status) box office success, and also to garner the Academy Award for Best Picture in 2009 and the Best Director Oscar for Bigelow. Those markers of achievement are not inconsequential, for they have the potential to draw attention through the years to come, although there have been more than a few Oscar winners that have not shown great staying power as time passes. There's an excellent chance, however, that if Americans show any interest in war films from the Iraq conflict—in, say, fifty years—Bigelow's *The Hurt Locker* is one of the two films to which they will turn (with *American Sniper* being the other option). Both of these films show American warriors who are superb in their designated combat roles.

Before digging into the story that Bigelow's film presents to us, it must be recognized that this film managed to draw a good bit of attention as it worked its way through festivals toward general release, with considerable acclamation from a wide array of critical voices, as shown in the following sample of reviews: "A great film, an intelligent film, a film shot clearly so that we know exactly who everybody is and where they are and what they're doing and why"—Roger Ebert for the *Chicago Sun-Times*; "Like every war before it, the US invasion of Iraq has generated its share of movies. But *The Hurt Locker* is the first of them that can properly be called a masterpiece"—Rene Rodriguez for the *Miami Herald*; "This one enters the pantheon of great American war films"—Mick LaSalle for the *San Francisco Chronicle*; "*The Hurt Locker* redefines war-film electricity"—Michael Sragow for the *Baltimore Sun*; "The best nondocumentary American feature made yet about the war in Iraq"—A. O. Scott for the *New York Times*; "Overwhelmingly tense, overflowing with crackling verisimilitude, it's both the film about the war in Iraq that we've been waiting for and the kind of unqualified triumph that's been long expected from director Kathryn Bigelow"—Kenneth Turan for the *Los Angeles Times*; "A near-perfect movie about men in war, men at work. Through sturdy imagery and violent action, it says that even Hell needs heroes"—Richard Corliss for *Time*; and "A first-rate action thriller, a vivid evocation of urban warfare in Iraq, a penetrating study of heroism and a showcase for austere technique, terse writing and a trio of brilliant performances. Most of all, though, it's an instant classic that demonstrates, in a brutally hot and dusty laboratory setting, how the drug of war hooks its victims and why they can't kick the habit"—Joe Morgenstern for the *Wall Street Journal* (http://www.metacritic.com/movie/the-hurt-locker/critic-reviews). Yet even with that kind of strong critical commentary, *The Hurt Locker* managed to generate only a little over $17 million in its domestic theatrical release; the worldwide gross of $49 million was just a little over three times its $15 million production budget.

In 2009, the year *The Hurt Locker* went into widespread release, it did not make the list of the 100 top-grossing films. While it did draw more viewers than any other Iraq- or Afghanistan-related film in the century's first decade (several of which will be accounted for shortly), the box office for this Best Picture Academy Award winner compares very poorly with the films taking that award over the past fifty years. It is one of just two films to win the Best Picture award and yet never place in the weekend top ten at the box office (along with *The Artist*).

If fantasyland America was not captivated by *The Hurt Locker*—was not eager to confront the realities of war in the Middle East—what *was* of interest for moviegoers in 2009? The box office results for the five top-grossing films that year provides a quick (and unsurprising) answer: *Avatar* ($760,507,625), *Transformers: Revenge of the Fallen* ($402,111,870), *Harry Potter and the Half-Blood Prince* ($301,959,197), *The Twilight Saga: New Moon* ($296,623,634), and *Up* ($293,004,164). While it must be recognized that a war film tightly focused on American soldiers doing dangerous duty in Iraq might not travel across international borders with the ease of the fantasies projected by *Avatar, Transformers,* Harry Potter, vampires, or a gruff old man in a cartoon balloon (thus depressing the worldwide gross), *The Hurt Locker* record clearly shows a weak appeal in the home market. America was in a war; Americans did not want to face the war in a film.

Nevertheless, partly because *The Hurt Locker* did garner film industry awards—and partly because its narrative arc represents the best possible means of generating at least a little bit of attention from the American movie audience—Bigelow's film must come early in this chapter. The last film to be explored, *American Sniper*, represents in two particular ways the opposite of *The Hurt Locker*—a mammoth success at the box office but seriously rejected at the Academy Awards ceremony.

The story of *The Hurt Locker* was developed by Mark Boal in a script that won him the Academy Award for Original Screenplay. Boal had been an independent journalist embedded with a bomb-defusing unit in Iraq five years before the film was released, so he had great material to draw from as he built a screenplay that adroitly steers clear of taking any overt political stance of either criticism or endorsement related to the war effort by Americans. From the opening scene onward, action is central to our viewing experience, and the narrative is extraordinarily tense, with very few moments of relief offered all the way through to the finish.

As soon as the film opens, a bomb-defusing unit is being deployed to investigate an apparent explosive device buried in debris along a roadside in an Iraqi urban center. Because this scene was part of an Iraq War story not included in the way the war was imagined by the Bush administration before the start of hostilities in March 2003, it could be taken as grounds for criticism of the buildup to war on less-than-solid evidence and without comprehensive understanding of the dangerously divisive sectarian rivalries within the Iraqi population. However, that angle of critical perspective is not exploited in the film; the dialogue of the soldiers featured in the action for the most part steers clear of any political judgment.

After the defeat of Saddam Hussein's army, Iraq almost immediately collapsed into bloody infighting among rival forces, and American troops were often the most readily available (and, unfortunately, preferable) targets for virtually all sides in the civil war atmosphere that emerged. The situation was hellish. Viewers of Bigelow's film can quickly determine that the reality of Iraq at war is ghastly, that American forces had to confront enigmatic but deadly threats constantly, that the fractious political landscape is unrelievedly treacherous. The treachery plays out in innumerable ways every day for the American military forces tasked with the mission of defeating the opposition. Most of the time, the people responsible for setting up explosive devices are not known. The bombs appear everywhere, with fiendishly clever and ever-evolving sophistication in terms of detonation.

To safeguard American bomb-defusing specialists wherever possible, robot devices (bots) were frequently deployed—but often enough, the situation would develop in a way that called for human intervention. The bots could do only so much—and sometimes malfunctioned. In the opening sequence of the film, SSgt. Matthew Thompson is seen going into action after a bot fails. He discovers one bomb device and acts to disarm it, but as he begins to make his way back to his fellow soldiers waiting safely out of blast range, he discovers wiring for other explosive devices. As he tries to outrun the expected explosion, the bomb is remotely detonated—and Sgt. Thompson, as experienced and careful as he is, becomes a war casualty. His replacement, SSgt. James (the Jeremy Renner character—and the film soon becomes a vehicle to stardom for him) is experienced but not inclined to be careful. He seems to love maximum risk, so all his bomb-defusing episodes through the rest of the film are full of heightened danger, to himself and to his fellow soldiers. It takes some getting used to, for his peers and for anyone faint of heart in a theater audience.

Most of the action takes place in densely populated areas. The bombs are hidden in trash, in cars by the roadside, in dead bodies, and near the end of the film, upon the body of a live person who is being sacrificed by the enemy against his will. In the intense heat, with sweat dripping fast and heavy, Sergeant James often discards his protective suit, choosing to confront the challenge of the moment with only his wits and expertise. He is superbly good when the risks are at a maximum level, and he clearly thrives on danger. His behavior lines up perfectly with the observation made in Joe Morgenstern's previously cited review about the drug of war hooking its victims, a point earlier driven home by Chris Hedges in his book *War Is a Force That Gives Us Meaning*; a quote from Hedges to this effect appears in the opening credits for *The Hurt Locker*. However, not everyone becomes enchanted by the risks inherent in the Iraq War scene.

Other soldiers around Sergeant James show signs of either sensible caution or weakness, in one form or another, with his closest working associate, Sgt. JT Sanborn, even considering killing James to eliminate the elevated risk linked to his unorthodox methods. Sergeant James is the iconic American loner male, a figure stretching from James Fenimore Cooper's Natty Bumppo on through many John Wayne and Harrison Ford film characters. This type of character operates best on his own, following his intensely personal compass to guide him toward success in a mission. Grace under pressure—the

Hemingway formula for courage in the face of danger—is an easy way to understand the role that Sergeant James plays in *The Hurt Locker*.

One action sequence stands quite apart from the rest of the film, and it does not ring true; it seems overly contrived, a plot device designed primarily to showcase yet another dimension of the Iraq conflict, one calling for employment of different tactics and different equipment. Sergeant James's bomb unit is directed to motor out to a remote desert area to dispose of explosives. In a vast expanse of sand and emptiness, they encounter others—first a roguish band of bounty hunters with British accents (a bizarre nod, perhaps, to the main "coalition" partner for the United States in the Iraq War mission) and then several members of an enemy force holed up in a building way out in the middle of nowhere (but deadly nonetheless, due to their skillful sniper fire). The answer to enemy snipers clad head-to-toe in black is a sniper in US Army camouflage armed with a Barrett .50 caliber rifle. As mentioned in an earlier chapter on creative nonfiction from the Iraq War, to date the great breakout book from Iraq is *American Sniper*, the Chris Kyle story, which quickly became a film directed by Clint Eastwood and starring Bradley Cooper as Kyle. Ironically, the sniper scene in *The Hurt Locker* may well have helped to set the stage for the appearance of Kyle's autobiography not long afterward—and for the Eastwood film that would not only generate astounding box office returns but also stimulate heated debate about the intentions of the film and its probable effects. Full discussion of *American Sniper* closes this chapter.

In the open desert scene of *The Hurt Locker*, with Sergeant James as spotter and Sanborn as shooter, the dark enemies in the isolated desert are soon dispatched. The action is sufficiently riveting to overwhelm any thought that it would have been entirely illogical for enemy snipers to hole up in an isolated building way out in the desert, where they would have no way to slip out of danger once they had fired their first shot. Urban areas were prime locations for sniper activity, because the sniper could readily find concealed locations from which to operate, with easy options to slip away into a dense warren of buildings should the need to escape arise.

Finally, the predetermined tour of duty for Sergeant James is up; he has a long list of successful bomb-defusing operations to his credit; and he can return to the United States where his wife and young son await him. He is shown briefly back at home—and in every scene in America, the tension for Sergeant James is greater than in Iraq. It is a different type of tension, of course. He is now very much out of place. He thrives where he can do his thing, confront death solo, live by his wits. Shopping for cereal (a whole aisle full of boxed packages, each one unique—and yet also just like all the others) totally unnerves him. His wife and her vigorous vegetable chopping unnerves him. His son's innocence unnerves him. He simply can't endure it. He is at home only in the war zone. It is where he belongs. So he returns for another tour.

If we remember the beginning of *The Hurt Locker*, we know where the story of Sergeant James will end. He is on a long suicide mission of his own. There will come a time when he will meet the same fate that took down Sergeant Thompson as the film commenced. A small mistake, a miscalculation of some kind, will bring his life to an end. The casualty rate in bomb-defusing units has been astronomical in every war that called for their deployment. You push your luck, your luck eventually runs out. One day, the bomb wins. Hence, in a very quiet but determined way, *The Hurt Locker* points us back to a statistic mentioned earlier regarding the suicide rate for veterans. Sergeant James has essentially assigned himself to a suicide mission. He is to be counted among that grim statistical category. Better to die on the job than as a discarded veteran wandering lost and lonesome as a kind of sorry outcast in fantasyland America. We do not have to witness the end-point for Sergeant James; it is there nevertheless, another facet of reality we would just as soon ignore.

The War Films Nobody Much Went to See, 2001–2013

As noted in the early part of this chapter, *The Hurt Locker* broke out of the general pattern in America of ignoring war films about Afghanistan and Iraq. However, this pattern in no way means that there were no worthy war films from this period; it only means that Americans by and large chose to look at other options in mass media and culture. Much of what was made into film texts about Afghanistan and Iraq contained daunting scenes—the very sort of thing that Plato would have excised from Homer's narratives. Americans in the twenty-first century appear to have an inner Plato operating on auto-function to edit out disconcerting or complicating film texts from their multiplex trips and their Netflix queues.

It bears remembering that the young teens are in the driver's seat in America for much of mass media these days. They are the ones with disposable income to support repeated trips to the movies. They are drawn like moths to the bright lights of blockbuster action-fantasy films, and the adults of today's America seem to be saying with their cinematic choices that if it's good enough for the kids, it's good enough for them. Hence, relentlessly roaring Spidey-Manned, Dark Knighted, Lord of the Ringed, Caribbean Pirated, Harry Pottered, Hunger Gamed, Avatared, Avengered, and Skyfallen stories race across the big screens and keep us enthralled, safe in fantasyland. The ostensible goal is to give audiences copious images of mayhem and gory deaths, all in a super-stylized Hollywoodish way, but in this process of finding the sweet spot to drive good profit, it is essential to steer clear of real-life downer subjects for the numbers to be good at the box office.

In exploring a representative sample of films from our most recent wars, the order of discussion is roughly cued to box office impact. When good films failed to catch interest from the domestic audience, I note the loss and ruminate on the reasons for it. And there is conjecture regarding reasons that determined where all the films landed when the box office opened for them.

A relatively recent film featuring American war activity (which includes the broad transnational war on terror) is *Zero Dark Thirty*, the follow-up to *The Hurt Locker* from the team of Kathryn Bigelow and Mark Boal. Although the film had its Los Angeles premiere in December 2012, it reached wide release on 11 Jan. 2013, all safely after the reelection of President Obama, thus quelling radical right-wing paranoid fulminations about how the film was being developed as a propaganda effort to push Obama over the top in the 2012 election cycle. But when the film finally reached theaters, it was the representation of the role of torture during interrogation of terrorist operatives that garnered most of the attention paid to the story about the long and frustrating hunt for Osama bin Laden, a pursuit that eventually led to his death in Pakistan.

Indeed, *Zero Dark Thirty* provides a rough, brutish look at the whole interrogation process; the film forthrightly opens up for scrutiny the cloak-and-dagger danger zones where American military and CIA operatives battle their terrorist opponents relentlessly to score ideologically driven hits against diverse targets on both sides of the conflict. This look into the dark side of humanity requires a hard heart and certainty that the end justifies the means; in many ways it is more ugly than most representations of standard combat in modern warfare. Much of what appears on the screen in Bigelow's second war film constitutes a direct challenge to the idea that Americans somehow manage to win battles by clinging to the moral high ground. This film shows that to eliminate a dreaded enemy, ugly things must be done—and will be done. In *Zero Dark Thirty*, ugly is done.

Consequently, a dimension of strident controversy attended the way the film shows torture as a necessary and successful means of gaining factual information and actionable leads in a deeply challenging detection process. All this debate did very little for the film on the Academy Awards stage, although Jessica Chastain did wind up with a Golden Globe award in the Best Actress category. The artistic merits of the film were pushed into the background behind the torture issue. Political pundits went back and forth over this nettlesome matter for quite a time while the film was in general release. The controversy probably helped sell tickets, with the box office benefiting from the free advertising spilling out from newspaper op-ed pages, the blogosphere, and talk radio. One further feature of the film was certainly a major contributor to the domestic gross for the film, which at $97,720,716 hugely exceeded the domestic gross for *The Hurt Locker* ($17,017,811): everyone who ventured to the theater could have the satisfaction of seeing exactly what had been deeply desired for a decade after the horror of September 11 2001—Osama bin Laden dead and gone. The American movie industry has always leaned toward happy endings, and *Zero Dark Thirty* delivers perfectly in that regard. Real-world events gave the movie a satisfying conclusion for American audiences, but a bizarre reverse twist on this happy finish totally upset the plan guiding the early production for *American Sniper,* where the projected feel-good ending was smashed by hard reality and sent in an entirely different direction—one drenched in pure pathos and copious audience tears.

A further surprise for Americans viewing *Zero Dark Thirty* involved the central role of a woman in prosecuting the successful search for bin Laden. The role of Maya, a CIA officer, is the key to the whole story *as the film presents it.* She may be working in a world largely associated with men, alternatively in beards with matching grunge-wear or clean-shaven with crisp suits, but the film puts the credit for a successful finish squarely on Maya. Jessica Chastain gives a gritty performance; her Maya is tightly focused, relentless in determination to find the pieces of the puzzle regarding bin Laden's location after his escape from the Bora Bora caves. When Bigelow and Boals began work on the follow-up film to *The Hurt Locker,* they had the botched Bora Bora job as a focal point—but when the Navy SEALs got to bin Laden's Pakistani compound, killed him, and brought his body out for certain identification before burial at sea, the project needed a massive script overhaul in order to deliver the good-news miracle that had emerged from massive embarrassment. It's not every day that a Hollywood film concept gets such a whopping good ending courtesy of reality. A cynic might see the happy ending of this Hollywood war movie as a case in point to prove true the satiric barbs about the film industry that vivified Robert Altman's film *The Player* in 1992.

In the main, however, the other major films dealing with the wars in Iraq and Afghanistan do not manage to wend their way to a happy ending any more than the conflicts they cover. The Iraq War concluded for Americans on a muted note with no glory attached—essentially a dreary operation obliged to gather up and remove an enormous cache of super-potent "stuff" so that it could not fuel sectarian rivalries after the American departure—and as it happened, plenty of other weapon sources were readily available for vicious sectarian conflict, which finally escalated to virtual civil war status in early 2014 and then the take-over of northern and western Iraq by ISIS in mid-2014—a grim destiny that governed subsequent honest films about the conflict.

Two films, both generally favored by critics, opted to bore deeply into the twisted, tangled "why do all these guys look alike?" web of terrorists, terrorist suspects, and assorted others whose agenda could sometimes be favorable to the foreign policy goals of America—and sometimes not. All you have to do is add a major Hollywood male star (or perhaps several) to the scene, arm him with many more questions than answers, and whether the setting is in Baghdad or Jordan or Washington, D.C., viewers in front of the movie screen will be lost and helpless. Who are the villains? Who exactly are the good guys? Does anyone here have a moral compass that can be trusted? Could it be that the American-led "alliance" charged into Iraq under less than truthful pretenses? And why do all the most questionable types look so much alike? If one is treacherous, might they all be? Except for the loyal driver, of course—the one who pays with his life for serving the Americans.

There in abstracted terms sits the gist of the plot lines that spiral through *Body of Lies* (2008; an American spy film directed by Ridley Scott, with domestic box office of $39,394,666) and *Green Zone* (2010; a British/French/American war story directed by Paul Greengrass, with domestic gross of $35,053,660). With director Greengrass (who also directed *United 93*, a documentary-style film about the hijacking and crash of United Flight 93 on September 11) and Matt Damon both coming to *Green Zone* hard off work on *The Bourne Ultimatum* spy drama, it is not surprising to find copious thriller-ish elements driving the story along—plenty of mysterious "who can you really trust?" moments with the list of potential villains extending up to the Pentagon and into the Paul Bremer–led transitional government during the days of discovery when the weapons of mass destruction cause collapsed into desert nothingness. The storyline for *Green Zone* manages to tuck in veiled references to the *New York Times* reporter Judith Miller and her role in lending credence to the whole WMD hype job in the buildup to war. Critics weren't thrilled with this concoction, but Matt Damon has a considerable following, which probably explains why the box office reached the level it did. "Bourne" by another name does not yield much value to artistic renderings of the Iraq War, although Greengrass indicated that he was purposefully doing a movie that veered into the political maelstrom that the toppling of Saddam Hussein created. His film thus would venture into territory not explored by *The Hurt Locker*.

Body of Lies also centers on political intrigue, with CIA officers crisscrossing the border of Iraq and Jordan—and suffering some double-crossing in the process. It is tough to trust anyone, even though the main American CIA officer, Leonardo DiCaprio as Roger Ferris, earnestly tries to get to the bottom of all the subterfuge. At the end, however, Ferris is tired and frustrated—thoroughly burned out—and leaves the whole sordid and twisted mess behind at the end (along with a couple of fingers lost in a brutal interrogation suffered along the way). Eager followers of DiCaprio, Russell Crowe—and maybe even Mark Strong, who plays, with critically acclaimed panache, a very slippery Jordanian intelligence chief—pumped a modest box office gross.

Fantasylanders do have a hankering for spy intrigue thrillers (witness the *Bourne* franchise), but the taint of Iraq served as a depressant on interest among the moviegoing American public for *Green Zone* and *Body of Lies*. It is bad enough to be lied to—but far worse to be confronted with the fact. Ignorance is bliss. A poll conducted by a Dartmouth government professor (Benjamin Valentino) between 22 April and 2 May in 2012 found that 63 percent of Republican respondents were still convinced that Iraq had weapons of mass destruction in 2003 (Froomkin); once a "fact," always a "fact"—at least in rigid sectarian terms, as only 27 percent of independents and 17 percent of Democrats held the same belief.

Two other films that dared to broach the truth about unpleasant factors in the Iraq War, however, fared even worse at the box office than *Green Zone* and *Body of Lies*. *Redacted* (2007; written and directed by Brian De Palma) and *In the Valley of Elah* (2007; developed from a story by Mark Boal and Paul Haggis and directed by Haggis) both evolved from cold, hard factual cases of ugly, murderous behavior on the part of US combat soldiers.

The straight-from-real-life circumstances shaped by De Palma into a tough-to-watch film involve the rape and murder of a young Iraqi girl (and the killing of others in her family) by a small group of soldiers who become unhinged in their combat tour. It was not a unique, isolated phenomenon. For example, in Afghanistan, a combat-hardened soldier, SSgt Robert Bales, left his post, entered a nearly village and systematically killed sixteen Afghan civilians in their homes; his crime was settled with a murder conviction by a military jury and punishment of life in prison. Beyond the incidents involving degradation of foreigners (for example, the rough treatment of Abu Ghraib prison inmates by American soldiers), there has been a steady stream of stories involving the sexual predation of male American soldiers upon their female comrades in arms. Contrary to claims from conservative quarters in America, stories of ugly behavior on the part of Americans have not been overreported by the press. If anything, these matters have been shunted out of the limelight, perhaps because they have become rather commonplace—hence, not as newsworthy as they once might have been.

Redacted works aggressively to showcase a brutal scene of war, an incident far beyond the bounds of decency, of humanity, of goodness—infinitely distant from everything noble and sweet in the notes we sing in carried-away moments of patriotic enthusiasm. Viewers of this film are certain to be discomforted by all they see—from the ubiquity of cheesy porn and vulgar discourse right through to the horror of the rape/murder scene. The historical record makes the ugliness inevitable. There is no way to steer this story toward a happy ending.

Only by recourse to life and reality outside the film can we escape, contentedly thinking that there were a great many American soldiers in Iraq who were not involved in high crimes against humanity like rape and murder. Redaction, the striking of certain details from the record in order to preserve or protect something—national honor, the idealized image of America's military, the mythology of exceptionalism wherein Americans can only do good and never stray over to the dark side of depredation—is a natural impulse when confronting the terrible events shown in De Palma's *Redacted*. And ironically, the film produces in real life the very concept featured in the title. Fantasylanders redacted this movie by staying home. Domestic gross at the box office topped out at $65,388. Redacted, indeed!

In the Valley of Elah is another film with a dark and discouraging center. The family at the center of this narrative seems to be the sort that would be impervious to moral failure. The dad, a character named Hank Deerfield, played by Tommy Lee Jones, is gruff and proud in his American patriotism; he is a war veteran, having served long and well as a military criminal investigator. Yes, crimes are committed in the military, thus warranting a police force and detection expertise. Susan Sarandon is the mother—steady in her own way—although not as overtly patriotic and stoic as her husband. These parents have already lost one son—to an accident involving the crash of a military aircraft. Well, bad stuff happens—and there's no use crying over any spilled milk. Hank still cares deeply that the American flag be flown properly; early in the film he stops at a school where the janitor (not born in America) sloppily raises the flag upside down, but Hank is there to make the necessary correction. He knows how to do the job right.

Soon he has another job that needs doing right. Hank and Joan Deerfield are shocked to get the news that their other son, Mike, has gone missing. Nobody knows where he is—only that his unit recently returned stateside after a tour in Iraq. Hank is puzzled, knowing no reason why his son should suddenly drop out of sight, with no hint of a problem to his parents. Hank gets in his truck and drives off to the military base where his son was last known to be. Because of his veteran status and his particular service as a military cop, he is able to get deeper into the base culture than most fathers would—but he nevertheless runs into a certain level of officiousness and cold shouldering. Whatever happened, perhaps the military is hesitant to find out; perhaps something very bad happened, bad enough to create serious public relations problems for an armed force tasked with meeting daunting recruitment targets and continuing to prosecute an increasingly unpopular war effort.

Hank manages to get his hands on Mike's cell phone. It has considerable video footage stored in it, but the images are distorted; the file has been damaged. Hank gets the phone to an expert in salvaging damaged cyberfiles—and some improvement is eventually made, although the context for the images is not clear. Still, the scenes from Iraq show Hank that the war there was wretched—that American soldiers endured the usual horrors of combat and at times probably lost their moral compass as well. Their sense of decency seems to have been compromised. Experiences they shared together would haunt them for a very long time. There would be post-traumatic stress consequences for these American soldiers, including Mike, the good soldier's son.

Getting nowhere with the military in the search for his son, Hank tries his luck with the local civilian police. There's a problem here, for neither the military police nor the unit commanders appreciate civilian interference in matters they would prefer to keep under wraps. However, a police detective named Emily Sanders (played by Charlize Theron) eventually comes to sympathize with Hank in his desperation, and together they work to solve the mystery. Mike's body is found, chopped into pieces and burned far from the military base. Hank redoubles his investigative efforts, persistently questioning the fellow soldiers in Mike's unit. At long last, the truth comes out. Mike got into a foolish scuffle with a few comrades in his unit, the fight turned violent, and Mike wound up dead. His fellow soldiers tried to hide the evidence.

None of this action looks particularly good for the American military. Combat tours in Iraq bring back traumatized and morally challenged young men and women. The brute ugliness of the war zone comes home—just as it did in Robert Stone's extraordinary Vietnam War novel, *Dog Soldiers* (1974; winner of the 1975 National Book Award for fiction), which culminates in a blood-drenched apocalyptic battle in the California hinterlands. The war zone images, retrieved in somewhat distorted form from Mike's phone camera—testament to the social media coverage of every human activity—are shocking, not the sort of thing to raise patriotic goosebumps. Grotesque violations of America's best values shadow soldiers from warfare in Iraq back to their home bases—where they compound into the lies that Hank has to penetrate. When Hank gets to the bottom of it all, his patriotism has bottomed out. At the end, in passing the school with the flag, he lowers Old Glory, puts the stripes up and the stars down, hoists the flag, and then applies duct tape to secure the ropes to the pole. The symbolism needs no expertise to comprehend. Hank's faith in his country has been compromised by experience. He is disgusted with it all—and commits his act of civil disobedience to make his point clear.

America in 2007 was not of a mind to go where Hank Deerfield went. It would be best to leave those ugly images scrambled on the phone, to leave necessary public relations campaigns to the military, to see if maybe—just maybe—a miraculous surge could pull off victory at last. Although Richard Corliss (2007), *Time*'s veteran film critic, applauded *In the Valley of Elah* as a top 10 movie of 2007, as did another *Time* film reviewer, Richard Schickel (2007), box office results were dismal, with a very meager domestic gross of $6,777,741 falling way short of the $23 million production budget (although the overseas gross did put the film's return above the cost). Before moving on to consider a very different kind of film response to the Iraq War, it should be noted that public rejection of *In the Valley of Elah*'s storyline (where the title summons up the mythic encounter between David and

Goliath) was drawn from the public record. Mark Boal had written a non-fiction account of the murder of an Iraq veteran by his fellow soldiers—and this truth from life served as the basis for the film. As with other years and other Iraq films, fantasyland was caught up in enthusiasm for *Spider-Man 3* ($336,530,303 gross), for *Shrek the Third*, for *Transformers*, for *Pirates of the Caribbean: At World's End*, and for *Harry Potter and the Order of the Phoenix* ($292,004,738). Anything but tough truth serves fantasyland best in time of war.

One final film from 2007 will round out the truth-avoidance pattern reflected in *Redacted* and *In the Valley of Elah*. *Grace Is Gone* is a very quiet and modest project that passed through America almost entirely unnoticed upon release (a scant $50,899 domestic gross), despite receiving the Audience Award for Drama at the Sundance Film Festival in 2007. The film stars John Cusack, who also produced it and worked on the storyline with director James Strouse; the whole project evolved out of the anger Cusack felt in reaction to the Bush administration's decision not to show footage of caskets returning to the United States from battlefields in Iraq and Afghanistan. This decision certainly protected the privacy of the dead—but it was also a form of truth suppression.

Grace Is Gone works to open up the deep pain and stress involved in combat deaths as they are eventually experienced by survivors on the home front. Cusack plays Stanley, father of two little girls and husband of Grace, who has gone off for a tour of duty in Iraq; Stanley had also tried to enlist, but his terrible vision kept him at home. Grace has gone in his stead to represent the family in war. Soon, though, Stanley is faced with two military survivor assistance personnel at his door bearing news that Grace is dead. Stanley has been hard-pressed to manage his children's lives in his wife's absence, and the idea that she will never come back to the family to guide them all with her love and wisdom practically shatters Stanley's existence. He knows what Grace meant to him—and what she meant to the girls. Grace is gone. Grace is gone. Grace is gone.

Not knowing how to break the devastating news to his daughters, Stanley resorts to desperate tactics. The family (what is left) will go off to a long-promised amusement park, way down south and east from the Midwest, a place quite well known and much visited, a destination where one would not be at all surprised to find Fantasyland (even if by some other name). The girls are thrilled—and off they all go for one last glorious immersion in the grace of a fantasy vacation. What fantasyland can ever measure up to that which is fantasized? Earthbound redemptions clearly have their limits. The film finishes in a scene by the sea, in a muted moment on the sand as waves break nearby on the shore, and all must finally confront the hardest of hard truths—Grace is gone. Perhaps the very few people who saw *Grace Is Gone* breathed a sigh of relief that Stanley could finally bring closure to his wife's life when he finally summons the courage to carry the news to the ears of his little ones. By all ways of counting, though, the comfort was cold indeed. Americans would see neither caskets of dead soldiers nor *Grace Is Gone*.

The war in Iraq had a distinct beginning, but as we look back at it, it is easy to see that point of origin actually had nothing at all to do with Iraq. Rather, there was the awful shock of September 11, 2001, endlessly playing images of planes smashing into the World Trade Center, and then the devastating collapse of Tower 1 and Tower 2. Another plane crashed into the Pentagon. And then there was Flight 93, the one destined to plummet into a field in central Pennsylvania, a weapon of opportunity seized by terrorists but ultimately thwarted in its intended target by the brave resourcefulness of its passengers, who somehow realized what was going on that day, saw that they were captive players in the drama, and determined to control their own fate—charging the cockpit, wresting control away from their enemy near at hand, and dying as the plane spiraled down toward the earth. It's a story of heroism, of a sort—giving up life in order to realize a greater good (in this case, avoidance of some larger-scale murder in the plot hatched by bin Laden and carried out by his suicidal followers).

Legends are made of such stuff, and *Flight 93* works to push the passengers of that plane into myth-dom. They gave their lives to save others. The film develops in a documentary style, looking to track what was knowable about the flight and its perilous end from the fragments of information that escaped in cell phone calls and flight tracking data. Paul Greengrass, already mentioned for his work on *Green Zone* (and yes, the *Bourne* films), provides skillful direction—and relatively speaking, for the films noted here, audiences in fair numbers (with a domestic gross of $31,483,450) summoned the courage to travel along with those fated to die in Pennsylvania on that day which will forevermore be large in the American chronicle. For 2006, the year of the film's release, the gross was unquestionably modest—pure piffle compared to *Pirates of the Caribbean: Dead Man's Chest* ($423,315,812), *Night at the Museum* ($250,863,268), or *Cars* ($244,082,982)—the top three at the box office five years after the fateful day of shocking loss in September. The number five film (*The Da Vinci Code*, $217,536,138) might have unsettled a few of the most conservative and über faithful in the Catholic flock, but it nevertheless attracted filmgoers at a rate sevenfold that of *Flight 93*.

That film may have aspired to lift up the spirits of America with a tale of unselfish effort, but it was no *Seabiscuit* (2003; gross of $120,277,854).

The shocking events of 9/11 very quickly got American boots on the ground in Afghanistan. The home turf of Osama bin Laden had to be liberated from the evil-doers, and an international coalition, naturally led by the US. military, soon made short work of the Taliban, putting bin Laden on the long run that would eventually end in Pakistan, in the successful sneak mission detailed earlier in *Zero Dark Thirty*. It strikes me as more than slightly peculiar that virtually all of the texts (books or films or poems or novels) showing up here for scrutiny involve the Iraq War, not the still ongoing drama of combat in Afghanistan. America's longest war is on track to becoming its most obscure in terms of artistic representation.

Five diverse texts dealing with the Afghan conflict attempt to correct this, although with mostly negligible audience impact, and we will examine them before we contend with the blockbuster Iraq story, *American Sniper*. One of them, *Lone Survivor* (2013), stands alone, by itself. The other three are linked texts, from two different genres (creative nonfiction and film documentary): they are Sebastian Junger's book *War* (2010, Twelve, Hachette Book Group), *Restrepo* (2010, National Geographic Film documentary), and *Korengal* (2014, Goldcrest Films documentary). Junger's creative nonfiction book could well have been included in the chapter devoted to that genre (which has provided much of the most powerful artistic response to the American wars of the twenty-first century), but it seemed best to address it here, as it completely complements *Restrepo*. *Restrepo* is the film version of the story at the heart of *War*.

Sebastian Junger and Tim Hetherington (a photojournalist later killed covering the conflict in Libya) were embedded with the Second Platoon, B Company, Second Battalion, 503rd Infantry Regiment, 173rd Airborne Brigade Combat Team, a US Army unit that operated in the Korengal Valley, northeast Afghanistan, south of the Pech River in Kunar Province. The physical environment is brutal—virtually unreachable mountains with lethal valleys slicing between the heights—the kind of place that makes large-scale (or even small-scale) military operations extremely difficult. The terrain is hostile, especially to outsiders. Americans were definitely outsiders in this remote region. In opposition stood smallish but determined bands of people whose motives may have diverged in some particulars but joined in the desire to see Americans leave Afghanistan. The goal for US military forces entering what was often called the "deadliest" place on earth was straightforward: find the enemy, engage the enemy, defeat the enemy. It is amazing how one simple mission fits so many situations. Junger was there, he captured the whole operation in words, and he and Hetherington put together an astounding film record of the experience.

To find the enemy, you must go deep into enemy territory. Such was the Korengal Valley. Getting there was not easy. It's a long slog from anywhere. Helicopters provided some help—for troop insertion and provision of supplies and building materials. But at a certain point, nothing but walking will do. The slopes on the valley sides are steep and unforgiving. Narrow paths must be followed, but the paths are well known to all the locals, so movement is hardly a surprise. You can't risk being caught on the low ground of the valley floor; in military terms, low ground is always dangerous, and high ground must be captured and controlled. Second Platoon is dispatched far into the valley, first to OP Korengal, then deeper into danger to create and hold OP Restrepo, which is named for PFC Restrepo, killed very early in the maneuver to set up a position far, far, far in treacherous territory.

You are obviously deep in enemy territory, but knowing exactly who is your enemy is another matter. There are indigenous people, tough and resilient folks whose families have been in this daunting location for centuries, almost from the beginning of time. They lead simple lives, with not much need (or opportunity) for commerce with the world defined by American values and lifestyles. The American leadership team (of the platoon and the company) tries to be friendly, tries to gain the confidence and support of the locals, but it's a dicey business. If you accidentally kill an animal in an operation, you are instantly in a deep hole. Livelihoods hang on precious resources, and a goat or cow looms large in these equations of survival. Americans hold out the promise to build a road—a route out to the world. How was the great American West conquered? By building railroads and highways—that's how it's done. So shall it be done in the remotest parts of Afghanistan. When the proposal is floated, however, it doesn't get much traction. When you watch the DVD of *Restrepo* (and very few people got to see the film in theaters, where it grossed a paltry $1,330,894), the whole road deal sounds like a colossally hard sell. Here's this simple, rudimentary, survivalist form of life—a model of human existence that has operated for a much longer time than America has been a country—and there has never been need for a great road to connect the Korengal with anyone elsewhere. There's never going to be an intersection here anchored by a Walmart and a Starbucks.

The year at OP Restrepo creeps along. Patrols seeking enemy engagement are initiated regularly. You have to defeat the enemy, and that means shooting them, or hitting them with the payload of an American fighter jet.

There are some firefights—some enemy killed, some American casualties. The neighborhood chiefs are beseeched to aid the American effort. They listen and then go back to their homes. Some of them could be the enemy. Who can tell for sure? The days go on, tedious and downright stinky.

Finally, there is a last mission, much like all the others, with sophisticated technology and massive American firepower trying to find elusive and minuscule enemy forces. And then the post is abandoned. The Korengal goes back to what it was, what it will always be. Junger's book wraps up with a visit to the platoon in Italy as it moves inexorably toward dissolution, the end of unit cohesion, which had served so well to keep the troops focused and supportive of each other in a time of dire necessity. That support is at an end. The conflict in Afghanistan continues. These particular American soldiers are no longer there, but the parting scene suggests they will be on a long Odyssey before they reach home safely.

With its release in late May 2014, *Korengal* serves as a muted coda to *Restrepo*. Junger developed this documentary as a complement to his earlier effort. He had plenty of extra film footage to go back over to create this video portrait of the Korengal region, a place where Taliban activity intensified in 2014, as well as in many other Afghanistan locations. If the time ever comes for the US military operation to be finally declared at an end, with just a small residual force remaining (mostly to provide training for the Afghan army), ownership of the Korengal will be virtually the same as it was in 2001. There has been much, much, much ado; little has changed. Americans in 2014 showed the tiniest interest in Afghanistan. News headlines and obsessive CNN coverage went off in new directions: ISIS in Iraq and Syria, Ebola in Africa and America. A month into its limited United States release, *Korengal* had a box office tally of $55,200. *Transformers: Age of Extinction* (2014), on the other hand, pulled in $100 million on opening weekend (by October 9, 2014, *Box Office Mojo* put the domestic total for *Transformers* at $245,439,076). Things that change easily—with absolutely no meaning or consequence—Americans love. The hard-to-change things are just not popular.

Lone Survivor is a Hollywood film (Universal) based on a true incident in the Afghanistan conflict. Mark Wahlberg plays Marcus Luttrell, a Navy SEAL who undertook a mission with a small team to eliminate—in one way or another—an important Taliban commander, Ahmad Shah, in June 2005. The title is a spoiler alert. The mission does not match the success of *Zero Dark Thirty*. Indigenous people complicate the mission, with significant

American losses as the team tries desperately to get out of danger once they are discovered. The Wahlberg/Luttrell character survives—but only through the generous assistance of a friendly Afghani at grave risk to his own life. The violence shown in the film is true enough to the actual mission, and the thrill of seeing one dauntless American emerge alive from the jaws of death was sufficient to drive a decent box office return: *Box Office Mojo* puts the total at $125,069,696 domestic by 4 Apr. 2014. The magic of happy endings still pulls in an American audience like nothing else.

Even with the Taliban resurgent in 2016, steadily applying pressure to the Afghan army and other security forces, as well as the US advisor units still remaining in Afghanistan, the war scene there was almost completely absent from the 2016 presidential election campaign. With virulence running amok in the Trump campaign, and Clinton trying to keep the lid on questions about her private e-mail use as secretary of state, there was precious little space for any attention to be given to the unremitting stresses and strains of conflict in Afghanistan. Against that backdrop, it is hardly surprising that when *Whiskey, Tango, Foxtrot* opened on 4 Mar. 2016, it went flying through the multiplexes with almost no notice and a box office gross of $23,049,575, falling far short of covering the estimated $35 million in production cost.

This film was a fairly accurate adaptation of Kim Barker's memoir in 2012, *The Taliban Shuffle: Strange Days in Afghanistan and Pakistan*—and Barker's spunky, witty, quirky, irreverent account of her efforts to be a successful journalist in a place where women have almost zero cultural standing seemed on the surface like a perfect fit for Tina Fey, who was quick to take an interest in Barker's book and pushed relentlessly to get the film made. The film's title, three words derived from the military's phonetic alphabet, played Feyishly off a bit of military argot appropriate for a surprising situation that is not going well: in brief, WTF, standing for WHAT THE FUCK? The biggest overall point being made by Barker and by *Whiskey, Tango, Foxtrot* is that Americans really don't give a flying Fandango about conditions in Afghanistan. There were some clever lines to spice up the action, but despite Tina Fey's following and her obvious deep commitment to correcting American avoidance of thought about this sad place on earth, American audiences would have virtually none of it. WTF was the net result, and this film had not a prayer of reaching an audience of decent size. A little over a year earlier, Americans had found the film they wanted to represent war in the twenty-first century.

American Sniper, 2015

If a happy ending is one sure-fire route to box office success, then when Chris Kyle's memoir *American Sniper* was optioned by Warner Brothers in 2012 for a film project (in conjunction with DreamWorks and with Bradley Cooper on board for the lead), the story looked to have excellent prospects for a feel-good finish. Kyle had completed four tours of duty in Iraq, and as his memoir reached its conclusion, he was out of the military, back at home with his wife and children: Odysseus returned to Ithaca—or, better yet, Texas, where valor in war is always celebrated, never questioned. Just ask Audie Murphy.

American Sniper was initially set to be directed by Steven Spielberg, but he dropped out fairly early, and the directing task moved to Clint Eastwood. Bradley Cooper was an integral part of the project from the beginning, as one of the producers and also as lead actor playing Kyle. Cooper was seriously enthusiastic about the story and has reported having a very positive conversation with Kyle himself about the project. As Cooper noted in a *Fresh Air* interview with Terry Gross about two weeks after the film's big opening, Kyle jokingly observed to Cooper "that he's going to strap me to the back of his truck and get the pretty out of me" (2 Feb. 2015). The Cooper/Kyle exchange was positive, with all signs pointing to a very satisfying production. Cooper would go on to add forty pounds of bulk to his frame, thereby drawing closer to Kyle's physical stature, and he assiduously studied all available voice recordings in order to accurately intone everything Kyle would say in the film.

But then everything changed, just as it did with the killing of bin Laden while *Zero Dark Thirty* was being developed. In this case, though, there was no joy or happy relief to anchor the film's finish. Just the opposite occurred, for on 2 Feb. 2013, Eddie Ray Routh, a mentally disturbed Iraq veteran, shot and killed Chris Kyle and one of his friends, Chad Littlefield, at a firing range where Kyle had taken Routh to try to help him combat the demons linked to his service. Suddenly, the film's lead figure, a Navy SEAL sniper with 160 confirmed kills and the genuine conviction that every kill had been justified (and would pass muster in God's review at the gates of heaven), falls dead at the hand of a fellow ex-soldier. Instantly, at the speed of a bullet, a radically different film becomes necessary. The bullets at the firing range that day blew apart the happy ending, the one designed to leave everyone in the theater feeling relieved and satisfied—the one featuring a masterful killer in war, a warrior who believed in America absolutely, who wished only to have done more to protect his comrades and further the American cause in Iraq, who negotiated the perilous return to civilian life and intended to be more of a family man. Odysseus, home again.

Of course, not everyone would be happy with that ending. Protesters who had resisted the Iraq War at every turn would not like the virtual celebration of killing reflected in the story of the most skillful sniper in American military history. However, for American patriots who never want to hear a discouraging word about their country—in war or in peace—*American Sniper* was nearly perfect. Yet bullets would have it otherwise. When Chris Kyle met Routh's bullets, the film version of *American Sniper* was forever altered. Reality provided the main substance of the project from its origins; reality also wrote the conclusion, and the pall of death would hang heavily over the reality-driven new resolution.

In the year before Kyle's death, as I worked on this study and reflected on the plan for a movie to be based on *American Sniper*, it seemed very likely that this film would prove to be easily the most-watched war film in American cinematic history. The narrative was tight and clear, with a hero unambiguous in purpose and rather simple in character. The exceptional sales of Kyle's memoir—his book's best-seller status—were certain to drive a huge box office. The audience was well prepared. Here was a distant cousin of Forrest Gump—but with unquestioning faith that God loves America most of all and that whatever America does is right and needs to be supported by warrior guardians; here was a regular guy from the Southwest who fitted himself perfectly into a role never before featured so prominently, so centrally, so successfully in a big American war movie. Sure, Kyle sometimes left his overwatch protection assignment (as a sniper) to insert himself in the house-to-house clearing operations needed to flush insurgents out of their sanctuaries, but his claim to fame resided in his kill count as a sniper. The sniper function produced "The Legend." *American Sniper* was the title; sniping was the story.

The sniper role in war has sometimes been a bit vexed in American culture. Winslow Homer created a famous Civil War image of a Union sharpshooter perched high in a tree, patiently waiting for a rebel Southerner to move into his crosshair sights. True as the image was to Civil War combat, and significant enough to be included in a 2006 special show on Homer at the National Gallery of Art, it proved unnerving to Homer, who wrote in a letter to an old friend, "I looked through one of their rifles once. . . . The . . .

impression struck me as being as near murder as anything I could think of in connection with the army and I always had a horror of that branch of the service."

While Audie Murphy was never a designated sniper, both his memoir *To Hell and Back* and the film based on it stress his exceptional marksmanship, a skill he had honed as a young boy hunting rabbits for the family dinner table in Texas, long before he joined the Army. In the south of France, on 26 Oct. 1944, Murphy was wounded in the hip by a sniper, who was then killed by Murphy in a clean shot to the head. Murphy recovered from his wound and returned to action early in 1945, soon to engage the enemy in the heroic action that earned him the Congressional Medal of Honor.

Much more recently, a sniper role assumed a very large place in the concluding combat sequence of Stanley Kubrick's *Full Metal Jacket* (1987). Near the end of the film, the Lusthog squad under command of Cowboy is moving cautiously through a burning cityscape meant to represent the Vietnamese city of Hue, which was taken over by North Vietnamese soldiers and Viet Cong fighters in the 1968 Tet Offensive—and which required several long weeks for American forces to recapture. When the character Eightball slips between two buildings while trying to find a safe way forward to the squad's next checkpoint, a sniper's bullet fells him, although he is clearly still alive. While Cowboy and the others try to determine their best course of action and seek tank backup—not forthcoming—the sniper hits Eightball with another wounding round. Cowboy is worried that the sniper just wants to lure them one by one into a killing zone as they try to bring back their fallen squad-mate, but Doc Jay ignores Cowboy's stand-down order and goes out to tend to Eightball's wounds and drag him to safety. However, Doc Jay becomes the sniper's next target of opportunity and is shortly wounded on the ground beside Eightball. Seeing the trap clearly, Cowboy is ready to pull back from engagement since the sniper clearly has the advantage, but Animal Mother continues the insurrection, charging ahead with machine gun blazing at his hip. He manages to determine the sniper's perch high in a burning building, and gathers the others in what seems to be a protected location. Unfortunately, as Cowboy works the radio, his upper torso is revealed through an opening in the protective wall, and the sniper strikes once again, killing Cowboy.

The surviving Marines then pursue a "payback" hunt for the sniper, who is finally discovered by Joker and his photographer buddy Rafterman. The film presents a huge surprise in this confrontation, for the sniper is a woman. As she turns to fire on Joker, whose rifle malfunctions, Rafterman shoots her down before she can kill Joker. Earlier in the film, Vietnamese women have twice been represented as aggressive prostitutes, eager to pick up some cash from American soldier customers. Now the aggression takes an extremely different aspect—a shock to the Marines and also to viewers of the film. Who could have imagined a woman being so skilled and so deadly in a sniper role? But then, the whole Vietnam War episode revealed countless gaps of understanding in America's venture into full-scale combat in Southeast Asia.

As it turns out, the film's ending incorporates one further surprise twist—this time in its radical departure from the last scene of Gustav Hasford's *The Short Timers*, a novel that provided much of the storyline presented in Kubrick's adaptation. In the last segment of the original story, the Lusthog squad is on a patrol in the jungle. The point man is hit by a sniper, and eventually it is Cowboy who goes out to help the wounded man and is in turn wounded—acting on the credo that live Marines will not be abandoned on the battlefield. An argument then ensues between Joker and Animal Mother about command of the squad. Joker assumes charge—and, to break the daisy-chain, shoots and kills Cowboy (at Cowboy's request). In the novel, one good Marine kills another good Marine in cold-blooded self-preservation. Kubrick and the scriptwriters (including Michael Herr, whose name shows up in quite a few Vietnam film projects) could not film that dark murder and expect much of an American audience to watch it, so the conclusive sniper action was moved to Hue—and the jolt of seeing a female sniper.

Steven Spielberg's 1998 film *Saving Private Ryan*, perhaps most notable for the graphic depiction of the D-Day landing on the French coast, also includes two sequences with an American sniper foregrounded. In a French town not far inland from the beaches, Captain Miller's select team from the Second Ranger Battalion, dispatched to find Pvt. James Ryan and get him safely out of danger and home to his grieving mother (three of her sons had been killed in combat already), is targeted by an enemy sniper in a bell tower. Pvt. Adrian Carpazo is killed, but the team's sniper, Pvt. Daniel Jackson, dispatches the German sharpshooter with a shot that passes right through his long-range telescopic sight. Jackson is a Christian, even more devout than Kyle, and his backcountry origins in Tennessee match up rather remarkably with another famous Tennessee sharpshooter, Davy Crockett, who is shown taking deadly aim with "Ol' Betsy" from the parapet of the Alamo and killing Mexican soldiers at great distance in the 1950s Walt Disney version of that battle.

Later in *Saving Private Ryan*, in the battle of Ramelle, Private Jackson and another soldier, Private Parker, are themselves up in a tower to spot the German advance. Jackson kills quite a few German foot-soldiers before a Panzer tank round destroys the tower, killing both Jackson and Parker.

Next in line to showcase the sniper's expertise would be *Jarhead*, the 2005 film based on Anthony Swofford's 2003 memoir of the same name. Swofford was a Marine at the time of Gulf War I, and as a member of a scout/sniper platoon, he took part in the military action to free Kuwait from Iraqi occupation in early 1991. Sam Mendes directed the film, and Jake Gyllenhaal assumed the role of Swofford. In an actual combat mission in Kuwait, Swofford has an Iraqi officer in his sights; his spotter seeks command approval to fire, but the request is denied by the officer-in-charge, and very shortly thereafter, the target is hit by an airstrike. Having never put to use all of his specialized sniper training, Swofford is left frustrated.

American Sniper would seem to be the perfect antidote to the aggravation experienced by Swofford in his sniper inactivity. Chris Kyle pulled the trigger many times; his training and expertise were not wasted. He laid claim to a record likely never to be topped; he became famous to his peers; his memoir made him a kind of positive icon for a war that generated many more negative images than were ever anticipated when the Iraq War commenced in the spring of 2003. If America desperately needed a warrior guardian of exceptional skill and simple, defiant determination to execute by bullet as many enemies as humanly possible, Chris Kyle, sniper extraordinaire, was just that person. His story would resonate like no other. It would keep American exceptionalism on life support for a very long time.

The film version of *American Sniper* hews fairly close to the memoir, although as Bradley Cooper has noted, with Eastwood as director a certain tilt toward the Western genre was almost inevitable. On an early ride into Fallujah, one of the soldiers even calls it the "new Wild West of the old Middle East." In order to sustain dramatic tension through the battle sequences that make up the center of the film, the film postulates an escalating competitive rivalry between Kyle and a counterpart on the other side, a sniper called Mustafa. In the memoir, Mustapha is given very brief mention:

While we were on the berm watching the city, we were also watching warily for an Iraqi sniper known as Mustafa. From the reports we heard, Mustafa was an Olympics marksman who was using his skills against Americans and Iraqi police and soldiers. Several videos had been made and posted, boasting of his ability.

I never saw him, but other snipers later killed an Iraqi sniper we think was him. (139)

In reality, Kyle did not go up against Mustafa, but in the film much is made of this one-against-one contest. Unsurprisingly, it climaxes in a shoot-out at a rooftop corral somewhere in Iraq, and sure enough, it is the American sniper Kyle who gets the kill. American Westerns for decades featured this sort of white hat/black hat shootout; these particular genre conventions are intact in *American Sniper*.

Nevertheless, this confrontation, even as it serves the film's need for dramatic tension, is a complete fiction—a pure fabrication, just the sort of falseness that, if it had been included in Kyle's memoir, might well have dispatched his story to the realm of memoir hell into which James Frey's *A Million Little Pieces* fell when it became known he had tucked in some experiences that were not true to reality. Kyle's memoir does not lie, but the film version seriously misrepresents reality as detailed in print. However, the huge box office for *American Sniper* (as of 24 Mar. 2015, *Box Office Mojo* put the domestic total at $344,276,641) indicates that American audiences are very comfortable with cinematic distortion of truth. The memoir accounted for an American sniper's expertise and success in his role; the film delivers the same expertise and then richly spices success with the Mustafa bit—all of which has proved to satisfy Americans desperately seeking to affirm American competence and superiority. The Mustafa fabrication is a simple, easy-to-grasp story: our best guy beat their best guy. Advantage America. In this regard, it is worth remembering that *American Sniper* was delivered in limited release as a 2014 Christmas present for America.

Because the sniper role is tedious, with long hours of waiting and look-ing between sightings of possible enemy targets, the film obviously could not relentlessly focus on Kyle and his spotter on various rooftops in over-watch protection mode. Just a few scenes of this activity would be quite sufficient to make the point. Even then, variety must be included to sus-tain audience interest. Differences come in the identities of actual target figures, and the film does not shy away from putting women and children in hostile war roles that warrant a kill shot from the sniper. Civil wars are brutally ugly, typically enlisting everyone in the effort to defeat an enemy. To significant chunks of the population in Iraq, Americans were the en-emy. Young and old, men and women alike were all drawn into the con-flict in horrific ways. Looking through the rifle scope, an American sniper would need to have a hard heart to do what the job required. Fairly early on, this grim reality is made manifest as Kyle shoots first a young boy and then his mother, both of whom are trying to lob a grenade in the way of an advancing American unit.

In the memoir version, Kyle is steady and unflinching as he accounts for his sniper work, but the film treatment brings in some shading. In one instance, fairly far along in the narrative, Kyle shoots an insurgent aiming a rocket-propelled grenade launcher at a nearby Humvee—but when a young boy then picks up the same weapon and tentatively moves into position to fire it, Kyle quietly (with words heard only by the film's audience) pleads for the boy to drop the weapon so he will not have to be killed. At the last moment, the weapon is dropped, the boy runs off, and Kyle is able to breathe again. The audience breathes too. Clearly the film wants the audience to feel Kyle's natural humanity, to sense some compassion still alive despite all that he is called upon to do in an unspeakably ugly war.

When the professional media reviewers sized up *American Sniper*, the film was treated respectfully. A tally at metacritic.com shows that of forty-eight major reviews, thirty-six were "positive" and twelve were "mixed." No reviews were judged to be "negative." A short sampling will show the various ways in which reviewers found satisfaction in *American Sniper*: "It shows Eastwood, at 84, in his finest directorial effort since the 2008 *Gran Torino,* while painting on a much broader canvas. Utterly in command of his epic material, he films the Iraqi action in terse, tense panoramas with little cinematic editorializing, as if he were an old Greek or Hebrew God who is never surprised at man's ability to kill his fellow men, or to find reasons to do so. . . . Skeptical viewers may pick at the particulars of *American Sniper,* but they'd have to admit that Eastwood, like Chris Kyle, is a superb shooter" (Richard Corliss, *Time,* 31 Dec. 2014); "*American Sniper,* like Eastwood's 2006 World War II films, *Flags of Our Fathers* and *Letters from Iwo Jima,* captures the rattling adrenaline rush of battle, the visceral shock of close-quarters combat. Like those films, too, American Sniper is both a war movie and an antiwar movie" (Steven Rea, *Philadelphia Inquirer,* 16 Jan. 2015); "Throughout the film, adapted for the screen by Jason Hall (*Paranoia*), Kyle comes across as a man gifted not just with the ability to shoot, but with a remarkable—and, at times, almost incomprehensible—moral clarity. Despite an opening scene that shows Kyle hesitating to pull the trigger on an Iraqi woman and a small boy who appear to be preparing to throw an antitank grenade at a convoy of Marines, *American Sniper* presents Kyle as someone with an almost superhuman ability to bear the same doubts that weigh so heavily on others in his job" (Michael O'Sullivan, *Washington Post,* 15 Jan.

2015); "*American Sniper* is at its best when it deals with the assembly-line-of-death relentlessness of combat for Kyle, how it simultaneously consumes him and wears him down, and how, to his wife's distress, it turns the civilian life he returns to between tours of duty into the aberration, not the norm" (Kenneth Turan, *Los Angeles Times*, 24 Dec. 2014); "*American Sniper* may be the hardest, truest movie ever made about the experience of men in war. Why? Because there's no glory in it. Glory is for civilians, politicians, patriots, home-front blowhards. Glory is the reason supplied by those who weren't there, when those who *were* there know too much, have seen and done too much, to put it into platitudes. The movie is about Chris Kyle, the late Navy SEAL and military marksman, whose 160 confirmed kills (out of a probable 255) over four tours in Iraq remains a record, for those keeping score. As played stolidly and inwardly by Bradley Cooper, he is a hero to everyone except himself. He'll say he was just doing his duty in that tight, polite Texas drawl, but his eyes reveal the immensity of damage he has done to others and to himself" (Ty Burr, *Boston Globe*, 15 Jan. 2015).

As this quick check on the professional reviews shows, *American Sniper* was taken seriously as a well-made film, one with abundant gravitas. It was credited with representing the sniper combat role accurately; some reviews made more than others about the way the effects of combat are shown to shadow veterans as they return to the home front. There are scenes back home with Kyle and his family that clearly indicate he is haunted by his war experience, and he is shown being interviewed by a counselor at a veteran's hospital facility after an outburst at a backyard family barbeque. When Kyle indicates he is bothered that he could not help more of his combat mates avoid wounds or death, the counselor says he can help heal the veterans who have come home but are deeply unsettled by their time in combat—a suggestion that led to Kyle's fateful encounter with Eddie Ray Routh. In sum, though, mainstream media reviewers found mostly satisfaction in what *American Sniper* presented to viewers, and hence, those reviews generally added a boost to the film's box office success.

Yet the professional reviewers were not the only people to weigh in about the film. Both Michael Moore and Seth Rogen fired up their Twitter accounts to lodge a bit of discontent with the spirit of *American Sniper*. When that sort of thing happens these days, millions of tweeters and hashtaggers pile on, and as sure as there is a mad mama moose in Alaska, the *American Sniper* advocates went to war for their side, happily knocking down Moore, Rogen, and any other real or imagined left-leaning, war-questioning non-patriots—which would include Bill Maher, Chris Hedges, and Noam

Chomsky, all accounted for by Cara Buckley in her splendid *New York Times* "Carpetbagger" story, "*American Sniper* Fuels a War on the Home Front" (29 Jan. 2015). Once Sarah Palin weighed in via Facebook to chastise Moore and Rogen for disrespecting a true patriot, it was clear that *American Sniper* would enjoy a spike in box office activity by folks over on the far right politically. It happened.

I myself was loath to see *American Sniper*. From the memoir, I knew exactly how Kyle would have to be represented, for he was unequivocal about his need to fight for freedom and his country. He had no questions, no qualms, about the justification for Americans going to war in Iraq. It was enough that there was a war, and his skills could be put to good use. He excelled in shooting the enemy ("bad guys," anyone who was trying to do harm to American soldiers), and as noted earlier in this chapter, by the end of his memoir, he is content with what he had done with his weapon. The only surprise I received from the movie came from the few scenes that indicated how Kyle had experienced some degree of PTSD himself—but the quickness with which his troubles seemed to dissipate runs counter to my general understanding of the ravages of stress deriving from combat experience and indelible memories.

My theater viewing experience matched up thoroughly with what one of my students had reported—that the audience was visibly shaken by the film's ending, with viewers quietly sobbing, rooted in their seats long after the final funeral scene. Well, the movie sure did play the pathos card to maximum effect in the last few minutes. Kyle is at home, seemingly all better after his brief PSTD episode, playfully pointing a handgun at his wife while telling her to drop her underwear—good for a laugh, since their two kids are just a few feet away at the time—then playing a bear to give a fright to his young daughter, and finally, portentously, telling his son to take care of the women while he is away. He is going to a firing range to help a suffering veteran, who is seen at the roadside by Kyle's wife; her face registers alarm as she exchanges looks with the Routh figure. Then the screen goes black, except for the news, in white type, about Kyle being shot by Routh later that day at the firing range. Cue the funeral procession in the rain (shades of Catherine Barkley's death at the end of Hemingway's *A Farewell to Arms* in 1929) with the highway lined by flag-waving Texas patriots who also fill the Cowboys Stadium in Arlington, Texas, for a massive tribute to their fallen sniper hero—and the theater scene across America is perfectly prepped for tears to fall. The emotional stops are pulled out to full effect as *American Sniper* concludes.

The American military forces will never have a recruiting problem in the future. Generations of young people will watch *American Sniper* on Netflix, on a DVD—somewhere, anywhere, everywhere—and a great many will be called to follow in Chris Kyle's estimable footsteps. They will not question their country on the threshold of some future war, wherever it might take place, any more than Kyle did. They will eagerly assume the warrior guardian role that Kyle's story so potently represents for them. If there are eager warriors aplenty, it seems more than a little likely that there will be wars. The little bit of PTSD that edges into Kyle's story will be no deterrent; his death at the hands of Eddie Ray Routh is to be processed as no more than a sad accident. It will not stand in the way of war, of warriors, or of future suffering veterans.

Finally, any viewing of *American Sniper*—now or at any point in the future—will not draw out the point that *Americans* messed up Chris Kyle's life . . . and the life of Eddie Ray Routh . . . and the lives of many, many thousands of veterans, quite a few of whom will commit suicide sometime in the next forty years as a belated consequence of their service in combat. More precisely, following the direction of thought initially broached in this study, the film will never serve to show that Americans broadly and generally are responsible for everything relayed in *American Sniper*, responsible by not paying careful attention to the affairs of state, by being too distracted, too bothered to care, too wrapped up in the wide array of fantasyland stuff— March Madness, Cinderella, *Dancing with the Stars*—distractions without end . . . but with disastrous consequences. This distraction tendency will be more fully explored in chapter 6, following further investigation of all that creative imaginations have wrought from the war experiences of Iraq and Afghanistan.

CHAPTER FOUR

Poets Capture War in Brief—for a Small Audience

When Americans gathered their resolve and acquiesced in the necessity of war early in the twenty-first century—sending military forces first to Afghanistan in 2001 and then to Iraq in 2003—everyone in uniform was a volunteer. All of the citizens-turned-soldiers had made a free-will commitment to serve their country, in peace and in war. The volunteer-force concept had been in place since 1973, late in the Vietnam War era, coming just four years after a lottery system replaced the previous Selective Service system of recruitment through local boards that managed registration and various deferment issues; home-front dissent regarding the war effort and draft system finally reached a point of intensity that drove the need to find a different way to populate the military. Always there are people who have a significant inclination to put on a uniform, and today that spirit includes women as well as men.

The military has appeal for those with deep patriotic feelings. It offers the possibility of extraordinary excitement. It holds promise for a level of dramatic tension and risk lacking in ordinary citizenship. Furthermore, in communities where poverty levels are a menace to young and old alike, the steadiness of a military paycheck and an escape from the clutches of desperation are attractive, to say the least. It looks like salvation, and recruiters from America's military regularly visit poor neighborhoods; as noted previously, they flash handfuls of cash, and the message is delivered with startling clarity: Join US and escape this place.

Given the subject of this chapter, the question must be asked: What are the chances that the volunteer nature of today's armed forces would draw in people whose zest for language would impel memorable poetry as they worked to cast their experience into words? Would the volunteer system attract a Wilfred Owen or Siegfried Sassoon, a Randall Jarrell or James Dickey, a Bruce Weigl or Yusef Komunyakaa? Surely this possibility could not be denied on the face of it; it might be tempting to think that the stereotypical "poet" types would be loath to venture off to war, but it is not acceptable to settle for lazy thinking, and indeed there is sufficient evidence at hand to prove the possibility that warrior-poets still volunteer—enough to warrant this chapter.

However, while some striking poetry from twenty-first-century war fronts has emerged, there is no indication yet that the contemporary war-poet population will be sufficiently large to fill a collection like the fabulous one assembled by W. D. Ehrhart, a gathering with a perfect title: *Carrying the Darkness: The Poetry of the Vietnam War*. Ehrhart was a Marine veteran, having joined up immediately after high school, just brimming with youthful eagerness to prove himself on the field of battle and to kill the enemy in Vietnam. A year in Vietnam yielded a very different Ehrhart, and during his PTSD struggles in the 1970s, writing poems proved therapeutic. A wide variety of other veterans found the same outlet for feelings and insights valuable. Once the fall of the South Vietnamese government sealed in despair for generations, the release of dark spirits through the medium of poetry became increasingly significant.

The range of poets and styles represented in the Ehrhart collection is remarkable, and many different kinds of war experience are accounted for. John Balaban was a conscientious objector, and his alternative service took him to Vietnam to work with war victims; as a consequence, he has for many years written with a depth of knowledge about Vietnamese language, mythology, and culture that extends far beyond the reach of the typical soldier dispatched to Vietnam for a year's tour of duty. Walt McDonald was an Air Force pilot, so he brings that perspective to his Vietnam experience. Basil Paquet was an Army medic; his poetry reflects the urgency of life/death moments on the battlefield as encountered in desperate moments of attention to wounds. David Huddle had the vantage point of army military intelligence. Ehrhart himself reflected the details of Marine combat operations. Bruce Weigl worked in army communications. Because Yusef Komunyakaa's army position in Vietnam involved gathering material for military publications, he had a writer's perspective even as his year in-country unfolded, and his experience was sufficient to yield several poem collections—memories long-lasting enough to catch fire in his imagination even decades later.

A few of the poets gathered in Ehrhart's collection did not serve in Vietnam (for example, Denise Levertov and Robert Bly), but the tumult of Vietnam engaged many people on the home front on a deep and moving level—a pattern not nearly so evident in the years of Afghanistan and Iraq, where America seemed simultaneously engaged and detached, almost as if we were watching a film that could not be edited, or beholding an experience beyond reach of meaningful comment. Nevertheless, when Laura Bush attempted to gather poets for a White House symposium, "Poetry and the American Voice," more or less scheduled to coincide with an invasion of Iraq commanded by President Bush and authorized by Congress, Sam Hamill determined to enlist fellow poets, if they were so inclined, to raise poetic voices in opposition to the war on the horizon. Hamill received a huge contribution of poems from his peers—more than thirteen thousand in total, the work of eleven thousand poets. Hamill gathered 262 poems for a collection called *Poets against the War*, which was published by Thunder's Mouth Press/Nation Books in 2003. Included are poems from Bly and Balaban, as well as many other luminaries in the world of poetry: Kim Addonizio, Lucille Clifton, Robert Creeley, Rita Dove, Lawrence Ferlinghetti, Joy Harjo, Galway Kinnell, Carolyn Kizer, Stanley Kunitz, W. S. Merwin, Robert Pinsky, Adrienne Rich, W. D. Snodgrass, Terry Tempest Williams, and C. K. Williams. These poets raised their voices in alarm; their voices went out, but they were most certainly not heeded. Perhaps their marginalization could be attributed to the fact that they did not write from direct experience with war. Soon enough, though, there would be voices raised in poetry from veterans of the most recent combat experience engaged in by Americans. The soldiers who went into the cauldrons of either Afghanistan or Iraq could not help but be affected—indeed to have searing experiences that would last a lifetime in memory, with shadows long and haunting. They would have words to share, something to say, whether an audience ever materialized for their words or not.

Operation Homecoming: Iraq, Afghanistan, and the Home Front, in the Words of U.S. Troops and Their Families was a project organized in expectation that people who had been directly affected by war would have a need to deal with the experience by writing about it—just the sort of thing that happened with the poets in *Carrying the Darkness*. The effort had the backing of Dana Gioia in his tenure as chairman for the National Endowment for the Arts. While Gioia's own inclinations are strongly biased in the direction of formalism in poetry, he certainly understood that the raw and real reflections of returning soldiers—and those of families greeting them—most likely would not measure up to the strictures of formalist composition. It was not a time to worry about form; people needed to have an opportunity to release the anguish, to find solace in the face of ruinous experience.

Andrew Carroll edited *Operation Homecoming*; in his introduction he notes not only the rich variety of genres (letters and e-mails, personal narratives, accounts of action, journal entries, fiction, and poetry) but also the broad spread of attitudes (from steadfast satisfaction with the war effort to blunt criticism of it). As Carroll reflected on the contents of the collection and the diverse positions represented, one of his observations squares rather precisely with the prime concern of this study—that Americans in fantasyland mostly opted not to be troubled with paying attention to war: "And some, in words that are more pained than angry, cannot believe that as two major wars rage overseas, claiming the lives of American men and women on an almost daily basis, the conflicts are often overshadowed by the latest movie-star gossip, celebrity wedding, or reality-show winner" (xxv). The conflicts in Afghanistan and Iraq quickly proved to be murky, a mess of contradictory purposes and counterproductive practices, not the sort of thing to inspire confidence or compel attention. Looking away seemed the best option, and pop culture creations like the Kardashian clan and Justin Bieber generate frequent headlines, always available for distraction. Hence, most Americans turned their attention elsewhere.

As the words of soldiers and military families fill the 377 pages of *Operation Homecoming*, a stalwart exercise in foregrounding recent American wars and their consequences, poetry occupies only 17 pages, with a total of just twelve poems. Most of the volume is prose. Given the abysmal experience that many students have with poetry in their high school English classes, it should be no surprise that poetry does not occupy the same high place of greatness and importance it once did in our culture. While poetry writing workshops are still helping to keep college English departments afloat—and plenty of extraordinary poetry is written each year in America, with a reasonable number of small journals available to publish good work—the ratio of poetry to prose in *Operation Homecoming* does not seem surprising.

The poems that are included in this effort are quite strong. Not surprisingly, the physical features of the war zone made deep impressions, for the terrain set the stage for combat action. Captain Michael Lang's short poem "Reflections" represents this tendency to catch the details that defined the location: Lang highlights the physical environment, offering a sand-swept landscape as backdrop for him standing, smoking, revealed by a flash of lightning. It's a spare eight lines, and the poem clearly looks to establish the desert as a factor in the war experience. Where Vietnam poets provided specifics of jungle, of torrential rain, of rice paddies, the Iraq poets cue on sand and wind and dry heat. Physical impressions are indelible. We catch life through our senses, and our most recent war poetry often draws attention to the atmospheric qualities. of the setting.

The opening stanza of 1st Lt Stephanie Metzger Harper's "Solidarity and Our War" poem continues in the same pattern Lang used—the desert again, a seemingly endless expanse out beyond the fencing of the base; it's certainly not a comforting place, all that desert, unforgiving. The desert in itself is not a threat, but there is nevertheless something important, perhaps quietly ominous, about the huge open space filled with sand. A colossal stage is set—and the stark bigness serves notice that developments of life-and-death import will transpire in this vast domain. Nature in the place will not kill you; but some of the people to be found in the towns and cities set off against the desert are primed to kill. Indeed, they want you dead.

The enemy forces would prove enigmatic. Who they were and why they were bent on killing American soldiers frequently was unknown, except in broad, vague terms. Closer at hand, though, was something both knowable and valuable—the intense connectedness that would develop between soldiers as they faced the certainty of uncertainty—and Sgt. Dena Price Van den Bosch addresses this phenomenon in her poem "Brotherhood." Where Lang and Harper present isolated witnesses of place, Van den Bosch addresses the way soldiers share their life experiences—good, bad, ugly—all of which powerfully serves to forge a commitment to others, a bond that could mean braving death to save a fellow soldier. At the end, the poem suggests this sort of sacrifice might be foreign, perhaps incomprehensible, to those without the bonding experience of combat.

Among the many ironies of war is the remarkable attachment that combatants can feel for each other, links that drive seemingly irrational behavior in the face of death, as Van den Bosch's poem avers, links that amazingly hold up in the hell of war but leave gaping emptiness when the soldier leaves war and faces a return to civilian life. This particular pattern is not, of course, unique to the conflicts in Iraq and Afghanistan, although the loss of connectedness (brotherhood) is especially acute for soldiers heading back to fantasyland, where large numbers of the population are in worlds of their own; these veterans have no connection to others in the community, save—perhaps—a small number of family members. Brotherhood intensifies in war; in peace it dissipates.

If we crave knowing the reality of war as hell, specific to Iraq combat action, then the selected poems of *Operation Homecoming* have that to offer too, as "Clusters," from Capt. Robert Schaefer, shows. Schaefer was there in

Iraq. He saw a minefield disaster unfold before his eyes—all-too-innocent soldiers being blown up by mines—and then others are blown up as they try to help their fallen comrades. It happened. Irrationality intruded: the childlike curiosity that proved deadly, the racing of many in brotherhood toward death's embrace in order to save someone/anyone, and then the blood memorial on a uniform preserved, a last marker of a life ended too early.

The reality of war in Iraq was explosive, and it could be surreal too, especially when the whole picture is exposed to a generation of Americans raised to measure everything in bytes of digital activity but suddenly plunged into a realm where the only digit that mattered was the one on the trigger. In his first of three deployments to Iraq, Marine PFC Allen Caruselle worked up a short poem that focused on the new oddity of war, children of video games and the information age confronting a darkness not made of pixels. Like the other poets already mentioned, Caruselle wrote in free verse, which seems absolutely appropriate to catch the reflections of soldiers in war in the twenty-first century. As Caruselle indicates, young Americans were called to duty, dispatched to the strange lands of Afghanistan and Iraq, and in the process they had to morph from virtual, video game fighters into the real deal; but as this poem from a professional soldier indicates, the leap from onscreen scenarios to actual nightmarish experience was really just a matter of brute chance, with no known algorithm for success.

The poem selections from *Operation Homecoming* examined thus far would have to be considered the work of amateurs, people for whom poetry is a potent mode of expression and who have good command of language but whose lives are not centered on the making of poems. They have not defined their existence as wordsmiths, even though their poem texts cited here bristle with energy and insight. Nevertheless, they have served well to open the door to the poetry of the Iraq War.

The final three poems in the *Operation Homecoming* project were collected from Sgt. Brian Turner, who has become the best-known and most widely published poet of the Iraq War. Turner's two collections from Alice James books—*Here, Bullet* in 2005 and *Phantom Noise* in 2010—have led to his being a frequently featured reader at poetry conferences and writers gatherings. For example, he was one of the keynote readers at the Massachusetts Poetry Festival in Salem, Massachusetts, in late April 2011—and he delivered his war poems with intense force. The three Turner selections in *Operation Homecoming* deftly cover the spread to be seen in his books;

"Ashbah" and "The Baghdad Zoo" reflect a measure of learned reference to indigenous culture as it would bear upon the American presence in Iraq, and the "The Hurt Locker" zeros in to register the intensity of combat action and the literal trauma it delivers to soldiers. This range suggests erudition, and indeed, when Turner deployed with the Third Stryker Brigade of the Second ("Indianhead") Infantry Division for eleven months in Iraq beginning 3 Dec. 2003 (with action in Baghdad and Mosul), he brought with him the language sophistication of an MFA in creative writing (University of Oregon, completed prior to his seven years of military service). Because the three poems noted above are distinctly more sophisticated and nuanced than the other poems featured in *Operation Homecoming*, they will be analyzed as they appear in the initial section of *Here, Bullet*.

Turner the professional writer/scholar is evident in "Ashbah," for the title appropriates an Arabic word for "ghosts"; and the poem's eleven lines draw together American and Iraqi dead, ghosts of diverse cultures lingering in the detritus of war, "desert wind blowing trash" as the minaret sends out a "soulful call" (18), a clear sign to the American ghosts that they are far, far from home—but offering no particular benefit for the Iraqi dead either, although the date palms are "leaning toward Mecca when the dawn wind blows" (18).

Turner knows, too, that relentless pounding away at the details of *American* combat activity—the weapons, the tactics, the fear and loathing, the flashes of heroism and even shades of depravity—runs the risk of becoming tedious, a dreary, all-too-predictable echo of poetic notes sounded in response to previous wars. All of that has been featured previously, from World War I forward, especially in Vietnam War poetry. In his book collections, Turner does go to the well of past American war experience frequently, but his impulse to reach out to the particular context, to weigh in on the culture and history of Mesopotamia, the Fertile Crescent where civilization in the West first flourished, gives his poems an intellectual heft seldom appreciated in fantasyland. On many levels, we see signs in Turner's poetry that the war reality before our eyes, ears, and nose is located in Iraq. It is not Stephen Crane's Civil War. It is not Ernest Hemingway's or E.E. Cummings's First World War. It is not Norman Mailer's or James Dickey's Second World War. It is not Tim O'Brien's or Bruce Weigl's or Bill Ehrhart's Vietnam War.

Turner's "The Hurt Locker" serves handily to set up deeper analysis of what he set out to achieve with two book-length collections, and that discussion is followed by exploration of two chapbooks by Hugh Martin, a Wallace Stegner Fellow, plus two other book-length collections from MFA-trained poets: *Shortly Thereafter* by Colin D. Halloran (MFA from Fairfield University) and *Letter Composed During a Lull in the Fighting,* from Kevin Powers (MFA from the University of Texas, Austin, where he was a Michener Fellow in Poetry). "The Hurt Locker" not only provided Kathryn Bigelow with a title for her movie but also forthrightly presents us with a jagged open wound that will refuse to heal for decades to come, hurt that will not abate when America turns its attention elsewhere, as it already has, whether to *Despicable Me* (or any other of its multiplex ilk—charming and distracting but utterly inconsequential) or to yet another military conflict:

> Nothing but the hurt left here.
> Nothing but bullets and pain
> and the bled-out slumping
> and all the *fucks* and *goddamns*
> and *Jesus Christs* of the wounded.
> Nothing left here but the hurt.
> Believe it when you see it.
> Believe it when a twelve-year-old
> rolls a grenade into the room.
> Or when a sniper punches a hole
> deep into someone's head.
> Believe it when four men
> step from a taxicab in Mosul
> to shower the street in brass
> and fire. Open the hurt locker
> and see what there is of knives
> and teeth. Open the hurt locker and learn
> how rough men come hunting for souls. (11)

Hurt, bullets, pain, death—plenty of angry curses—an enemy who could be just about anybody, young or old, near or far—dangers discriminate and indiscriminate. Rough and raw men . . . hunting for souls. Who has lost a soul? Who has a soul to give for the cause? The hurt locker is full to overflowing. And fantasyland? Well, never mind. Not too long after *Here, Bullet* was published, there was a badly botched home mortgage system threatening to drown the economy and dash American dreams, and angry elements of the citizenry carrying Tea Party flags who wanted to just get rid of government as the route to "a more perfect Union"—never mind the "establish Justice" bit, which takes a lot of government action to realize.

The poems of Turner's first book-length gathering (winner of the 2005 Beatrice Hawley Award) frequently link together in one way or another. For example, the collection's title poem ("Here, Bullet") powerfully draws upon the bullets/pain line at the beginning of "The Hurt Locker" by focusing on the ungodly intimacy of bullet and body, as if each was made for the other.

Here, Bullet
If a body is what you want,
then here is bone and gristle and flesh.
Here is the clavicle-snapped wish, the aorta's opened valves, the leap
thought makes at the synaptic gap.
Here is the adrenaline rush you crave,
that inexorable flight, that insane puncture
into heat and blood. And I dare you to finish
what you've started. Because here, Bullet,
here is where I complete the word you bring
hissing through the air, here is where I moan
the barrel's cold esophagus, triggering
my tongue's explosives for the rifling I have
inside of me, each twist of the round
spun deeper, because here, Bullet,
here is where the world ends, every time. (13)

The stance taken by body to bullet is taunting—a "here I am, you want me, come get me" challenge—all of life denoted and prepared to be found, thus bringing the world to an end, "every time." Bullets have been the instruments of combat death for many centuries now, but Turner is the first poet to address that fact, explicitly by name, calling the bullet out in a head-on challenge. The originality is breathtaking, a staggering presentation of the life–death battlefield partnership. Score one for the bullet. But then there is the riposte, a firing back.

The response from the human—the body—is equally brilliant and true. What force can a body throw back at the approach of an "I'm coming to get you" bullet? Can anything answer such a threat? Well, yes. It's a sound . . . the sound surging up through a throat, spinning to gain accuracy in the process, and then launching itself out into the world . . . in the fierce form of a word. In the beginning was the word. And in the end, too, was the word as this ferocious poem roars to its finish. Human utterance, the province of a poet, comes along to meet the bullet, undaunted. Who shall have the last say? In this case, Brian Turner, poet.

As mentioned previously, Turner's style extends beyond the usual war phenomenon—the weapons, the tactics, the fears, the deaths. He situates his poetry unmistakably in Iraq, in a war where the conditions were often enigmatic, and so the poetry slides often and knowingly away from America-centered matters over to reflect on and contend with the details of Iraqi language and culture. We see this pattern directly in his sequence of interpretations of diverse Iraqi phrases in "What Every Soldier Should Know," which comes, quite appropriately, early in the collection, although for a great many soldiers—at all levels of rank—the knowledge store was frequently insufficient as the fighting in Iraq evolved. Right away, there is a bit of language training, for it is always good to know the words of the people where you are making war:

> *O-guf! Tera armeek* is rarely useful.
> It means *Stop! Or I'll shoot.*

> *Sabah el khair* is effective.
> It means *Good Morning.*

> *Inshallah* means *Allah be willing.*
> Listen well when it is spoken. (9)

Iraq was a strange place—foreign in a great many ways to the average American soldier—and infinitely remote and far off the radar for the average American citizen. The languages were not known; the culture was alien. Ignorance of fundamental matters, such as the Sunni/Shite schism, proved disastrous once the regime of Saddam Hussein collapsed. Turner digs away at the profound gulf between Americans and their Iraqi hosts, many of whom took on the additional role of enemy. We are clearly meant to be wary regarding the "Listen well when it is spoken" line—and later in the poem a very short scene amplifies the full meaning and consequence of the "*Inshallah*" interjection: "Men wearing vests rigged with explosives / walk up, raise their arms and say *Inshallah*" (10). Indeed, listen well, but even if you master a few words, it may well not be enough to save you.

American soldiers deployed to Iraq had much to learn on the fly, and fast. As with the case of Vietnam a generation earlier, Iraq was an enigma, foreign beyond belief. Different language. Different history. Different culture. Different smells. Different food and drink. Different religion. Different gender politics. In a schoolbook taken up somewhere in high school, maybe there had been a Hammurabi question on a quiz, so perhaps there was knowledge running one question deep as troops flooded into Iraq. Only in the first few weeks was the war "conventional" in any sense of the term, a fleeting moment when it didn't matter so much what you knew about the country and the people where you were sent to fight. The Iraqi military was quickly in tattered ruins. Soon enough, there was a guerilla situation, a civil war—although it was heresy to admit to such terminology at the time. And guerilla wars, wherever fought, devolve into a realm of treachery and uncertainty that is bluntly accounted for in the last few lines of "What Every Soldier Should Know":

Small children who will play with you,
old men with their talk, women who offer chai—

and any one of them
may dance over your body tomorrow. (10)

Kids at play. Old men talking. Women with good things for the table. There's a culture in short form, and it looks appealing. However, add an outsider and everything changes. The joy of dance now involves death for the outsider.

Think of all the countries where Americans might be tempted to send military forces on the ground. Syria? Iran? Pakistan? Korea? Where do we know the language? Where do we understand the culture? Where do the religious notions line up with mainstream America? Nowhere. Nowhere. Nowhere. Where is the peril of outsider status guaranteed? Everywhere. Frances Fitzgerald's revelatory *Fire in the Lake*, about Vietnam, came too late to do Americans any good in that conflict, but that book could have served as an abstract primer for other equally "strange" places where Americans might venture in combat. Unfortunately, cultural ignorance was the order of the day as American forces were sent into Iraq to wage war.

Here, Bullet arrived in the middle of the Iraq War, in 2005, and it served notice that Brian Turner was a fine poet—and also that he sure knew both the brutality and the subtlety of the war Americans experienced in Iraq between 2003 and 2011. His book was too late to deter the start of the war, but as we look at a number of other poems in his first collection, we might ponder the potential impact on history if every person elected to Congress or to the presidency going forward had to read through the entire sequence—just so the architects of any future war would better understand what we're getting ourselves into. This would mostly involve older people, people who would not be going off to do the dirty work of war, a variation on the point of concern raised by Plato in *The Republic*. We would not frighten future guardians—so soldiers would continue to step forward voluntarily to serve country and to advance liberty; rather, we would seek to enlighten the political decision makers, making sure they had some depth of understanding about war—with details extending beyond simple clichés. Even rethinking something as simple as a road might be useful.

Everybody knows roads. You want to get somewhere, you hit the road. In war, this one fact of life does not change. One of the big roads in Iraq was Highway 1. There was a Highway 1 in Vietnam too. Both of them were long and treacherous—at least in war. Highway 1 in Vietnam now carries plenty of American tourists eager to explore the land where danger once lurked at every turn. One of Turner's early poems in *Here, Bullet* is titled simply, "Hwy 1," but the first line quickly amplifies the most salient feature of this route: it is the "Highway of Death" (6). As the poem moves along, most of what we learn involves time past, time before an American incursion. But in the last stanza, an American makes his mark on the place. In fantasyland, Americans always go off to war to do noble things, to fight honorably, to make the world—not just a nation—more perfect. Turner gives us a cautionary alternative option, though, to this innocent and naive fantasy. There is a crane, a bird, and the bird has nested high above Highway 1. This crane is shot, for no apparent reason other than that it was possible, by an American sergeant. The shooting takes place on a beautiful morning, not long after sunrise, one of those eternal moments of hope and promise. The crane is "amazed that death has found it" (6). Stupid bird! It should have known death would come on a battlefield. It is what death does in war, and in this provocative poem, we see a new kind of road kill.

Just a little bit later in the collection, in "The Al Harishma Weapons Market," the ugly commerce of war is explored as the story of an Iraqi gun dealer, Akbar, develops even as his young son, Habib, is terrified by nighttime sounds of gunfire. To comfort his son and help him slip into the comfort of sleep, Akbar lies. Lies abound in war. Everyone pitches in with some form of untruth. In the false telling, the gunfire is just part of a cosmic musical extravaganza, a sound and light show (weirdly paralleling the football game halftime show where Billy Lynn and his squad mates were to be given a fantasyland celebration), and the tracers show "how each bright star travels / from this dark place, to the other" (8). Imagine that, lying to your young son, hiding your very ugly killing business from him with a fantastical narrative. It's actually a variation on "Here, Bullet"—the ending of this arms dealer's deceit—as bullets race across the earth, always looking for a target, always bringing death, the migration of lead from dark place to dark place, with a searing bright arc between.

"Two Stories Down" brings another death scene into close focus, a dramatic fight pumped high with irony. Here the combat is hand-to-hand. As the poem begins, an insurgent named Hasan jumps to the ground from two stories up, breaking his legs in the fall. An American soldier approaches quickly, full of uncertainty. What has happened? What does it mean? Does the fallen man need care, comfort? The situation is ambiguous—right up to the moment when the insurgent "steals the knife from its sheath" and a life-and-death struggle ensues, with the knife ending the story sunk into Hasan . . . and then the final turn of irony as Hasan thanks his adversary. It all makes sense—for Hasan is out of excruciating pain, out of life, and yes, into a wondrous heaven for a servant of Allah. If E.E. Cummings were trying to represent this twist, all your downs are ups.

War and irony are mated forever. The astounding irony of war is worked out in "Ferris Wheel," which focuses on riverine death. The setting is Mosul, where once there was a tourist complex, complete with a Ferris wheel, that idyllic enchantment of bygone childhood fairground experience in fantasyland America. It is now, however, an artifact of some earlier and presumably happier day, just an inchoate witness to the bizarre drama of war. An American helicopter goes down in the Tigris. Navy divers are dispatched to recover the pilots; they bring up bodies, an "Iraqi policeman" and "a college student from Kirkuk" (55). In the last stanza, the poem avers that "the history books will get it wrong"—with nothing about the rusted Ferris wheel, nothing about how one pilot tried to save the other, with both drowning as a consequence. It is cold and brutal, that water—dumb in this history—and no one will get it, get the full import of such lunacy. This is no *American Sniper* sort of scene, no simple wish just to kill the bastards shooting at us in their country. This particular Ferris wheel has absolutely no place in fantasyland.

Then of course there was sex. There's always sex, even with soldiers off at war—especially with soldiers off at war, desperate to do something connected with regeneration of life, not just its termination. "Last Night's Dream (for Ishtar)" brings sex to the fore near the end of Turner's first collection.

It's not the clearest or cleanest sex ever. It is a dream, after all, and moreover, all of the copulatory action is related in combat terms—"azimuths" shot to the navel, UFH radio transmissions, flashbang grenades, Arabic kissed "into skin," translated "backwards into cuneiform and stone," an orgasm that "destroys a nation" leaving medevac helicopters to "fly in the dark caverns of our lungs in / search of the wounded, and we breathe them one to another, / a deep rotorwash of pain and bandages" (58). Turner here delivers a new take on the Eros/Thanatos intersection as sex and death mingle intimately, nightmarishly, in the Iraq of an American combat veteran. For the denizens of fantasyland, voraciously devouring *Fifty Shades of Gray*, this quickie dream (for Ishtar) may not measure up. Why must the shadow or specter of war loom over everything? Is there no escape into pure sex?

With *Phantom Noise* (2010, also published by Alice James Books), Turner provides a split-screen consideration of the Iraq War—sometimes still there, grasped tightly by the clutches of memory in the combat zone, digging around for perspective; and sometimes back in America, digging around for some way to fit in, to complete the journey home of this Odysseus. In "Lullaby for Bullets" (67), for example, we are once more tossed into conversation with a bullet on the receiving end. This bullet is fired, is headed toward some unsuspecting American, and then is encouraged "to lean to the right, / if you lean back and look as hard as you can / for that mountain you came from, sunlight / warming the pines, clouds approaching / from the north with a gift of silence, / if you do this you might just graze / the man's temple, so close you might hear / his name, the humming of blood / over bone, the many voices / within, the years to come." Whoever had such an extended discourse with a bullet? The original one-shot wonder—Hawkeye, Deerslayer—James Fenimore Cooper's proto-American on the war front, he had plenty of strange and awkward colloquies, but never was there any talking to a bullet on its mission of death. In the Vietnam film deeply indebted to Cooper, Michael Cimino's *The Deer Hunter*, the Michael character portrayed by Robert De Niro has a brief moment of strange talk with his companions about the rifle bullet in his fingers, high in the mountains for a final deer hunt before Vietnam becomes the land of the hunted. Michael is distressed by Stanley, one of the film's homebound chicken hawks, who waves a small handgun around with silly bravado. Glaring menacingly toward his foil with the tiny gun, Mike holds up the long round and spits out "*This . . . is this.*"

And so it is, indubitably. Cryptically. A perfect tautology, just the sort of thing to introduce a war that would baffle Americans for a decade. Just the sort of thing a man of few words would say—which is entirely typical of mythic Americans at war—from Cooper's Natty Bumppo to Hemingway's Nick Adams to John Wayne's many characters (all the same, really). Regarding guys who are loners, "isolatoes" in Herman Melville's lexicon, their numbers are legion in the American landscape of imagination, and they typically are men of very few words. In Hemingway's treatment of the male loner type, it is a sacrilege to explain or explore feelings or emotions. It is best to do what is required—and speak little of it. Turner is pushing back, trying to find more to say, working hard to give the war experience a full and complete interrogation. It's a mighty effort, that business of trying to deflect a bullet ever so slightly with some words. The result is a version of the old pen vs. sword contest, dressed up as a lullaby.

Some of the poems in *Phantom Noise* sketch in background for the soldier at war: the first flash of terror at age four, in 1971, carrying a cup of tea over a gangway with a guard dog snarling furiously underneath ("Lucky Money"); and "Homemade Napalm," a multigenerational meditation extending back through a father's heavy drinking to a grandfather's flame-thrower experience on Guadalcanal, and then settling in to brood on the old man's late-night record playing, listening to plaintive songs in the loneliness of "blue dark," all leading to the insight that "to be a man is to carry things inside, / no one would ever understand, things better left unsaid; sung about, / maybe . . ." (41). These words could be the mantra uniting Natty with the Hemingway code hero, the male emotional emptiness that continues to bedevil many relationships that require communication beyond the statistics of sports or the economy.

Set off against the long past are recollections that rise to the surface in the aftermath of the Iraq War experience—the near history. In "VA Confessional," scenes from the war invade all hours of the day and night, especially the night, even the sex, which is not called love. Recollections of killing are the constant. You'd think it might go easier in "At Lowe's Home Improvement Center," the happy shopping ground for fantasylanders looking to make the good life better aisle by aisle, a relentlessly material pursuit of happiness—but in this poem, at every turn—from the hammer and anchor section through plywood, ceiling fans, and even paint, vivid scenes from the destruction of war intrude upon the construction impulse. The profusion of decorator choices is rather overwhelming, maybe most so in Aisle 7, which offers practically every kind of light imaginable. So much light! Suddenly "Each dead Iraqi walks amazed / by Tiffany post and Bavarian pole lights" (7). This catastrophic immersion in American material excess, here fleetingly joined by the dead and living of Iraq, is comparable in some ways to the moment in *The Hurt Locker* when Sergeant James is caught in panic, paralyzed in the long cereal aisle at the supermarket—facing just too many choices, confronted with so much that it is not really possible to make any good sense of it all. Americans transport their excesses everywhere they venture, and then sometimes the ghost spirits of people in other cultures come home with our veterans. The last quick scene from the Lowe's/Iraq conflation has a young Iraqi boy putting a "*T, for Tourniquet*" on the forehead of the representative veteran—painted in "Retro Colonial Blue" (7). Retro to the max. Once upon a time, America had its own civil war of independence—a long and often ugly struggle that brought the colonial era to an end. But the past comes back, often in very strange ways. It's a grotesque mash-up.

In any full accounting of the Iraq War, the American vice president in office at the time when the pretext for combat activity was fabricated should make at least one appearance, for no one at the time was more vociferous in pressing to get American soldiers into battle again. As it happened, Dick Cheney made a visit to the Air Force Academy in Colorado Springs—nothing at all unusual for a vice president to do. He was accommodated at Rampart Lodge, an inn that operates to serve guests at the USAF Academy. Then later, Brian Turner found himself in the same place, even in the same bed as the one occupied by Dick Cheney. Hence the poem "Sleeping in Dick Cheney's Bed" (15). Turner was there, as a sergeant, to speak to "the officer corps in a theater / filled with 1600 listening faces—as I spoke / about rape, death, and murder" (16). Later, in Cheney's bed, he really, really, really needed the escape of sleep. The literal situation here, the sharing of a bed by disparate people, necessarily opens up the idea that the bed Dick Cheney made—getting American soldiers into war in Iraq—was a bed that Brian Turner shared during his Iraq tour of duty. As quite a few of the poems in *Phantom Noise* show, that particular bedding frequently did not provide restful sleep. Getting out of such a bed would not be easy, at least not for the soldier types. However, it wasn't such a big deal for the vice president (retired), who over the course of a long and multi-heart life has owned large chunks of fantasyland real estate in places as far apart as Wyoming and St. Michael's, Maryland.

While most of Turner's poems are short lyrics, in most cases a page or slightly more, on occasion he works in a longer piece. "Al-A'Imma Bridge" runs to five pages. Given the span of time that the poem covers, so apt for a poem on a bridge, twenty variable-length stanzas is not really long. Still, the history packed into the poem is daunting. The history Americans cherish extends only a few centuries into the past; Iraq is different, as this bridge poem makes clear in every detail. The river is the Tigris. The present scene is not pleasant; bodies topple off the bridge, frantic and desperate, as war rages around them. A few stanzas deep in misery, we move back a few decades to the "one million who died fighting Iran" (28)—then ratchet way off to the past where "Alexander the Great falls," and soon the lines are filled with the "walled ruins of Nineveh: / the Babylonians and Sumerians and Assyrians" (28)—then Scheherazade and Ali Baba, but quickly the movement on the bridge goes the other way, and we are confronted with "pirated Eastern European porn videos" full of the "freaky" (28). Some years are noted quickly in passing (1956, '49, '31, '17), the "snowfall in Mosul," and then 1967, 1972, 2001, and 2002. To these signposts in history—and to us, far away, knowing not so much in intimate terms of these dates and their significance—questions are posed: "*What will we remember? What will we say of these?*" (29) For Americans, of course, we haven't had the key operative year mentioned yet; that would be 2003, when American soldiers entered Iraq to topple Saddam Hussein. We have a very tight historical scope.

The poem then shifts, though, to a time long before in this foreign place. It is the year 1258. Not a single American could attach an event to that particular year. We might have something for 1066 or 1492, but 1258 is enigmatic to the nth degree. We are empty there. But in Iraq, not so. It was a year of terrible bloodshed as the siege of Baghdad ended with conquest by Hulagu Khan's Mongols; something on the order of a million citizens were killed. The Tigris was full to overflowing with the dead. Who could forget that? War has been here before, with death on a horrific scale. And now, again, "the Tigris is filling with the dead, filling / with bricks from Abu Ghraib, burning vehicles / pushed from Highway 1" (30). This place is once more ugly and wretched with killing, but "Gilgamesh can do nothing" (30) as all of this present mayhem moves along into oblivion, soon to be "forgotten in American hallways." But here, "where mourning has a long history" (31), flowers must be gathered and offered to "light the darkness" (31). Americans often are full of the fantasy of omnipotence—of being all-important—but this bridge poem presents a very different viewpoint; in the long bridge of time, our passage through Iraq is a very small blip. To see this, however, is not easy; it takes a bigger scale of human history than we are generally inclined to provide. We were not mindful of this history going into Iraq, and we surely are not ready to pay attention after getting out. Turner pushes back against this mainstream pattern, but he labors mostly alone. We can't keep our own short history straight; why bother with somebody else's past?

Every day humans leave behind a little record of our existence. Bodily eliminations follow us wherever we go. "Wading Out" takes us to this rancid realm of reality. It is a poem "after Bruce Weigl," and the key Weigl poem to remember is "Burning Shit at An Khe," which is included in *Carrying the Darkness*. Weigl's poem comes to a pungent finish, which is perfectly obvious given the title and the activity described throughout. Turner's soldier in Iraq is on patrol, the day is hot, and he starts to slog through "a patch of still water" (47). But it's a cesspool, and soon he is deep in it, and so too with his platoon and all their gear/missions/casualties . . . and his lieutenant as well. Can he wade through it, come out the other side? And others? Uncertainty covers all, like a certain smell. For any survivors, "poolside in California, / the day as bright as this one, how will we hose ourselves off / to remove the stench, standing around a barbeque / talking football—how?" (48). Sports, sports, sports—the lifeline of fantasyland. Turner's "Wading Out" puts the return to sports-talk fully in doubt for veterans. It's too much a world of shit—distantly echoing the exchange between Pvt. Joker and Pvt. Pyle in the barracks head at the end of the first half of *Full Metal Jacket*.

If sports may not work to transport Iraq veterans home safe, Odysseus back in Ithaca after many years of trials and travel, perhaps a better answer resides in the potency of art. Homer himself suggests this solution—by giving to Odysseus cleverness with words, one of the always-important arts. "In the Guggenheim Museum" comes close to the end of *Phantom Noise*. Two lovers are making their way down through the "curving ramp of galleries" (9) in Frank Lloyd Wright's rotunda. In the foreground for our attention are intimate kisses of two lovers even here in the midst of an art-loving crowd, all out in the grand open space with others and "conversations trailing behind them like multi-colored scarves" (90). The lovers finally reach the "Sound and Light exhibit" (90), which is exotic and electric, "the unified theory / of color conjoined with sound" (91), and they are transported, as if by magic of word and sensation to the night before when they enjoyed a lover's tryst in the park, getting drenched in their act of love by sprinklers on full blast. The memory of sex in nature infuses memory even as the lovers now stand in the midst of artifacts, "petrified" in "their fossilized stations" (92), and so "yet, here we are / walking among them—*alive*" (92). ALIVE. Such a potent word for the end of this poem. In the presence of art, in the act of love, it is possible still to be alive, even after war. So it was with Penelope and Odysseus—long, long, long separated—and here Turner reaches the same endpoint. *Alive.*

Brian Turner's poetry is quite well known. As mentioned earlier, he appears frequently at poetry conferences and all sorts of programs for writers. Hugh Martin's published work now matches up with Turner's—two chapbook collections in print (*So, How Was the War?* in 2010 and *The Stick Soldiers* in 2013)—but he is not at all so well known. In subject matter, his poetry is way less likely to incorporate the deep history or culture of Iraq; instead he hews close to the experience of American soldiers who found themselves being hastily prepared for combat in Iraq and then enduring actual combat exposure as best they could. The curve to writing and poetry for Martin is different from the one in Turner's life. Martin pursued his MFA degree *after* service in Iraq. Many of his poems have been crafted for his graduate program, in workshop activity. His poems are tightly built— and they pack plenty of punches.

For example, early in *So, How Was the War?* there is "December in Fayetteville," an accounting of attitude and disposition in two soldiers soon to be off to the Iraq War. It's a prose poem. The setting is antiheroic; they are huddled in the cold under semitrailers parked in Fayetteville, "a town one soldier describes as, / strip club, pawn shop, strip club, pawn shop, strip club, pawn shop" (3). That is Fayetteville all right—and many other military towns as well. These soldiers-in-training are not within the daunting fenced expanse of Fort Bragg, a very serious staging ground for war in any year. They are off duty, so to speak, chilling with some beers in the cold of December. And then the situation is fleshed out: "In two months / we will leave for Iraq; we have been leaving for Iraq for four months. / If we'd have wanted to talk about it then, under those trailers, / neither of us would've given a damn since all we wanted was to go, / get over there, to begin, what they call, 'boots on the ground,' / which would last a year and then we could finally go home, stay home" (3). Nothing glamorous here, nothing of the hero spirit—just a desire to get it over with.

Sure enough, in Iraq there were "boots on the ground." And one year/one tour for quite a few soldiers turned into several years/several tours. It was a bad time, to echo the opening of Tim O'Brien's first big Vietnam novel, *Going After Cacciato.* And before this December moment ends, there is the confession that "all we wanted / was to feel a buzz, maybe just enough to forget where we were going" (3). Cheery Christmas might be coming—but this poem is all dreary December, a time saturated with anxiety from the fear of being lost or alone.

Martin went off to Iraq; others were dispatched to Afghanistan. In "Sampson's E-Mail with Attachment," the two wars bleed together, thanks to the Internet and cybercommunication. The opening is provocative and re-velatory: "I accidentally deleted the e-mail / of the head you sent me / from Afghanistan" (11). The image of a detached head gives significant weight to the title, for Sampson of the ancient world's mythology lost his head. Here the loss has been compounded—a head first lost from the body, and then lost from the digital record. It's almost as if nothing happened. But the picture had indeed loaded, before deletion—and there was a detached head, pathetic on "the bloody sand"—and the written note made the whole situation clear: "guy threw grenades at main gate, / hit him with SAW and 240" (11). It's glossary time, but this first book has no explanatory notes to bring everybody up to speed with the military lingo. If *SAW* and *240* leave us scratching our heads in bewilderment, it's a sure bet we're secure in fantasyland. We did not have to work up a new vocabulary of military nomenclature; hence, we do not have to build up our word supply in the aftermath—and will seldom get help from the veterans who are in the know by virtue of hard experience. (Turner appended a very brief set of "Notes" to *Here, Bullet*, mostly to explain references to details of cultural background in Iraq.) The end of the poem provides a fuller account of the head loss (the decapitation, not the digital deletion): "back home, you'll tell me / after dozens of bullets had entered / his collapsing body, / it was his own pinless grenade / that fell like a stone from his hand, / and took off his head" (12). Sometimes the irony, not just the devil, is in the details.

Martin's second collection, *The Stick Soldiers*, has much of the same mix as *So, How Was the War?* The title poem for the collection illustrates in the simplest of images the distance separating American soldiers in Iraq and the homefolk in fantasyland. In support of the war, children back at home—in elementary schools and Girl Scout troops—have mailed off Christmas cards, filling them with wishes for presents (a doll here, a dog there), some-times with stick-figure illustrations. One innocent young correspondent draws a death wish for three "Iraki" stick-figure insurgents, about to be done in with the toss of a grenade-like thing from a US soldier. And then, as it turns out, there is stick-figure art on the streets of Iraq. One cartoon shows: "In white chalk, on concrete walls, / a box-shaped Humvee, with two antennae / rising like balloons from the hatch" (17–18). In the wall image, a fellow soldier with rifle offers a wave to others, real soldiers, passing in their Humvees. So far, so good. But down the street, the cartoon develops further, as "a stick man holds / an RPG / aimed toward the Humvee, the waving soldier's head—" (18). The poem's conclusion conflates wishes by children—some wishes for Christmas presents, other wishes for dead Americans.

"First Engagement" lives up to its title. It develops in the second person, a deft use of the all-inclusive "you." You are there. You are in a defensive posture, trying to hold your place against hostility—an unclear threat yet expected from any direction, at any time. As it turns out, three mortars had come in from somewhere earlier in the day. And now, here comes a white utility truck, bearing down on your unit's position. It plows blindly in your direction, sparks flying behind, and when it does not stop prudently when any prudent driver would stop—since no one wants to risk death by truck-borne IED—it is met with a barrage of gunfire from the Bradley's cannon and from your weapon as well. You fire until your lieutenant tells you to stop. The truck is full of holes, a wreck. The driver and passenger are full of holes. Who could know the desperate and ill-advised effort to drag rebar home for a rebuild project, a father-and-son project? But one fact is known for certain: "the man falls to the road for you, for the Bradley, / for all the men, to show just how you've done" (26). To prosecute a war, you engage the enemy. You kill the enemy. Engagement has begun—and so has killing. This war will last an incredibly long time for many soldiers who went there and engaged in it. Odysseus will not be safe at home for a great stretch of time.

Martin gives us an "aubade," in his first gathering; for the second he moves on to "nocturnes." The dawn comes—but, inevitably, so does darkness. Martin's representation of the Iraq War has plenty of darkness. Details of experience in that four-letter-word place (Iraq) accumulate, poem by poem. There are lots of "Ways of Looking at an IED," maybe not the thirteen of Wallace Stevens's meditation on blackbird variability, but nine is surely enough. Just one would be enough. One would be too many. Three hours are lost to the anxiety and caution generated by the mystery of a "black plastic bag" by the roadside—eventually discovered to contain "six ripe tomatoes" (76). The landscape is routinely treacherous, with much to be avoided, and it doesn't take long for soldiers to "hate the ground" (77), a point emphatically represented earlier in Kathryn Bigelow's *The Hurt Locker*.

Eventually there is demobilization, the story of a return. The longest poem in the collection is the last one, "Nostros: Quinn's Bar, Cleveland Heights," with the date line of January 2005. There are nineteen sections, stretching out over ten pages. Being home is no easy matter. Gone is the weird clarity of being a target, being hunted; now it's a matter of just fitting in again, just being regular. All you have to do is process the news:

Iraqi Violence Intensifies as Election Nears
U.S. Ends Search for Weapons
Ohio State 34, Notre Dame 14
Largest Passenger Plane Launched in France (90)

It is the end of one year, the beginning of a new one, life (Notre Dame football) goes on, and family members are glad to have their soldier home for
the New Year's Eve dinner. Lobster bisque, a waiter suggesting salmon—the
good life. But then arrives a section of memory, recollecting some favorite
saying of a fellow soldier—but one who died "in Kufa / from a young Shiite
boy's RPG" (91). There is once-upon-a-time certainty about the weapons
of mass destruction—"*before you went in, a convoy of trucks crossed / the
Syrian border. / We know*" (92). There are questions: "*Were you scared? You
pop any A-Rabs?*" (93). Later, a fellow soldier shows off his "postdeployment
gift / to himself: / Semi-automatic Bushmaster M4 Carbine" (96). Later
yet, with three guns out and being nuzzled intimately, there is almost an
Odysseus-back-in-Ithaca massacre when "Tom's mother walks in / holding
three bulbs / she wants us to hang, we turn—cheeks tucked to stocks, three
muzzles / pointing" (97). And then it's out to confront the cold of "the black
Cleveland skyline" (97) and an iced-over Lake Erie, the three isolatoes walking into the snow, feet crunching frozen whiteness below.

An earlier section (#6) had put the war-zone-to-homeland separation
into tight perspective: "Back there, I wanted to go home / and have / the
whole world. Here, / the crowd smells of cherry vodka and sleet" (91). Sassoon said it for the World War I warriors: "Soldiers are dreamers." O'Brien
stretched the dream out over eight thousand miles in *Going After Cacciato*,
a dream that collapsed into violence in Paris, the City of Light, with escape
from Vietnam looking like a project extending far into the future beyond
peace talks and the return of US soldiers to America. Hugh Martin adds
another twist by acknowledging the gulf between having "the whole world"
and being thrown in the midst of "smells of cherry vodka and sleet."

Before we transition to analysis of fiction, two more poets merit exploration. After an army tour in Afghanistan, Colin D. Halloran pushed to get
his life in order by completing his bachelor's degree and then an MFA from
Fairfield University. He has worked as a teacher and poetry workshop facili-
tator, with particular interest in poetry focused on understanding war experience. His 2012 poetry collection, *Shortly Thereafter*, centers on that subject and works the territory with significant range. While his poems do not

attempt to match the depth of detail Turner uses about the land and culture he visited in uniform, Halloran nevertheless makes perfectly clear his presence in an experience that stands in stark contrast to what is known by people back home. The poem called "Echoes" features a dramatic split consciousness, an awareness of two radically separated worlds, one dominated by "The call to prayer: / a five times daily reminder / of where I am, what I've become," the other a dream vision of wilderness Maine, complete with "birch flecked island perched on the edge of a northern lake" (21). "The call to prayer" defines a place of violence just waiting to happen, the imperfect function of human malfeasance mystically counterbalanced by the purity of a faraway and pristine sanctuary of island, lake, and raging rivers all "under Katahdin's shadow" (21). A similar sense of foreboding surfaces again in "SPRING OFFENSIVE I. I HAVE HEARD THE MULLAH SPEAK," where a prophetic voice speaks of the past in multiple layers of fathers and sons and brothers, over and over again, reaching way back to Cain and Abel, all punctuated with one recurrent phrase, *Allahuakbar* (25–27), which serves universally as warrant for war while diverse weapons are readied for action and lives are prepared to be lost—such an old story in this very old place.

The almost unbridgeable gulf between the experience of war in Afghanistan and life back in the United States is shown especially well in two poems, "Morning Commute" and "4th of July." For the past century, most Americans with a job have had to contend with a commute to work in the morning. Traffic snarls and trains behind schedule can make the commute quite miserable. But Halloran provides a fast-moving commute story that makes the typical American going-to-work challenge seem inconsequential by comparison. All it takes is a young boy full of innocence, eager to greet the traffic: "That's the spot he ran to, / Where he came to say hello: a wave and a salute" (30), and then the scene turns ghastly with the boy's "arteries so cleanly cut / as shrapnel raced from ground to chest." The boy gets the best available trauma care, and he fights for life. "Then he falters. / Machines are reattached. / The smile in his eyes / begins to fade. / That's the spot. / I drive by it every day" (30–31). In just over a page, Halloran provides a glimpse of hell to put to shame all ordinary complaints about a morning commute.

"4th of July" takes us back to reflections in the first chapter about the propulsive power of the Declaration of Independence with its "acquiesce in the necessity" of war as a steady force working on generation after generation of Americans. So here now is an American soldier deployed to Afghanistan, and it's the Fourth of July, a matter of no consequence to any Afghan but loaded with emotion and implication for someone in hostile territory a world away from home. Fortunately, marvelous devices of communication became readily available for use in the twenty-first century; it's officially a "day off," whatever that might mean in a combat zone, so a phone call home is easy to arrange. Back home, all is normal: "The picnic's at my mother's house / and I can almost see them gathered / poolside, bare feet against the deck / that hostas try their best to breach, / plumes billowing from the grill / I don't much like the sight of smoke now" (38). The ordinariness and high predictability of the home-front scene is eerily unsettling in this circumstance, and the following two stanzas add immeasurably to the discomforting distance that shrouds this war-zone-to-home telephone chat.

The whole family's there, even great-uncle Pat,
who asks with interest
if I've had the chance to
shoot any gooks?

His was a different time,
a different war.
It still persists within him,
Shaping his perceptions of mine. (38)

What do the folks at home understand about the conflict and war action going on in Afghanistan? Halloran's "4th of July" poem makes it excruciatingly clear that even the little that might be "known" is sadly mistaken, far off the mark. Of course, all wars are the same in the soldier's essential goal—to engage the enemy and kill him, with the derogatory label being a matter of little consequence.

In such a light, the soldier's response to ignorance is understandable: "I laugh it off, / take in their telescopic voices / what could be one last time, / then head to the tower. / It's never really off, after all" (38). A holiday, even the one for the Fourth of July, can mean different things in different places—carefree picnic at home . . . wary guard duty in war. By poem's end, the soldier is pondering "what this will look like / when my mind's had / sixty years to shape it" (39). Given the intractability of the Taliban cause in Afghanistan, it is possible that this soldier will himself receive a call on the Fourth of July from a grandson deployed to this forever war zone, but even across all that time, the depth of knowledge and understanding evident at home in America is likely to be about on par with what is presented in Halloran's poem.

In "The Tragedy of the American Military," James Fallows details a host of reasons why most Americans have but scant awareness regarding the wars in Iraq (once thought finished, now just a nettlesome work-in-progress) and Afghanistan (ongoing, with no end in sight). He very astutely notes that World War II was impossible to ignore; the war was intimately experienced by Americans all across the population. Vietnam, while never reaching the massive scale of citizen involvement required by war in the 1940s, was nevertheless brought home through the antiwar protest movement, and by the time combat troops were withdrawn in 1973, the Vietnam War had come to define a generation (or two). War in Iraq and Afghanistan never in any way reached that level of common knowledge, shared experience, or serious consequence for any generation in America early in the twenty-first century.

Poetry is about ready to give way to fiction in this study, just as the progression took place in human evolution from epic poems in the time of Homer to the rise of the novel in English from the eighteenth century on, and extending the novel's literary primacy right through the end of the twentieth century. Kevin Powers offers a perfect pivot text from poetry to fiction in his "Letter Composed During a Lull in the Fighting," for this poem serves to provide not only the title for his 2014 poetry collection but also the name of a key figure in *The Yellow Birds*, his widely acclaimed novel published two years earlier.

Estrangement might be the best word to describe the typical issue of concern in the poems of Kevin Powers. His various surrogate figures are isolated for the most part, struggling to move forward under the weight of experience almost too heavy for words to bear. "Elegy for Urgency" presents a kind of worst-case scenario for a veteran/poet:

> But you have noticed nothing in a long time,
> holy or otherwise, so it is not remarkable
> that you spent the rest of the day listening blankly
> as your friends and loved ones chattered on,
> unable even to speak,
> the whole time dizzying further, only aware
> of the futility of trying to fix yourself in the world
> with words you cannot remember. (19)

A poet without words is no poet. The people who did not go to war—as Powers had done—have abundant words. The fact that they "chattered on" suggests an emptiness at the core of this too-too-too much conversation. The overwhelming din of noise from everyone else bears unmercifully down on the one who most needs to work with words.

A profound sense of loneliness and estrangement simmers throughout "Meditation on a Main Supply Route." The title plays off against a bit of war lingo; the main supply route (MSR in military shorthand lingo) designates a very important part of the war terrain, crucial for successful replenishment of supplies to wage war, with an on-the-ground road being the route for trucks to make their deliveries. The enemy easily figured out the route, which immediately became a prime target for improvised explosive devices as a way to disrupt resupply activity. Any US troops involved in movement along the MSR would be in peril, thus giving ominous overtones to the opening line of the poem: "I recall Route Tampa going / in a straight line all the way / out of the war" (21). As the poem moves quickly along, the destinations outside the war span the country (Virginia, California, Ohio, Texas, North Carolina, New York), and then we are introduced to the wounded veterans whose MSR duty got them home in really bad shape physically— and rather ragged psychological condition as well. Finally, focus turns to the poem's persona, whose condition is different, at least initially: "I am home and whole, so to speak." However, a few lines later, we hit a hard wall of reality: "But I can't remember / how to be alive. It has begun / to rain so hard I fear I'll drown" (23). For veterans shattered or whole, in sum, the MSRs are roads to hell, in one form or another, all across America.

Reading through *Letter Composed During a Lull in the Fighting* is really tough, for each poem adds a new dimension of torment, unrelentingly bringing far away wars into the evolving landscape of America. "Photographing the Sudden Dead" reveals the indelibility of war experience as understood through the lens of documentation. An ugly scene in Iraq unfolds: a car racing toward a checkpoint barrier, and its occupants riddled with gunfire because they refused to stop as ordered—and a photograph of it is taken, evidence to be carried forever as the witness moves along fitfully through life.

> We no longer have to name
>   the sins that we are guilty of.
> The evidence for every crime
> exists. What one
> must always answer for
> is not what has been done, but

for the weight of what remains
as residue—every effort
must be made to scrub away
the stain we've made on time. (49)

The stain made on time—what a powerful way to capture the permanence
of war experience. The human bearer of that experience, as represented
by poem after poem in this collection and accounted for most achingly in
"Photographing the Sudden Dead," will not rest easy for a very long time,
with most of that time suffered in self-imposed isolation:

Nor would it be enough
to have myself for months secluded
in the dark rooms
of an apartment
I'd wound up paying for up front,
Desperate for anything
To keep out light, a sometimes
Loaded gun,
and whatever solitude
I needed to survive
the next unraveling,
undocumented instant. (50–51)

Of course, as noted early in this study, writing about horrific experience
can be therapeutic. Words matter intensely, and poets put them to use to
solve problems and to heal wounds. In "Improvised Explosive Device," Powers aggressively interrogates the potency of language, relentlessly equating
the power of a poem with those explosive devices that ruined so many
American lives in Iraq (and Afghanistan): "If this poem had wires / coming out of it, / you would not read it" (27). Over and over, the features of
the poem are aligned with the IED—metal/wires/deafening sound/blinding
light. At the end Powers has one last provocative explosion waiting for us in
this poem/IED comparison:

If this poem had wires coming out of it,
you would not read it.
If these words were made of metal
they could kill us all. But these

are only words. Go on,
they are safe to hold and put into your pocket.
Even better, they are safe
to be forgotten. (32)

Words safe to be forgotten: with this wryly ironic twist at the end, Powers
has thrown down a challenge to his fellow Americans. War veterans know
war. War veterans who become poets know how to improvise explosive
word devices. But will readers dare come near? And even if they do, perhaps they will be all too ready to rush the poet's words into the wasteland
of "forgotten."

The final poem by Powers to be considered, "Letter Composed During
a Lull in the Fighting," first appeared in the February 2009 issue of *Poetry
Magazine*. The place of initial publication alone bespeaks the importance
of this poem gesture, and it also indicates that the efforts by veterans to
reach American readers with their explosive words was supported by the
poetry establishment. Through the determined and dedicated—and very
creative—editorial leadership of Christian Wiman over the first decade of
the twenty-first century (his ten-year editorship ended on 30 June 2013),
Poetry surged again to the highest level of importance in the domain of
poetry. Wiman's approach brought many new readers, increased circulation
hugely, and introduced long-form journalism pieces to round out the intellectual ferment that brought excitement to new heights at the magazine.
But as always, the heart of the project was publication of shimmering new
poems—whether by well-established poets (Kim Addonizio, Stephen Dunn,
and Virgil in his *Aeneid*, II, line 692 to the end) or by poets new to the genre
and most certainly new to the revered space of *Poetry*.

Kevin Powers would be in the latter category, a veteran of Iraq combat
now fighting it all again in words. The poem features a natural form for
bringing the war home. It's a letter. But as we know from the letters of Sa-
mantha Hughes's father in Bobbie Ann Mason's novel *In Country* (1985), the
missives to loved ones back home often prove to be very evasive—on many
levels. In the name of love—and in the zone of war—some lying is often
well warranted. The impulse to protect loved ones from dark and unsettling
knowledge is natural. Shield them from truth; keep them safe. Against that
backdrop of dissembling via truncated and nuanced communication, however, this poem from Kevin Powers serves up a rougher portrait of war than
the one provided in Hugh Martin's poem "So, How Was the War?"

The opening from Powers is predictable enough: "I tell her I love her" (5). Of course! Millions of missives home from soldiers on foreign battlefields have borne this simple sentiment of love. We all know how absence can add to fondness. But with this sweet part immediately noted for dispatch, the rest of the poem must deal with all the unpleasant stuff that the home front does not really want to receive. So loving becomes immediately compared to "not killing / or ten minutes of sleep / beneath the low rooftop wall / on which my rifle rests." The luster of love is suddenly dulled—or driven to new heights of intensity by the linkages introduced in this poem.

Then the poem turns to the physical sensations carried by the letter, the raw, intense smells of battlefield reality: "that will stink, / when she opens it, / of bolt oil and burned powder / and the things it says" (5). Inchoate though they may be, the smells of war will sneak through under the surface of subterfuge. What can be said, so as not to throw the good folks back home into a tizzy of despair? Perhaps we could quote a fellow soldier, one with enough cleverness in language to make the death dance of war into something more like a ballet. Powers deftly executes just such a move in the last stanza of this letter poem:

I tell her how Pvt. Bartle says, offhand,
that war is just us
making little pieces of metal
pass through each other. (5)

That's manageable—just thinking about little pieces of metal passing through each other. There is no blood, no terrible screaming in pain, no slipping away into unconsciousness and then way out there to death . . . to a body bag . . . a flight to Dover AFB . . . a military funeral with all the trimmings . . . and then the drop down into American soil. Add a few hundred thousand "Support Our Troops" stickers on SUV rear doors across the land, and all will be well, not to worry, for fantasyland is safe and secure. Pvt. Bartle really knows how to render brute ugliness into sweet grace. Who is this private, anyway? As it turns out, it was just a name that came to Powers as he worked up this poem, but once Bartle had appeared, he stuck around. Private Bartle eventually became the central figure in *The Yellow Birds*, the highly (and justly) acclaimed 2012 novel by Kevin Powers, a story that opens the following chapter on the fiction that has emerged from our recent war experience.

CHAPTER FIVE

American Fiction (and Hellish Truth) from Wars in Afghanistan and Iraq

Responses in literary fiction to the wars in Afghanistan and Iraq have developed rather slowly. This pattern is not inconsistent with Vietnam. James Webb's *Fields of Fire* and Tim O'Brien's *Going After Cacciato* (Webb's novel sold over a million copies in a few years; O'Brien's won the National Book Award) appeared in 1978, a full five years after the withdrawal of US forces and three years after the collapse of the South Vietnamese government in April of 1975. The whole issue of how soon we might expect to see major fiction dealing with the Iraq or Afghanistan War experiences was broached aggressively as early as 2008, with a *New York Times* "ArtsBeat" blog piece by Gregory Cowles, "Shock and Awe: A Novel." Cowles led off by mentioning that two other literary critics, Tom Miller and Gregory McNamee, had wondered as early as 2004, in a *Kirkus Reviews* query, how it was that the Iraq War had yet to produce a response in fiction (2).

As we look back at the first decade of the twenty-first century, it is clear that 2004 would have been an absurd time frame for a serious work of fiction to emerge from the Iraq War. Even 2008 was pushing plausibility awfully hard. The blog post responses quickly pointed out that good fiction takes time, that the memoir responses had already flooded the market of curiosity about American efforts in Iraq, that the volunteer status of all returning veterans might well diminish the pool of writers who would have either inclination or talent to develop a strong work of fiction. One response to Cowles, by Tony Aiello (6), an experienced broadcast journalist, highlighted the memoir phenomenon and also sagely added that Brian Turner's poetry had already emerged—because short-form writing can more readily be completed close to the actual action of combat. In sum, the memoir method of getting an experience out in words proved particularly efficacious, as already shown in an earlier chapter, and Brian Turner was fully primed, with an MFA in hand before venturing off to Iraq, to react quickly with words honed into striking poetic form. As we know from some of the scatological details incorporated into Evan Wright's *Generation Kill*, the shit of Iraq was quick to hit the fan. A big dump was thus taken quickly, and pungent reality rocked readers wondering what this new war might be all about. It would take significantly more time to regroup and find the special perspective that a work of fiction can offer. As is detailed later in this study, a full decade would be needed for two writers—Matthew Gallagher and Roy Scranton—to work out a novel-length treatment of war experience in Iraq.

Before zeroing in on a reasonably comprehensive exploration of fiction from the Iraq conflict, it might be useful to note two fairly recent, and appropriately acclaimed, works of fiction that emerged from the Vietnam conflict right in the midst of the ongoing battles in both Iraq and Afghanistan—first Denis Johnson's *The Tree of Smoke* (2007), which won the National Book Award for Fiction and was a Pulitzer Prize contender, then Karl Marlantes's *Matterhorn* (2010), which was high on the *New York Times* best seller list for sixteen weeks. Johnson's story took readers to the bizarre CIA side of the Vietnam conflict, complete with Vietnamese double agents, something not previously known to large numbers of US soldiers or the American public (apart from readers of Ward Just's early Vietnam novel, *Stringer*)—but from the opening scene where one of the key Americans emerges at dawn to empty his bladder and then enjoy a system-refreshing fart, readers know that Johnson's complex and convoluted yarn is going to be raw and real at every turn. Johnson probably picked up some impetus to create *The Tree of Smoke* from the ghastly accounts of dubious allies and dangerous civil war dimensions coming home in stories from Iraq. Certainly readers of his novel could find parallels with the reigning confusion of Iraq, where insurgents from diverse oppositions converged only in the desire to kill Americans; psyops types from various US intelligence agencies in Iraq were severely tasked day in, day out to determine exactly who the enemy was—and where they might strike next. Attacks mostly came faster than answers.

To this stew of uncertainty, Karl Marlantes had deep personal disillusionment to add. He had done his Marine officer tour in Vietnam, fighting with Marine distinction, Marine pride, Marine honor. He served to the best of his ability. His Marines fought tenaciously, carrying forward with every step of every patrol mission the Marine traditions of valor proved in the jungles of Guadalcanal and other islands of the Pacific in World War II. He survived and returned home.

For Karl Marlantes, the Iraq War may well have provided the final per-
mission and even imperative to work out a story that could help put Vietnam to rest in his own life. On his return to civilian life after combat in
Vietnam, Marlantes had plenty of commendations to show that he had
been a stellar warrior—the Navy Cross, two Navy Commendation Medals
for Valor, two Purple Hearts. He had done his duty and done it very well.
But all was not well, even as he went off to Oxford University to complete a
master's degree that he had begun on a Rhodes Scholarship before Vietnam
intervened, even as he developed a successful career in business, even as he
became a family man. Quietly, Vietnam was still with him, and by the 1990s
he was in need of help, suffering from PTSD, the haunting shadows of horrors witnessed, of dreadful things done, of mistakes, of recriminations, of
survivor guilt, of recurrent psychic pains that have intimately been known
by so many of his generation. Years of counseling were necessary for Marlantes to recover from his time in Vietnam—that and a novel that in its own
way would lay out the nightmarish experience for all to witness. *Matterhorn* presents Marines in battle near the Laotian border, specifically a unit
of Marines being led valiantly by Lt. Waino Mellas. His Marines are given
one ghastly mission after another as real estate in the mountain highlands
changes hands, each time at the expense of soldiers whose lives should not
be lost so pointlessly.

The story shows that at the command level, future stars on the shoul-
der were in the offing, for the Marine Corps is clannish and small enough
for everybody to know what everybody has accomplished—or not accomplished—whereby the grounds of promotion are established; Mellas himself eventually comes to recognize the staggering futility of the sacrifices
made by himself and his men. They were brutalized for naught. When the
battles for Matterhorn are finished, nothing has been gained. Yes, they did
their job; they have their hard-earned pride; but beyond the wounds and
the deaths, there is no sense of purposeful achievement to carry forward.
Forty years later, the hollowness of the whole Vietnam episode must finally
be confronted, and the narrative delivered by Karl Marlantes serves that
purpose directly and honestly.

If a reader should turn aside from the rain that drenches Mellas and his
fellow Marines as they slog through dense jungle to find the high ground
they have been assigned to take—at all costs—and suddenly shift attention
over to the grotesque battles waged before, during, and after the surge of
American warriors into the dark quagmire of west/central Iraq (particularly Fallujah) or virtually any valley or mountain pass in Afghanistan, such a

reader might justly conclude that Marlantes had a kind of double vision operating. Commanders looking for promotion . . . leaders looking to be valorized in future history books: and a great many ordinary citizens turned soldiers turned citizens again and left to carry torturous burdens deep into the aftermath. In a glance aside, looking out from deep in the dreadful, perilous terrain of *Matterhorn*, Vietnam becomes Iraq . . . or Afghanistan . . . and when Americans soldiers finally go home, chaos and depredation reign in the wake of their departure.

As the combat role for American forces in Afghanistan edges inexorably onward, there has been no striking work of fiction to emerge from that conflict, and while the Iraq War finally stumbled to an end for American troops in 2011, only a handful of notable novels have as yet emerged. The novel that managed to catch the most attention critically is Kevin Powers's *The Yellow Birds*, which appeared in 2012; and as the preceding chapter concluded with consideration of a poem by Powers that featured the name of a key figure in *The Yellow Birds*, this novel provides a useful entrée into the Iraq War in fiction.

To make a novel, you need characters, you need a plot, and you need a setting. Powers began *The Yellow Birds* with one character, Private Bartle, just as he emerged from imagination to deliver the final words of "Letter Composed During a Lull in the Fighting," the poem showcased three years earlier in *Poetry Magazine*. The novel that grew from this seed is spare; not many characters are needed to drive the action on its arc from start to finish. Add one more man, another private—this one named Murphy—and one woman, Murphy's mother, all bound inexorably to one another by a promise made by Bartle to Murphy's mother, but a promise destined for failure by the treacherous and deadly setting of Iraq in time of war . . . and there's the story. The architecture is simple. As soon as Private Bartle promises Murphy's mother that he will bring her fragile son home safely, the end is almost too predictable. The fates have always loved this sort of pact, and this is not the first time an American war story has hung on a promise that we know in an instant will be impossible to keep. The worst time to make promises is when you are going off to war.

At the end of the long wedding sequence that opens Michael Cimino's *The Deer Hunter* (1978), Michael (the Robert De Niro character) has chased the newlyweds' car down the streets while stripping off all his clothes. In darkness broken only by a streetlight, Michael's close friend Nick (Christopher Walken's character, who is soon to be a fellow soldier in Vietnam) joins him, and they have a brief, breathless exchange about the future they will soon enter—combat in Vietnam. Nick wants only one promise from Mike—that Mike will not leave Vietnam without him. Mike assures him he will live up to that promise. We all know immediately that the promise will bedevil Mike, and it does. For deep background on this point, it is useful to remember Frost's provocative poem about stopping in woods on a snowy evening—especially the concluding stanza with its unremitting focus on "promises to keep," and how that will postpone the release of sleep. A promise is always an ominous thing. In the run-up to a war, it is wise to be especially wary of the promise impulse. While Mike is eventually true to his word, he only manages to bring Nick home in a casket. This twentieth-century war epic has much of the flavor of fatalism that has spiced war narratives from the beginning of human time.

And now we add to Mike's *Deer Hunter* promise the one that seals the fate of Bartle and Murphy. Murphy is perfectly named. A law goes with the name—Murphy's Law: "Anything that can go wrong, will go wrong." Take a character named Bartle (and his closest literary ancestor would have to be Melville's Bartleby, who would always "prefer not to" do whatever was required), mix in a promise fated for doom, combine with a Murphy character, and then send this package off to Iraq under the darkside auspices of Dick Cheney (let's be Nixonianly clear about this: an American president should be able to act in any way necessary to meet any danger, real or perceived, to protect American lives—and if we should secure a friendly supply of oil and endless business for Halliburton through the ages, so much the better), Donald Rumsfeld (the American military fighting force can put any third-rate, Third World army to rout in a flash of shock and awe), and George W. Bush (Saddam never should have tried to off my dad). A tragic end is inevitable. Fate could have it no other way. An astute and subtle novelist, Powers refrains from making any allusions to the overarching political cloud of the Cheney-Rumsfeld-Bush triumvirate and focuses steadily on a very small sample of representative combatants (a kind of restraint similarly represented in Stephen Crane's *The Red Badge of Courage*), but any imaginative work dealing with Iraq must somehow carry with it the shadow of politicos muddling around furtively in the murky background while American soldiers suffer in the foreground.

In this light, *The Yellow Birds* might seem all too formulaic. But while the narrative indeed builds with forces that cannot deliver a happy ending to us, forces that can seem true and believable if they hew close to the honesty of earlier incarnations, those forces nevertheless hold us in thrall. When a colonel opts not to get his boots into the action, choosing instead to be "with" his troops through contact via the Operations Center, the skepticism about "command" motives that suffuses *Matterhorn* breaks into the open here as well. Mostly, though, like Marlantes's narrative, the story that Powers offers to us belongs to soldiers. The grit of training for war here is real and true. The devotion of Bartle to Murphy warms us, as we all would like to have a guardian. The singular and personal guardian here in *The Yellow Birds* might even morph into Plato's "Guardian," the force that rises to preserve the Republic from attack by its enemies. Anything good is sure to have enemies.

Then there is the ghastliness of Iraq, to which Bartle and Murphy venture. The enemy seems to be everywhere, but it is still hard to be sure exactly who the enemy is. The uncertainty in the midst of butchery is enough to challenge the most stalwart of soldiers, and Murphy is anything but that. He is witness to horror upon horror, and before long, his weakness overcomes him. After seeing an idealistic, lovely young nurse killed by a mortar round right outside the door of the chapel where she was headed to ease her soul after having a young life slip out of her hands, Murphy's limited resilience breaks down entirely. He goes forth naked into a desecrated urban battlefield. He is captured . . . he is tortured . . . he is brutalized—and then he is put on display as an example of what should befall all American infidels.

As the hand of fate presses hard upon the action in Iraq—and Bartle can in no way safeguard Murphy—the narrative goes as grim and bleak and dark as any war story to date. What happens to Murphy is not for the faint of heart. And then Bartle takes on the obligatory role of revenge. We drop down further into darkness and the realm of nightmare, but readers are likely to be sympathetic, even as horror begets horror. To keep the heart of darkness in *The Yellow Birds* uncertain for as long as possible, the storyline flips back and forth between duty in Iraq and the post-Iraq days. Bartle survives. He comes home, but he bears the dreadful secret of a war crime. The weight of the world seems upon him, and he nearly drowns in the James River near his postwar Richmond apartment hideout. The yellow "Support the Troops" ribbons infuriate him; he is ready to burn them, filled with anger at the idea of being welcomed home. He is physically back, once more on American soil—but he is not home, not by any stretch of the imagination.

Would anyone want to place bets on Bartle's life once he returns to the homeland? The darkness follows him, layer after layer, plot twist after plot twist. His murderous revenge is eventually detected, and justice must be reached. You simply cannot kill a hapless Iraqi witness to the river burial of a totally lost and brutally mutilated young American—Private Murphy—without consequences in the court of military law as well as in human conscience. Bartle does his time, but while still in prison, he has a cathartic reunion with Murphy's mother, the woman to whom he made his fateful promise before setting off to Iraq. She is compassionate; in the light of her sympathy, he sheds at least some of the horror wrought by the war on his spirit. Before the last page of his weariness is written, he has looked at the end from a prison window. And then he has been set free, free to continue on the long slog to get back to wholeness. He seeks solace in the solitude of nature, the sort of thing promoted by Thoreau and echoed, albeit hopelessly, by John Wade (and his wife, Kathy) in Tim O'Brien's darkest novel, *In the Lake of the Woods* (1995): "I've allowed myself the gift of a quiet quarantine in a cabin in the hills below the Blue Ridge" (223).

There in the isolated cabin, Bartle has only a few meager possessions, the bare necessities, including an army surplus cot . . . and also a map of Iraq that Mrs. Murphy had brought with her for her prison visit with him. With the map for reference, he can go back over the hard land where the Tigris passed through Al Tafar. And there, too, he sees Murphy. Murphy's body rides downriver, finally reaching the place where Tigris and Euphrates converge, just at the point where Western civilization was cradled so long ago. Murphy's body breaks apart in the ocean, his bones entering the waves that break on and on and on, timeless. Bartle had reflected earlier in the story, "half of memory is imagination anyway" (186), and in the last notes of this novel, memory is fully blended into imagination. Powers gave us a mighty strong novel to help us all have some memory . . . and to have some imagination. The way out of war will not come easy, will not happen by accident. We must attend to it, and novelists can provide assistance.

In addition to *The Yellow Birds*, two other novels clearly make 2012 the break-out year for major fiction dealing with the Iraq War. Each of these alternatives to *The Yellow Birds*—Ben Fountain's *Billy Lynn's Long Halftime Walk* and David Abrams's *Fobbit*—opens up significantly different ways of seeing into the bizarre mess that the war in Iraq became. Fountain's story, like the one spun out by Powers, has some intense lyrical passages, and by the second page, words of an inchoate poem are spread out all over the page . . . Texan sprawl, Texan drawl, Texan patriotic pap that wants to blow past the borders of the page and mushroom-cloud the world, inebriate bellicosity, a few simple words deemed sufficient—at least when you are liquored up and have on your "fancy cowboy boots"—to send American boys off to war again. It looks like this:

          terrRist
             freedom
   evil
           nina leven
         nina leven
             nina leven

troops
          currij
       support
            sacrifice
         Bush
   Values
God

(2)

A huge number of Americans feel very uncomfortable when they run into poetry, or anything that even remotely resembles poetry. Most unfortunately, they have been turned off to poetry by disastrously bad encounters with the genre in their schoolroom experience. They fear the mystery that poetry seems to throw in their face. They have no confidence in getting the meaning right to suit a teacher. American public schools try to do many things. Occasionally, things go well and students learn something well. But such is often not the case with regard to poetry. Many students come to hate poetry. We teachers should do better by them—and by the poets too.

The words above look like a postmodern poem of sorts—certainly something done after the modernist efforts of E. E. Cummings—and perhaps done with an eye toward Cummings as inspiration. Cummings expended his imaginative resourcefulness in language as a response to the grotesque horrors of World War I. In fact, his radical wrenching of words and lines into perplexing new shapes has everything to do with his concern about the failure of people (including Americans) to see beyond the surface of propagandistic slogans, the giving in without thought to the simplistic reductions of politicians and national leaders that produce potent (but ultimately empty) phrases in order to arouse desire for war and then sustain it even in the face of daunting and devastating setbacks. The propaganda initiative and nationalistic phrases send men off to combat, where they meet reality, a world apart from the propaganda slogans. Cummings tore apart standard language patterns in order to drive readers to pay more careful attention to the effect of words. It was a shake-up, wake-up gesture on his part.

But here in the opening of Fountain's novel, the words clearly position us in the twenty-first century: the era of the terrorist, the fateful time of 9/11, the excruciating simplicity of third-generation Bush politics. *Time* magazine had found God to be dead in the early 1960s, but now God has the last word. And the values pushed into the trench mud and gas-filled no-man's-land in World War I by Wilfred Owen—all that glorious but empty and mocking Horatian "pro patria mori" stuff—are here resurrected in full glory: courage (OK—"currij" in Cowboy talk) and sacrifice on the part of troops sent to battle, plenty of "support" for the troops on the home front. It may look like a weird "what the hell is this" poem at first glance—an example of the terrorism of poets attacking poor students in a high school English class—but it really doesn't take long (or the intervention of some expert English teacher) to get the meaning of this one. Two-thirds of a page, with plenty of blank space so as not to overtax our comprehension of a complex situation, is enough to explain the Iraq War in American history. OMG . . . a poem . . . one of those living nightmares in English . . . but we get it. Yes, we get it here. It works.

The rest of the story, of course, reveals fiendish complexity spinning out of the trajectory rendered so simply in the pretender "poem." We are introduced to a public relations event situated in Texas. Not surprisingly, since in Texas there is much ado about football, this event is staged to take place during the halftime show of a big football game. There's Dallas. Hence, the "Cowboys." There are sure to be comely cheerleaders. Friday night lights . . . Sunday afternoon swoons, football rocks and football rules. No question, Fountain situates his Iraq yarn perfectly. America and war are snug as a bug in a rug in Texas.

Yes indeed, America went into Iraq operating in a Simple, Simple, Simple mode, but the exit was all complexity. Complex trumped simple—even as a Fox News–promoted "Victory Tour" for a squad of returning Iraq War veterans moves through America to culminate on a stage to be shared with Beyoncé—halftime entertainment for football fans. It's Bravo squad, by the way. Not an actual squad, not one with that unit name, but for a Fox embed looking to make things look simple in a story from Iraq, to help keep Americans snug in fantasyland—"Bravo" seemed like an apt designation for the unit. Reality must not stand in the way of fantasyland.

"One nation, two weeks, eight American heroes"—the so-called Bravo squad flies unexpectedly out of Baghdad in order to serve a PR God. They are "home" but temporarily; when the PR tour is complete, they go back to the dirty work in Iraq. More than a little awkwardness attends this public relations extravaganza, and in some respects, it echoes the disquiet so palpably evident in the story of the three Iwo Jima flag-raising veterans who were brought back to pump up war bond sales in the waning days of World War II, a story not so long ago reinserted into American cultural consciousness by Clint Eastwood's 2006 film *Flags of Our Fathers*.

Public relations is involved in the Billy Lynn story because there's not just a war, not just a group of survivors of combat in war, but a war running amok; America desperately needs heroes, and to make the whole thing transcendently glorious, there's a tantalizing possibility for a film project, with a script being developed to showcase the "Bravo" squad. The script is being shopped around. The hunt is on to find financial backing. Money looms large in the land of football. There's a chance that all the pieces and possibilities will coalesce in one magical halftime moment at a football game in Texas. The money will be committed, the film will be made, and American heroes will walk from the sands of Iraq right out onto the multiplex screens of America, again with a nod to cinema history, for this kind of real-life to reel-life development is a cousin of sorts to the story of the three real Marine soldiers (PFC Rene Gagnon, PFC Ira Hayes, PM3/c John Bradley) involved in the iconic flag raising on Mount Suribachi, who later joined John Wayne in the cast of *The Sands of Iwo Jima* (1949). Billy and his squad mates may not make the big screen, but they are certainly prominent in the staging area for their war film's genesis.

However . . . always there is a "however," and the long halftime walk includes many "however" switchbacks, exactly as the war in Iraq had produced them. For example, in order for the film to get studio backing and financial support, a bankable star is needed. Hilary Swank is reportedly the top option to play Billy, who is a star of war, with a Silver Star to prove it— and also another member of the squad, Staff Sergeant Dime. It's a whopper of an invention, to have one woman play two guys blended together, but there's no denying a certain efficiency obvious in that choice, and also dark humor. Humor of that sort bristles throughout the story. The film business is full of metaphoric improvised explosive devices, and any one of them can ruin a project. It turns out that Hilary Swank will not commit until the studio commitment and financing is in place. Boom!

Maybe the Army can exert some pressure to get the movie deal done. An appeal is made to General Ruthven. Unfortunately, Ruthven is a Steelers fan; he hates the Cowboys. Another IED. Boom!

The whole whacky movie project is doomed from the get-go, a clone of the war itself. This little bit of fantasy collapses in on itself. Fantasyland is not yet ready for the movie. Yet the war goes on. Billy's devoted sister Kathryn would dearly love for him to desert, to walk away, to not be content with the long "halftime" walk, to realize that the war does not make any kind of sense for him, even if it did make sense for the American cultural leadership team responsible for its inception, a group summarily indicted by Kathryn for their lack of military service when they were young:

> Then she made a somewhat frantic speech about a website she'd found that listed how certain people had avoided Vietnam. Cheney, four educational deferments, then a hardship 3-A. Limbaugh, 4-F thanks to a cyst on his ass. Pat Buchanan, 4-F. Newt Gingrich, grad school deferment. Karl Rove, did not serve. Bill O'Reilly, did not serve. John Ashcroft, did not serve. Bush, AWOL, from the Air National Guard, with a check mark in the "do not volunteer" box as to service overseas. (98)

The novel form allows for such freedoms. As noted in the chapter on creative nonfiction, readers today are often tempted to engage more eagerly with memoirs and stories taken directly from reality rather than fiction, but Fountain's novel illustrates how all the possibilities open to the fictionist can combine to give a story greater cultural resonance and symbolic heft. Characters bursting out of imagination come alive in the passions of their beliefs. Kathryn wants to protect her brother. If those other people are crazy for a war, they should be the ones to go fight. Pretty much all of the soldiers in Bravo squad come from desperate family backgrounds, with almost nothing to lose by going to war. Billy's family has plenty of hardship. His sister doesn't want to add Billy to their misery.

As Kathryn pleads with Billy to find a different direction for his life, the movie concept becomes a full casualty. Death comes to it, just as death had come to Sergeant Breem, a casualty in the ferocious battle of Ad-Wariz on the Al-Ansakar Canal, which became a cover story for *Time* magazine and then propelled the movie idea and the subsequent PR tour through the homeland.

Different versions of the original "poem" are spread out through the narrative. One on page 38 adds "Osama," "Eye-Rack," "Eaaaar-rock," "Sod'm," "sooohh-preeeeme" (modifier for "sacrifice"), and "dih-mock-cruh-see." A few pages later (45), another one includes "double y'im dees" and the imperative "**PACK YOUR SHIT!**" A later variation turns on financial lingo—the stuff of film producer talk. Words from cheerleaders populate yet another "poem" (148–49)—which quickly leads to a more personal note as one cheerleader, exotically named "Faison," catches Billy's eye and feeds his own private fantasy (151–52). The Cowboys' owner, Norman Oglesby, delivers a tabletop, Thanksgiving Day "poem" speech of thanks to the glorious boys of the battlefield. Finally, near the finish, at the stadium as the game show wraps up, Billy hears, from a couple who are about his age, most of the words of the essential Iraq poem randomized again down the page, top left to bottom right, with a new phrase appended to put the whole grand thing in a summative perspective, "Kicking Ass!" (290)

America would want to see the Iraq War as "Kicking Ass!" Billy knows better. He's going back to Iraq. There will be more Shrooms. And there will be more ghastly two-hour firefights on the banks of canals and in small villages—and in large towns, places like Fallujah. In the winter of 2014, Fallujah fell into the hands of the very people so many American soldiers died trying to defeat. Mosul was overrun. Tikrit was almost lost to insurgents. By that summer, soldiers in the ISIS uprising laid claim to large chunks of northern Iraq and eastern Syria, an action that soon involved ongoing American airstrikes to hold these threats at bay. The scenes from Iraq these days are as bitter to take for surviving veterans of Iraq as the collapse of South Vietnam in April of 1975 was to veterans who had returned home from that conflict. All that sacrifice, all that loss. Here, alas, in this novel, there's not even an option to make a movie of the Iraq War.

At the same time that desperate trouble-spots of Iraq were slipping out of control of the dominant Shiite government, a "true" story from the battleground of Afghanistan opened with robust box-office numbers ($38.5 million on its opening weekend), a very impressive January showing for *Lone Survivor*. Ronald Grover and Chris Michaud noted in a Reuters piece after *Lone Survivor* debuted that the $40 million project from Comcast's Universal Pictures was hyped vigorously as a narrative strong on heroism and oozing patriotism. It clearly illustrates the real-world to cinema-world migration of stories that lies at the center of the territory explored in Fountain's novel. In fiction, at least in the offering by Fountain, the transfer was a no-go. In reality, the from-reality war film (represented clearly in *Zero Dark Thirty* and *Lone Survivor*) has fared rather well at the box office, and this pattern strongly continued when the film treatment of *American Sniper* opened. The final turn for Fountain's novel is drenched in irony, for as noted in the introduction, on Veterans Day in 2016, the novel about a failed Iraq movie project became a movie. But could it hold a candle to *American Sniper* in reaching a significant audience? Absolutely not!

The other big novel from 2012 has yet to draw film interest. *Fobbit* originates in another kind of war perspective, the one presented most vividly and originally in Joseph Heller's much-acclaimed novel *Catch-22*, back in November of 1961. At one moment of poolside craziness (a pool in one of Saddam's palaces has been commandeered for the relaxation pleasure of Australian officers), a soldier is reading *Catch-22*. The dark humor of Heller's take on US Army Air Force operations in the European theater was a shocker—not at all in synch with mainstream public images of the war—although not out of line with Norman Mailer's discomforting picture of war in *The Naked and the Dead* (1948). And if we look far back in the American fiction of war, *Fobbit's* debunking of American mythology follows in the vein of American war literature first introduced by Herman Melville in *Israel Potter* (1855), which almost no one has read, even after the robust Melville renaissance that evolved over the course of the twentieth century. Melville mocked heroism mercilessly in *Israel Potter*.

Nothing much goes well in *Fobbit*. The name plays on the Army predilection for acronyms, in this case designating someone in Iraq who is located at a forward operating base (FOB), and it also distantly echoes the Hobbit figures in Tolkien's mythology—those little folk who get caught up in larger-than-life experiences (and for aficionados of *The Hobbit*, in lieu of Smaug the fiery dragon, here we have SMOG, Secure Military Operations Grid, the linking of commanders by computer, which would be a first-rate way to avoid being Stonewall Jacksoned).

Where the Second World War offered "SNAFU" (Situation Normal, All Fucked Up), the Iraq War in this work of fiction proffers FOBBIT. In one way or another, all the characters introduced to us in the novel are aberrant, some of them way worse than others. One extreme example of dysfunction is Lt. Col. Eustace "Stacie" Harkleroad, who regularly embellishes his combat activity in letters home to his mother in Tennessee; in one such missive he avails himself of reference to the famous utterance of General Sherman—that "war is hell"—to make his own exploits seem to have consequences (and challenges) on a colossal scale. These extravagant lies go on even as any degree of stress in Fobbitland produces nosebleeds and bowel action beyond Harkleroad's control. Fantasy and reality are hidebound in Harkleroad, even as they are, in truth, exceptionally far apart.

Harkleroad is a standing joke on the commanding general's staff as he and Staff Sergeant Gooding wrestle counterproductively over every press release that his public affairs office is supposed to produce to give the world a positive, American view of everything that goes on in the war zone. Delays in finding the right wording often result in stories going out first from CNN or some other news organization. At the end of one such botched effort in public relations, Harkleroad asks Gooding how CNN could get such a detailed story out before the military was able to work up a report cleared through channels for release. Gooding's response goes to the heart of the problem: "Because they were there, sir" (75).

A dramatic counterpoint to the ineptness of Harkleroad is Lt. Col. Vic Duret, who hates Fobbits. Duret is trying to do a decent job, and he feels a personal need to serve well in honor of his brother-in-law Ross, who died in the World Trade Center attack, one of those who jumped to their death. Repeatedly, though, the incompetence of others causes Duret to have searing headaches. One such incompetent, a pure-bred Fobbit, is Capt. Abe Shrinkle, who winds up shooting a Syrian (or maybe he was from Switzerland) for pulling out a copy of the Koran—not a detonator for a possible bomb in a truck that had crunched into a tank. Shrinkle wanted to be able to tell the homefolk that he had killed someone. Later, after another idiotic action by Shrinkle (blowing up the cab of a fuel tanker), Duret gets him transferred out of the war. However, Shrinkle manages to get back, and while pretending to be a British archaeologist, he is blown to bits by a mortar round that falls right on him while he floats in the Aussies' pool (Australians were a minuscule part of the Iraq "coalition" force, but here they nevertheless merit a pool).

Fobbit is replete with bizarre characters and idiotic actions. If the war itself is packed with human folly and misdirection, what can be said of the home front? To settle that point definitively, Abrams has Duret slip into a quiet reflective moment on a Saturday at his desk, with sounds of a stateside football game wafting their way from a radio someone has on in the outer office. His initial thought postulates that those fans' cheers at the game are just as much for him and his men in their war work in Iraq. What a great feeling to have! But he knows better, as his continuing pensiveness shows:

> The reality was, of course, that of those thousands packed into the stadium, only a couple hundred knew what was happening over here in Iraq; and of those two hundred, only a dozen actually gave a shit—and those twelve were probably the wives of the men who were over here listening to the game on a Sunday morning. America, the beautiful ostrich—Oh, beautiful, for heads buried in the sand, for amber

waves of ignorant bliss. There were times when, given the choice, Vic thought he'd disown his country, chuck it all and live the life of an expat in some neutral country. (128)

In this passage of thought from Lieutenant Colonel Duret, Abrams voices a point of view very close to the one at the center of this study—and also to the conclusion of Matthew Gallagher's 2016 novel, *YOUNGBLOOD*. In fantasyland mode, America is indeed in "ignorant bliss," an appalling state from which veterans might well flee. Besides Duret, Sergeant Gooding is also sort of a positive counter to all the nuttiness and absurdity of Fobbitry. Gooding reads *Catch-22*. He reads *Don Quixote*. From this, we know he keeps the Iraq War in a kind of perspective. He is not just there, not just one fuck-up among many. He is sensible, and as a consequence there comes a point where he can no longer abide the nonsense he sees all around him. He feels compelled to get out. So he abandons his post, leaves his computer and desk, and makes for the main gate to find his exit from it all. He is about to execute the escape from a stupid war as illustrated in Tim O'Brien's best novel of the Vietnam War, *Going After Cacciato*, where Cacciato appears to lead a whole squad west from Vietnam to eventually arrive in Paris. At the end of O'Brien's night-watch fantasy, no one has left Vietnam—except to become one of the dead who are listed in the narrative's first paragraph. So . . . here goes Chance Gooding, looking to leave his part in the Iraq War:

It was only when he was within sight of the Main Gate, the dark mystery of Baghdad lurking just beyond the bristle of concertina wire, that Chance Gooding realized he had no helmet, no flak vest, no weapon. He hesitated for a second but then tucked his bare head to his chest and continued to sprint toward the guards at the checkpoint who were even now bringing up their rifles and shouting for him to "Stop!"

Somewhere to the north, a mortar shrieked across the sky, coming closer, ever closer. (369)

Chance Gooding is caught between rifles and a mortar: friendly fire, enemy fire. His life hangs in the balance, and while an extreme fantasy enthusiast might hold out for Gooding's preservation via ambiguity in the phrasing of this final scene, in this reader's eyes, Gooding is as dead as Robert Jordan is sure to be at the end of Ernest Hemingway's Spanish Civil War novel, *For Whom the Bell Tolls* (1940). Going into war is not difficult. Getting out is quite another matter.

Before turning to fiction dealing with the concerns of war as found on the home front, Nicholas Kulish's novel *Last One In* (2007) merits consideration. Kulish has worked for the *New York Times* since 2005, with postings to Berlin and, most recently, to East Africa. In 2003 he was a *Wall Street Journal* reporter embedded with a Marine helicopter squadron in Iraq. This exposure to war served as the basis for his novel, which is satirical to the core, particularly in its focus on the wide range of competencies brought to the war by all the correspondents who found themselves on assignment there.

Kulish's protagonist, Jimmy Stephens, is initially working the light entertainment beat for the *Daily Herald*, a fictional NYC paper. He goes off to Iraq in order to avoid the consequences of a libelous story he had produced; he shares the same name with a bona fide war correspondent at the paper and is whisked off to Kuwait to cover the Iraq invasion as an imposter of sorts. To say that Jimmy is a fish out of water, a beached whale, a man on a mission impossible would all be true—and would point to the central challenge of the book (and to all accounts of this era in American military operations): finding original ways to articulate and lay bare the whole mess. A cameraman, Woody, succinctly catches the originality challenge: "I mean, in imagery, evocative language. One NPR radio essay, and there isn't a metaphor left for the rest of us" (125). Quagmire, alas, had long since been appropriated as a fitting label for a military muddle. Nevertheless, occasionally the novel offers up an arresting image, such as when Jimmy reacts in horror to the sight of an arm by itself on the road. Homer's long-ago story provided the details of an arm being lopped off in combat; now we have just the arm—perhaps dragged to the road by a dog (205). Whatever happened here in Iraq, it is a grim footnote to Homer.

Jimmy finally leaves Iraq. His colleague Becky sums up the emptiness of the war for journalists desperate to contrive a story somehow but with nothing new to say: "They're hungry and waiting for electricity" (208). Same situation as yesterday. Ditto tomorrow. Fantasyland will not thrill to receive this news.

Staying home, not going off to a war zone, is yet another matter of concern in the fiction of the wars in Iraq and Afghanistan. Back in the film chapter, we took a quick look at *Grace Is Gone*, which features the experience of a husband/father whose wife goes to serve in Iraq and dies there—a story of spousal grief. Two very fine woman writers, Kristen Tsetsi and Siobhan Fallon, have worked to bring the story of wives left behind to light in their fiction. Tsetsi brought out *Homefront* initially in 2007, as an

Penxhere Press imprint; and in 2012 it was republished as *Pretty Much True* by Missouri Breaks Press. The novel grew out of a thesis project for the MFA degree Tsetsi received from Minnesota State University at Moorhead in 2003, the year her husband deployed to Iraq.

Mia is the main figure in Tsetsi's novel. She and Jake have been together for a number of years, since high school, and she is now twenty-six, but they are not married. Jake is a helicopter pilot, and as the narrative begins, with a dateline notice that it is 31 December, Jake and Mia are full of apprehension about his possible deployment overseas, for something involving Iraq looms on the horizon. Jake's friend William, another pilot, is married to Denise, who lives nearby, residing like Mia in off-base rental units. Almost immediately after Jake and William leave in the early stages of overseas assignment, Denise begins to go out with Brian, a rear-detachment serviceman who has schemed carefully in order to keep himself far from harm's way. Brian fills the "Jody" role completely, bedding Denise and presenting her with an eager, ready option should she decide to permanently jettison her husband—or should her husband be killed in action. With her husband far off, Denise does not lack for sex or other human comfort.

As mentioned earlier, every soldier sent off to battle with a wife or girlfriend left behind has an inclination to worry about the "Jody" figure. Ages ago, Penelope was never without suitors itching to fill the space once occupied so wonderfully by her husband Odysseus. The old story never gets old. It burns and sears with hot torment in every new generation of soldiers off to war with loved ones back at home.

Both Mia and Denise are unsettled by being left behind, anxious every day about the fate of their faraway loved ones, but as the separation grows in time, they move in different directions, each problematical in its own way. As noted already, Denise simply takes up with a new man. She is moving on, independently, albeit brazenly. Mia, in contrast, stays faithful, even when presented with options for cheating. She does spend a good deal of time with a Vietnam veteran, Donnie, and they provide for each other a kind of loving; their relationship skirts the sexual, but it is significant nevertheless. Donnie shows plenty of PTSD signs, barely holding things together, even many long and hard years after his Vietnam service came to an end.

Vietnam grew to be an unpopular war, with extensive protest activity, which sometimes turned from raucous to violent. Protest of the Iraq War emerges in Tsetsi's narrative as well, and Mia is drawn to it even though Jake is part of the war effort. A downstairs neighbor, Safia, is from Iraq, and she encourages Mia to join the antiwar campaign. By this point, William has died in a flying accident (hitting power lines), ironically at a moment when his wife is making love to Brian. Denise receives $250,000 in an insurance settlement, which provides her with a comfortable range of options for her future: buy a home or move away, send some money to William's family, continue her relationship with Brian. As we leave her at the end of the novel, her situation seems rife with ambiguity, for she is an impetuous character without clarity of purpose. She could represent a great many Americans, flailing about in the turmoil of a war that itself was developing chaotically in the absence of a compass.

Mia is different. What most defines Mia is her frustration and anger. She hates not knowing what is going on. Jake's mother seems closer to her son than Mia is to him, a point of distinct distress. When the anger swells, as it does frequently, Mia destroys things in the apartment—knickknacks accumulated in the building of a relationship and home, the TV (for all the bad news it presents and where the war in Iraq unfolds for her), and the Christmas tree that she sets on fire in May as she seethes with fury at the war, at Jake and his inattentiveness and unavailability, at all the craziness that swirls around her life; she has no benefits from Jake, as they are not married. She has struggled to pay bills by driving a cab, a job that sucks energy from her and provides significant aggravation. Time after time, she encounters frustration and the slough of despair.

By the end, Mia is fairly certain that William's death was not accidental, that he had received Denise's letter explaining her desire to move on in a different direction in her life and, in consequence, had committed suicide. Denise wanted to have as a keepsake a lighter that was William's, and at the end, Mia returns it, dropping it in her mailbox. Jake is coming back on leave, and there will be favorite snacks to greet him, thanks to Mia. But a dark chill hangs over the last scenes of the story. There's no happy homecoming—just another flavor of uneasiness. This representation of the American home front during the Iraq War is unremittingly bleak. From beginning to end, Tsetsi's novel is loaded with foreboding, drenched in varying moods of despair and disenchantment.

A short story collection by Siobhan Fallon, *You Know When the Men Are Gone* (2011), adds a different home-front twist to the one established in Tsetsi's story. The opening two paragraphs of the first story, "You Know When the Men Are Gone," bring the difference to the foreground:

> In Fort Hood housing, like all army housing, you get used to hearing
> through the walls. You learn your neighbors' routines: when and if

they gargle and brush their teeth; how often they go to the bathroom or shower; whether they snore or cry themselves to sleep. You learn too much. And you learn to move quietly through your own small domain.

You also know when the men are gone. No more boots stomping above, no more football games turned up too high, and, best of all, no more front doors slamming before dawn as they drudge out for their early formation, sneakers on metal stairs, cars starting, shouts to the windows above to throw down their gloves on cold desert mornings. Babies still cry, telephones ring. Saturday morning cartoons screech, but without the men, there is a sense of muted silence, a sense of muted life. (1)

Military bases are a world apart from American life. There is the Post Exchange (PX) for your Walmart needs; there is the commissary to supply all the family food needs; there is housing tightly scaled for everyone: single or married, couples by themselves, and families full of kids.

For officers and senior enlisted personnel, the housing spreads out in sinuously curving streets all named for famous generals and/or battlegrounds. The lawns are mowed to match stipulations promulgated by command. Like the haircuts given to recruits in basic training, every separate home looks like all the others. There are official parties of various kinds (and you really need to turn out for these orchestrated social events); there are daisy-chain phone setups to make sure everyone gets unit-related news as quickly and uniformly as possible. There are dress codes, behavior codes, protocol stacked upon protocol, with something regular and organized set up to handle every imaginable situation or turn of events. In the all-volunteer military force operating in America since the early 1970s, it is assumed that everyone on a base is on the same page. You are in the military (and spouses and children are included right along with actual service members), so you see things and do things the military way. You are committed. You are predictable. Your stuff is squared away. All through Siobhan's stories, these patterns of predictability are present, in one form or another. She has accurately and fully captured the feel and look of the military bases that are home to her characters.

However, just as combat quickly blows apart all the carefully honed battle plans once the weapons are blazing and IEDs are exploding, the unexpected makes its way through base housing. The absence of the men is the first such disruption, and as the epigraph for the collection (from Penelope's reaction upon seeing Odysseus returned at long last from his war sojourn) makes clear, the first disruption is certainly not the last in the order of life. Indeed, there are many more to follow.

In the lead story, Meg, whose husband Jeremy is away in Iraq, is childless, with a fairly uncomplicated life, and thus manages to stay safely within the norms of what is expected of on-base military spouses. She contrasts strikingly with Natalya, a refugee from Kosovo in a nearby apartment where almost everything seems to develop contrary to the normative military way. Natalya has young twins, a boy and a girl, a minifamily even in the absence of the father, but she refrains from participating in morale-boosting social activities designed to help those left behind cope with their forced separations (and eventually Natalya even has a mysterious male visitor staying overnight with some frequency). Meg lives close enough to keep a close watch on Natalya's errant behavior, and by the end, she has become a sort of surrogate parent to Peter and Lara, as well as a caretaker for the family's dog, Boris. As the story concludes, Natalya appears to have departed entirely, leaving kids and dog behind as she flees yet another war. Will the father recognize his children on the lap of Meg? And how will Jeremy react seeing his wife with kids? Before going to Iraq, he had been eager to start a family. These questions are not answered, but it is clear how much Meg appreciates the return of her husband. They have survived. They can rejoin life together again.

A similar—yet different—storyline is worked out in "Inside the Break." This story broaches the Jody concern, but with a gender twist. In this situation, the faithful one is at home in a Texas military base (where much of Fallon's own experience as a military wife was collected). Kailani met Manny in Hawaii, her native state; they moved to Texas before his deployment to Iraq. She feels quite estranged, on multiple levels, but she copes with her isolation until she opens her husband's e-mail account and reads a love note from Michelle Rand, a female soldier also in Iraq. Infidelity—on the field of battle, not at home. Of course, Homer had that variation covered, as Odysseus was a wanderer in the fullest sense.

In a quandary about how to react to her suspicions regarding Manny and Michelle, Kailani tends to their two children, Javier and Ana. Still, pangs of doubt cloud her days and nights. Manny comes home from Iraq. He denies anything adulterous. They resume a semblance of marriage, including the old familiarity of sex. At the end of the narrative, Kailani is at a base park with the kids and another mom, Christina, and her children. Christina is bursting with gossip about a blond female soldier with a reputation for sleeping with other women's husbands. She presses this information on Kai-lani, who turns it firmly away with "I said I don't want to know" (130). Turn-ing a blind eye (or deaf ear) is always an option. If Roger Chillingsworth had chosen that option in *The Scarlet Letter*, Hawthorne would never have had the makings of even a very tightly crafted work of fiction.

"Camp Liberty" draws our attention to another stress point in military service—the pull of loved ones who want their soldiers home, against the dedication of soldiers to stay tight with their comrades in combat. David Mogeson ("Moge" to his messmates, "Davy" to his girl) is torn between two magnets. There is Marissa, his girlfriend of four years, and there is his unit in Iraq. He has been to bed with both. The narrative moves back and forth, from Marissa's world and her appeal to the intense service role Moge plays with his fellow soldiers. The "Davy" world competes with the "Moge" envi-ronment. Eventually, David decides to come home. It was an awfully close call. But once the decision has been made, nothing else seems to matter. However, if the narrative had continued, if it had tracked "Moge" for years stateside, it is entirely possible to imagine the war coming home with him, refusing to leave him even as he rejoined Marissa.

One of the later stories, "Leave," brings back the Jody situation. CW Nick Cash is off in Iraq when he gets a worrisome bit of information from a friend about his wife, Trish. Seems she has been spending time with Mark Rodell—at home. This news is most unsettling, and soon the corrosion of jealousy burns deep into Nick. He makes a secret trip back to his home, sneaks into the basement, and hides there for a week, all in order to catch his wife with her lover. For several days his suspicions seem unfounded, as Trish and their daughter go through entirely predictable and unassailable routines of normal home life. Finally, though, as Friday night arrives, there is a male guest for dinner, a guest who winds up sharing Trish's bed. The story concludes with a cliff-hanger, as Nick hovers over the bed, his knife blade flashing ominously in the moonlight as it moves from hand to hand. Where will judgment land? The reader's imagination is given no hope that this domestic triangle will end in anything but horror. Again, think of all the suitors who are slain by Odysseus in the bloodbath that follows his re-turn—even with an uncorrupted marriage bed!

Fallon has been a military wife for many years. She has done her duty on quite a few military bases. She is obviously comfortable and at home with military life, including all the particular distress that it can present to the men and women who are caught up in the circumstances of war. Her stories cover a lot of the possible territory—and to her credit, not all goes well as these stories move to their conclusions. While some endings admit to a measure of contentment as a soldier returns home, some others open up into full disaster. Fallon's collection is honest in this diversity.

Two other recent story collections will serve to round out the investigation of fiction in response to wars of the early twenty-first century. The first is a gathering of fifteen stories, *Fire and Forget: Short Stories from the Long War*, collected and edited by Roy Scranton and Matt Gallagher, each of whom contributed one of the stories (and each of whom brought out a novel later). Here we find some familiar writers (for example, Brian Turner, with a tight, surrealistic narrative, "The Wave That Takes Them Under," featuring the ultimate of sandstorms, a blinding monster blast of sand that becomes a kind of living tomb for the American soldiers trying to make progress in the face of it; and Siobhan Fallon, with "Tips for a Smooth Transition," another narrative working the territory explored in her own collection—all the efforts expended by spouses and the military apparatus to bring soldiers home safe and intact). We also meet new writers (for example, Phil Klay, whose story "Redeployment" becomes the title narrative in a March 2014 Penguin collection of his own work, *Redeployment*, which is examined in detail toward the end of this chapter).

Fire and Forget evolved through the guidance of Scranton and Gallagher, plus three others (Jake Siegel, Perry O'Brien, and Phil Klay), all connected through their participation in the NYU Veterans Writing Workshop. In varying degrees, all of them represent some measure of benefit to be gained by putting war experience through the process of writing about it. The veterans who have regained their lives by means of literary activity in the past hundred years are large in number. Sometimes the therapeutic value is realized quickly; sometimes, as in the case of Tim O'Brien, decades of writing about Vietnam proved necessary. Colum McCann, who teaches at Hunter College and who in that setting encountered a war narrative by Phil Klay, a Marine veteran getting an MFA at Hunter, provides a provocative introduction to the collection. McCann talks with exhilaration about the imaginative work produced by Klay and all the others in the collection. As he says, "The war went literary"—a development that could serve as "harbinger of the novels and short story collections we will be seeing in the future, as those who served continue to try to make sense of our wars for us in the most rigorous way possible, through fiction" (ix).

Certainly we will see further novels and more story collections. Efforts to make sense of our wars will proceed apace. As forcefully shown by the contents of this early collection—and of Phil Klay's collection of his own work—the fiction will be rigorous, and the truth will burst out to any reader up for seeing it. Unfortunately, all the Americans ensconced in fantasyland—and that would be the huge majority—have no taste for literary fiction, or even literary nonfiction, for that matter. Their reading diverts in other directions. They will be reading *50 Shades of Gray*; they will be reading the gigantic, densely packed tomes of George R. R. Martin; they will be reading tweets; they will have sunk their teeth into many vampire yarns; they will be reading Chris Kyle's *American Sniper* (for reasons outlined in earlier chapters). They will be reading all the 100 best sellers at Amazon, where there happen to be *no* works of recent fiction that come within a million light years of the tough truths spun out in narrative after narrative in *Fire and Forget* and *Redeployment*. The readers of all-consuming nonsense in America will certainly not be reading this study either.

However, *if* some fantasylanders happened to stray from their zones of distraction and *if* they had a hankering for hard shards of reality based on the war experience of veterans who went off to Afghanistan and Iraq, the storylines proffered here would go a long way toward counterbalancing the American yen for high risk as it may be encountered on the battlefield. Here are veterans holding the line against the seductive lure of suicide and, in the angst-ridden process, showing everyone who dares to read plenty of good reasons for never again venturing innocently off to war.

Stories from fifteen writers are gathered in *Fire and Forget*. While the war experiences driving these stories mostly involve Iraq, a couple of them reference Afghanistan. Most of the protagonists are male, although one of the narratives centers on a female veteran, and there are women intimately involved with quite a few of the veterans. The story arcs often pass through a surreal dimension—moments where nightmarish images blend ambiguously with details drawn from reality. Those moments are especially effective in drawing readers into the mess that the wars have created—a mess that will last as long as veterans survive, even as they die of suicide at a troubling rate. The scenes and incidents we are forced to absorb from these stories are fantastical, shocking, disturbing, discouraging, daunting, and damning. And not one of them provides a chance to slip away to fantasyland.

So . . . where do the Iraq/Afghanistan story arcs take us? Consider Colby Buzzell's "Play the Game." There's an Iraq vet, pressured to re-enlist but determined to try to make it on the outside (outside the military). Yet as the narrative moves along, the actual nature and place of this veteran become increasingly unstable. His car is stolen, from right across the street where he lives in a cheap apartment. Cops aren't sympathetic when they come to check out the disappearance. The vet's day job involves holding a person-sized sales sign up on a street corner, one of the dullest and dreariest forms of employment a person can have. At the end of the day, after quitting the job, he finds his car, back where it was originally parked. The female cops who come to check it out are very skeptical about what is going on. There are fast-food wrappers in the car—from the "In and Out" chain—and the vet is stumped. How did they get there? It's all very mysterious, in a "Twilight Zone" kind of way . . . until there's a flash of memory . . . about being very drunk and furious at an "In and Out," from which he exited angrily as patrons watched—with that whole scene showing the way people looked at him when he came home from Iraq. Anger, hard drinking, forgetfulness heading toward oblivion—just try coming come from the war in Iraq. What a tough game to play! It is not hard to see why *Call of Duty* has many more players than ever contemplated signing up for real duty in the military—and the players of the video game are far less prone to suicide.

Could it be worse? Suck it up and take a plunge into Brian Van Reet's "Big Two-Hearted Hunting Creek." Here we are in Hemingway territory, most directly his "Big Two-Hearted River" stories toward the end of *In Our Time* (1925); Hemingway's Nick Adams, home from WWI, where he had been wounded, goes deep into the country back in Michigan to fish, passing through a desiccated landscape (an eerie reflection of the WWI battlefields) to reach the river where he will fish alone. He goes deeper and deeper into isolation in his quest for fish, finally reaching the edge of a dark swamp, a forbidding place from which he might never return; however, Nick decides finally to leave that possibility (the option of ending his life) for another day.

Now, in Van Reet's variation, with the Iraq War in the background, two veterans head off for a day's fishing. One, nicknamed "Rooster," is at Walter Reed Hospital, finishing up his painful recovery from horrible facial burns, the result of a suicide bomber's attack; the other, Sleed, was wounded at the same time in a way that explicitly references another of Hemingway's narratives, *The Sun Also Rises*, in which Jake Barnes has received a war wound that prevents anything in his lap from arising; Sleed lost his cock and balls, with no ambiguity whatsoever in this contemporary narrative about his war wound. Maxwell Perkins would not let Hemingway insert that kind of detail into his war stories. Decorum in the twenty-first century is not quite what it used to be.

Rooster will never have sex because his face is so terribly unappealing; Sleed will never have sex for obvious reasons that torture him daily. His wife has long since divorced him so she can have sex and more children. He hires a private investigator to take pictures showing his ex-wife having sex out in the open, all because he's trying to get custody of his child, but in the process his pain doubles down. The destination for this story is near Frederick, the city where Rooster grew up in upper-middle-class suburban comfort and where his father works at Fort Detrick testing biological weapons on monkeys. Given these details, what are the chances that a lovely day fishing in the Maryland countryside will end happily?

Rooster does catch a nice trout, but in trying to prepare the fish for cooking, breaking catch-and-release laws, he slices one of his fingers badly. Sleed helps bind up the wound, and they return to the bus to await the end of the outing (all arranged as therapy by the military). However, when two teenage girls arrive and head off along the paths by the river, Sleed moves to follow them. Rooster goes along to prevent any bad scene from happening—but in the Iraq War aftermath, bad scenes are hard to prevent. Sleed finds the girls, smoking dope, and pulls down his pants to show them his wound. Rooster tackles him, knocking off his prosthetic leg. Sleed is left sitting by a hickory tree as hailstones fall hard on the creek. World War I had hard consequences for some veterans, which Hemingway spent much of his life showing, and the war in Iraq has presented equally unsettling experience for its vets.

Roy Scranton's "Red Steel India" stays within Iraq for the whole story, which lays out the round-the-clock routines involved in trying to safeguard a compound gate. Iraqi workers (as in most stories, they are referred to as "hajjis") come in each day to perform diverse functions in the compound. Always they have to be carefully checked at the entrance, bodies frisked and bags opened for inspection. There are Iraqi guards, but sometimes they are Fedayeen or al-Qaida, so the threshold of trust is low. Some supervising sergeants are tight with the rules—fussing about always wearing protective armor, policing up cigarette butts; some are not. American soldiers love their Game Boys—and are loath to interrupt a game to attend properly to guard duties. Sounds of sex from a guard tower are distracting; most soldiers have to settle for masturbation. With the Iraqi passers-through, there are frequent exchanges about "ficky ficky." The story closes with one last reference to "ficky ficky"—tomorrow. And then, with a nod to the depth of darkness struck by Shakespeare in *Macbeth*, Scranton brings this story and the whole collection to a line that looks ahead: "Tomorrow and tomorrow and tomorrow" (227). Macbeth has done dastardly things, crimes for which he will be accountable in the end. Shakespeare's plays resolve themselves with a majestic air of finality—often with all the principal characters dead. The Iraq experience has spawned its own tortured messes. For example, Scranton's story accounts for the shooting of a boy who had a rock to throw at the American soldiers, an action that led to a Bronze Star for valor being awarded to the soldier who pulled the trigger to kill the boy and yet feels the world closing in on him, a nightmarishly unfinished bit of consequence. To what doom will that consequence bear out? In the context of all the stories in this collection that feature veterans in postwar scenes, it is easy to feel the implications of this particular "tomorrow" reference. They will get ficky fucked, no question . . .,

> Tomorrow . . .,
>   and tomorrow . . .,
>   and tomorrow.

In the background, ever so deviously and devilishly, there is the whole IED of Macbeth's act 5 soliloquy of despair: "all our yesterdays have lighted fools / The way to dusty death. . . . Life's but a walking shadow, a poor player / That struts and frets his hour upon the stage / And then is heard no more: it is a tale / Told by an idiot, full of sound and fury, / Signifying nothing."

When a tale goes out—and there is virtually no audience in fantasyland to receive it—we are mighty damn close to signifying nothing. These stories beg for an audience. They should be mandatory reading for every senior in every high school in America. But they are edgy. They are dark . . . dangerous . . . explosive. They do not drip with mindless "Support Our Troops" bumper-sticker patriotism, so, as a very sorry consequence, they will go quietly into the still backwaters of superstore Amazon.

Fire and Forget is rich and rewarding because it gathers fifteen different writers, each with a unique style and perspective; every story has merit. Collectively, these stories would put a shudder into fantasyland. For a knockout punch, we need only Phil Klay's stories in *Redeployment*. Here it's just one writer, but his range is phenomenal. His narratives will readily fill any remaining gaps in the way we could and should grasp the full import of the wars to which Americans have ventured in the twenty-first century.

Want to be in the know at the acronym level (and nothing loves acronyms like the US military)? Just read "OIF." Cryptic terms come flying your way, leaving you practically blind in the sandstorm of lingo kicked up by the war. And what is it like to have a kill story? You know, shooting a kid holding an AK, just after an IED was detonated by a mine-detector vehicle—a story you can tell, over and over, trying to own it, even if the details are unstable and it could be someone else's story, and after a while, the relentless retelling gets on everyone's nerves, and then more of your fellow soldiers get killed . . . or sometimes just lightly wounded, but still there's a story to carry around, take home or be haunted by. Officially, though, it's really just an "After Action Report." And in the end, "Whatever. It doesn't matter" (52). By the way, OIF is short for Operation Iraqi Freedom. How many fantsylanders know that?

"Bodies" is all about bodies, and the job of a vet who took care of getting bodies back home. This particular vet had a girlfriend, Rachel, before shipping out for his first deployment. She was a pacifist, so the war broke them up. One last "sad little blow job" (59), and he's on his way to duty in Mortuary Affairs. With the vet back home for a leave, he tells a mechanic he met at a party a particularly gruesome story about a horribly burned corpse—something he had considered telling to Rachel. But when the mechanic tries to express respect, the vet rejects that impulse immediately: "you didn't know that kid. So don't pretend like you care. Everybody wants to feel like they're some caring person" (71). Rachel becomes a Facebook friend—definitely a form of detachment—then marries on the vet's third deployment and has a kid on his fourth.

If fantasyland folks would like to know exactly where they stand vis-à-vis the war veterans, "Prayer in the Furnace" would work well. It's a chaplain's story, centered on the challenge of trying to find sensible things to say in the middle of a nonsensible war. That is no small challenge. Two short paragraphs from the chaplain's journal, though, strike close to the heart of the problem:

> But I see mostly normal men, trying to do good, beaten down by horror, by their inability to quell their own rages, by their masculine posturing and their so-called hardness, their desire to be tougher, and therefore crueler, than their circumstance.
> And yet, I have this sense that this place is holier than back home. Gluttonous, oversexed, overconsuming, materialistic home, where we're too lazy to see our own faults. (150–151)

Veterans are haunted by many things, and one of the scariest of hauntings is that there was more meaning and more honesty in the cauldron of war horror than can be found back in the homeland. One place is empty of all but Sisyphean effort; the other place lacks even that. Klay's work is relentlessly understanding of the diverse plights facing veterans, and his stories, in the process, excoriate fantasyland. Fantasyland knows how to handle this confrontation. Turn blithely away and watch the NHL Stanley Cup playoffs, the NBA playoffs, the Kentucky Derby, *Game of Thrones*, with occasional interludes of *Dancing with the Stars*. Leave *Redeployment* for the redeployed. Fantasyland is fantasyland is fantasyland.

As this chapter has demonstrated, some very strong and substantive fiction has emerged from the wars in Afghanistan and Iraq. If fiction has not, however, been at the pinnacle of response to the military conflicts in Iraq and Afghanistan, the explanation may involve two very contradictory developments in popular culture. The first one involves a shift reflected in television programming away from created-script entertainments and toward "reality"-based shows. The reality shows have a simple structure: there is always movement toward the declaration of a winner. The competition does involve uncertainty, but it is the sort of thing that can be worked out by votes of a "cast" (the *Survivor* series), or votes of the viewing audience (by phone or online at ABC.com and Facebook for *Dancing with the Stars*), or—worst of all—the achingly slow deliberations of a total narcissist vetting life partners in ABC's *The Bachelor* and *The Bachelorette* series. These shows prove that America has a colossal cast of folks eager to be fodder for risk moments that leave them completely open to view. Nevertheless, the winners are always happy, and America loves happy winners. Losers get to have a weepy moment, but then they get on with their lives. They have stories to tell. All of this comes at little production expense. There are very low costs for writers; the cast consists of rank amateurs. These shows make good money, and the feel of reality seems to excite viewers. It's cheap! It's brilliant! But what can writers of fiction, engaging the full measure of imagination, do to compete?

The other source of opposition to war fiction comes from a totally different direction. In terms of fiction that has had great traction for young readers, the essential component typically involves huge doses of pure fantasy, wild imagining, whether in *Harry Potter* or *Game of Thrones* plots, in cinematic translations of comic book superhero adventures, or in countless vampire variations. The undead are endlessly intriguing. A vampire story allows a viewer to process fighting an enemy who is uncertain. The engagement involves seduction.

For young people coming of age in the early years of the twenty-first century and looking to add a strong tonic of excitement to life, there were three big options: 1) be seduced by the sexy appeal of combat for the glory of the nation and go off to serve in Afghanistan and/or Iraq; 2) be seduced by the sexy appeal of video games in which you can be an immortal Chris Kyle, endlessly pulling the trigger to off some dreaded enemy; or 3) be seduced by the very sexy enticement to danger as found in a vampire. There looks to be no end to vampires. Video games with kill options in the billions await the next generation. And just as surely, some war will develop to seduce its quota of innocent Americans who find the thrill of war inescapable. Consequences for this last option are, of course, very different from the others. But you have to read *Fire and Forget*, *Redeployment*, *The Yellow Birds*, and all the other stories in this chapter to see and feel the full impact of that difference.

PART III

VETERANS LOST AS DISTRACTIONS RULE IN FANTASYLAND AMERICA

CHAPTER SIX

American Fantasyland in Time of War— the Hell Veterans Face at Home

New Fantasyland Represents the Magic of Disney Innocence, a Perfect Escape from Reality

On 6 Dec. 2012, Disney World in Florida opened New Fantasyland in the Magic Kingdom. The old Fantasyland had proved just too small to handle the hordes of Americans who wanted escape from reality. Of course, the whole Disney park experience, from the original Disneyland opening in Anaheim, California, in 1955, on forward to our time, is explicitly designed to provide escape from reality, but Fantasyland (new or old) best captures the American escape spirit in a word, in a place, in a concept.

When the world is full of challenge, and is really knocking you about, it's time to head out and get away from it all. The escape can take many routes (shop online at work, play solitaire during a dull meeting), as the diverse sections of this chapter show, but cumulatively, they all add up to proof that the quest for fantasy (and an attendant release from reality) is a key part of life for many people in the United States—and for much of the time, through the day and throughout the year. The evidence is copious.

Every year, millions of Americans use their precious vacation time and money (whether actual dollars in the bank or plastic funds from another kind of fantasyland that has broad reach in America) and devote—on average—a week indulging their yen for escape with time spent within the most carefully crafted safe zone in the country—a location without apparent dirt, without dissension, without frowns—and it is the same artful illusion, rendered by the titans of Magic, whether delivered at Disneyland (west) or Disney World (east). For the year 2010, the Themed Entertainment Association

(TEA) released statistics showing that 16.97 million visitors sought to pleasure themselves through the various delights of escape that are meticulously and very, very, very cleanly presented to them by the cunning genius of the Disney folks at the Magic Kingdom of Disney World. In the 23 Dec., 2012, Travel section of the *New York Times*, Stephanie Rosenbloom shared her recent visit to the Magic Kingdom in a piece called "Manifest Fantasy," which focused on the arrival of New Fantasyland. Rosenberg's relationship with the Disney theme parks is not atypical; like many other adults, she had made more than two dozen pilgrimages to the Magic Kingdom; clearly, Disney is not just for kids. She noted a point that is central to my concerns in this chapter:

> The Magic Kingdom is saccharine, expensive, and homogeneous. At the same time, it is a place where families can be silly together. It is a showcase for technological innovation and logistics. And, for better or for worse, it is a place devoid of responsibilities and heartache of the grown-up world. (6)

Imagine a nation at war—with soldiers engaged in grotesque battles in terribly complex places—and the adults back home are streaming off to find relief in "a place devoid of responsibilities and heartache of the grown-up world." Indeed! In a steady pattern stretching over many years, the favorite escape option has been Fantasyland, hence the need for its expansion and modernization. New Fantasyland is twice the size of the original, having grown from eleven acres to twenty-two.

Over the years following the opening of Fantasyland at the Orlando Magic Kingdom in 1971, Disney film projects proved to be amazingly successful at presenting new incarnations of fantasy, especially in female guise, as proved by Belle in *Beauty and the Beast* and Ariel in *The Little Mermaid*. As a consequence, New Fantasyland features Ariel's Grotto and Under the Sea—Journey of *The Little Mermaid*, as well as Enchanted Tales with Belle. Movies can serve handily to whet the appetite for fantasy, and they have worked wonders for Disney as a form of indoctrination, capturing young imaginations when they are eager to absorb stories that will bring sense to the world.

Religions work the same way, inundating the young with story material to keep them in thrall for a lifetime; so do cults, spreading stories out to entrap and entangle; and nations work along the very same line, with none so aggressive and formidable in this regard as America, which is built entirely of words and which depends for its survival on renewing the storyline end-lessly through successive generations. To see how this story propagation, this capture-the-imagination process all works, though, there's no example clearer and simpler than the Disney model. There's nothing like full im-mersion in enchantment, and for this, Disney is the lion king for all time. Join the tribe. Welcome to the club. My own exposure happened long ago, far away, when Disney found a clever means to sneak into homes all over America, a very welcome intruder for kids who could use a smidgeon of sweet and carefully packaged order to counterbalance a chaotic world.

When young men of my generation went off to fight in Vietnam, they carried with them a lot of both John Wayne and the Mickey Mouse Club. This was acculturation, American style, the nimble and you-often-don't-even-know-it's-working process of adding the US stamp on the postwar generation. Those young soldiers found that their Waynean swagger thing did not mean instant victory in the jungles and rice paddies of Southeast Asia; reality took its toll during their tour, and in the decades to follow for the many who were subject to the ravages of PTSD. Still, a shimmer of the Disney-driven fantasy lingered over and through the brutal reality encoun-tered in Vietnam.

Stanley Kubrick's *Full Metal Jacket*, a 1987 update for John Wayne's *The Sands of Iwo Jima* (1949), opens with explicit reference by the character James T. "Joker" Davis to John Wayne and his famous linguistic style (bare minimum of words, punchy delivery); implicit connections between these two films are established through the hard-assed drill sergeant roles fea-tured in both and the way they take the audience from harsh training on to the hard reality of combat; both films conclude with significant musical motifs. For *The Sands of Iwo Jima*, "The Marine Hymn," which accompanied the opening credits, is playing in the background as the American flag is raised on top of Mount Suribachi. There's no surprise about the prominence of "The Marine Hymn," for the film celebrates the sacrifices of Marines in World War II. The US Navy and Marines provided assistance in the mak-ing of John Wayne's movie; nothing comparable happened in the filming of *Full Metal Jacket*. Music at the conclusion of *Full Metal Jacket* splits in two contrary directions—a sure sign of complexity.

The first direction involves the Mickey Mouse Club theme song and is voiced by the surviving members of Joker's Lusthog squad and other Ma-rines who had been slogging their way through the city of Hue to reclaim it after its capture by the Viet Cong during the Tet Offensive in 1968; the last fifteen minutes of the movie are focused on street fighting by Joker and his fellow Marines, an engagement with the enemy that comes to a shocking finish as they blast their way into the redoubt of an urban sniper—who turns out to be a woman—in order to get some "payback" for their comrades who fell to the sniper's fire. While the sniper lies mortally wounded on the floor, Animal Mother and Joker have a last tussle of wills over the proper response to the woman's plea to be put out of her dying misery with a mercy shot. Animal Mother would opt to leave her to suffer.

Finally, though, Joker's hard Marine heart softens enough to deliver the woman to death, a scene that turns on ironic end all the Marine training and the terrors of Parris Island boot camp shown in the first half of the film. At the end, it is a soft heart that kills. What a twist! Slowly, against a backdrop of a city in flames, American soldiers march off to do battle again, somewhere else. They have known the hell of war, but they are united in song, a favorite from the childhood memory bank, and as they spell out the M-I-C . . . K-E-Y . . . M-O-U-S-E lyrics, it is manifestly clear they retain a deep-down lingering bit of innocence from their boyhood days in the company of the Mickey Mouse Club gang. The message here is implicit but clear: Look what innocence can do. Then, to accompany the credits, comes the last song, from the Rolling Stones, a ripping away from the lovely and safe realm of innocence so as to rock hard, roll harder into the words of "Paint It, Black." One song, battling another, proves to be an apt finish for a film that centers on the human heart in conflict with itself, the ultimate objective for stories, as William Faulkner averred in his 1950 Nobel Prize acceptance speech.

Back in the present of the twenty-first century, the Disney enterprise is still going strong, and the Magic Kingdom in Florida has a New Fantasyland commodious enough to handle all the visitors who want to be in a place where reality does not intrude. The hunt for bin Laden could go on for ten frustrating years, but the news would not break through into Fantasyland. Hundreds of thousands of American soldiers would serve tours in Iraq and pass through their own version of hell in the process, with long-term devastating results in the form of PTSD, yet none of that could break the bubble of Fantasyland. The economy could be wrung through a 1930s-style wringer, but the visitors to Fantasyland streamed in nonstop. If there was a go-to place in America for reality relief as a new millennium began, the numbers show that its name was Fantasyland.

That the Disney phenomenon should be so central in the way Americans manage stress and the hard edges of reality is no surprise. Right at the end of the last century, Henry Giroux's *The Mouse That Roared: Disney and the*

End of Innocence provided a sweeping array of examples to show that the business side of Disney had so possessed and manipulated the idea of innocence in American life that everything was contaminated. Profit had won; innocence was lost. The audience was in cahoots with Disney in the whole process. Americans had bought the rampant sexism of the early animated films, with female characters always in need of a prince to make things right. They had accepted the racism embedded in *Song of the South* in the 1940s. As Giroux argues, the audience for the Touchstone/Disney film *Good Morning, Vietnam* (1987) was enticed into another form of racism, this time against the Vietnamese people—which, of course, had been a rough factor throughout the years of American combat activity in Vietnam. But Americans chose not to notice any of these problems, so strong was their desire for the unfettered and uncomplicated innocent representation of the world that the Disney process produces for its consumers.

Over the years, these storylines from Disney etched themselves so deeply in the mythos of America that it is devilishly hard to erase and rewrite them. Along the way, of course, there has been a bit of pushback to the brutal norming pattern for girls that is driven by the whole "Princess/Prince" relationship embodied in countless Disney ways (*Mulan*, for example, opens up a different model for women, as did *Brave* and, most recently, *Frozen*). The reasons behind that belated effort to help women move forward toward equality are compelling, but New Fantasyland persists with storylines still clinging to the old templates, and the audience is huge and happy. Disney is not leading anything like a revolution. The chances for an Equal Rights Amendment (ERA) are no better now than they were when the ERA went down in defeat in Reagan's 1980s America.

Giroux's book pointed out serious problems with the influence and impact of Disney on the values and overall culture of America. His book presents a detailed and insightful history of the Disney operation from its beginnings to the end of the twentieth century. He was looking to set off alarm bells. In September 2014 his book sat, in the Amazon sales accounting system, at position #336,256, which means rather painfully that he is not having a whole lot of influence, even though his book shows up now and then on college course reading lists. In fiscal 2014, BusinessWire reported that The Walt Disney Company, largest media conglomerate in the world, had gross revenues of $48.8 billion—and a net income line of $7.5 billion. We have already considered the number of visitors to Disney World. The Disney Company has made many escape-from-reality films in the first decade of the twenty-first century. It is safe to say that Disney is winning the war against detractors. Deterrence of war in the realm of Disney is a lost cause, not even worth engaging. Disney came close to war more than two decades ago with Robin Williams playing Adrian Cronauer, an independent-minded disk jockey on the Armed Forces Vietnam Network in the film *Good Morning, Vietnam* (Touchstone Film for Disney); with the focus on Williams in manic mode, the film set in Vietnam was essentially a distraction from war. Distraction makes sense. People need an escape from reality. Disney helps solve that problem.

To keep the betting comfortably in safe territory, far from the ugliness of war, Disney went to extraordinary lengths to extricate itself from association with the 2004 release of Michael Moore's *Fahrenheit 9/11*, a scorching indictment of the premises involved in the run-up to the Iraq War. Miramax was the key studio in making the film, and at the time, it was a Disney company. As Moore's film headed through the final stages of post-production, Disney put great pressure on Miramax (and particularly on Harvey Weinstein, cochairman of Miramax) not to release the film. Eventually some difficult negotiations resulted in the film being acquired by the Weinsteins so it could be distributed to theaters. If war were to be challenged or interrogated in mass media in America, Disney would not be a party to it.

Television Fantasy; Or, 500 Ways to Go Where You Want and Avoid the Rest

What Henry Giroux was attempting to do with his stringent examination of the influence exerted by the Disney company over American life, Neil Postman matched in his assault on television in his book *Amusing Ourselves to Death: Discourse in the Age of Show Business* (1985). Postman's main focus was on the way news of the world becomes repackaged as it is presented through the medium of television; in the process, of course, entertainment trumps depth and meticulous seriousness. In his first chapter, Postman updated Marshall McLuhan's most famous observation, "The medium is the message," and argued that now "The Medium is the Metaphor" (7)—that "the news of the day is a figment of our technological imagination. It is, quite precisely, a media event" (8).

Television relentlessly pursues, packages, and presents image after image after image throughout day and night. One images follows another in a flash; as "media events" are rushed along to the audience, there is little if any resonance beyond the light, tinny quality of quick verbal commentary offered as a little flavor topping the cake of image. Sound bites predominate;

everything must be boiled down to fit the cascading progression of images that fill the screen. And no matter what the "news" might be in any given flash of a moment, no matter what level of gravitas might be otherwise warranted, the mood is sure to change in just another flash as some product or service is hawked for sale—often in dazzling images and verbal play that makes the "news" look horribly dull and unengaging by comparison.

Sometimes the packaging devised in order to foreground the dramatic impact of a "media event" actually alters the import of a television news story. Just such a situation occurred during the Tet Offensive in Vietnam in 1968. Tet was a huge surprise for the American military in Vietnam, and for audiences back in the United States following the war on television. When a country-wide attack on American forces and our ARVN allies took place, for a brief while Vietnam roiled in chaos. Nothing like this was supposed to happen; there had been strong assurances from General Westmoreland, MACV commander, telling Congress and the American people just a few months before that the enemy was weak, unable to match up to American forces. Such was the Vietnam "media event" in the fall of 1967. Then came the shock of Tet. There were plenty of news-people in Vietnam to witness and report the new "media event" as it unfolded, and one of its most famous scenes took place on the streets of Saigon.

The film presented on the evening news showed a street with ambiguous action in the foreground—some Vietnamese in various uniforms gathering around a man in a plaid shirt and plain dark shorts. As viewers in living rooms across America watched, the man seemed to be a prisoner; his hands were bound behind him. In short order, another man in uniform came in, directed others to move away from the prisoner, raised a small pistol, and shot the prisoner in the head at point blank range. The man who fired his pistol, killing the prisoner, was Nguyen Ngoc Loan, chief of national police for South Vietnam. Eddie Adams caught the scene in a still photograph that won him a Pulitzer Prize; all three major television networks featured the Adams photograph in their 1 Feb. 1968, broadcasts. There has been some debate about the origins of the film version, the one that soon became a hugely influential "media event" on the evening news when NBC ran its filmed version on 2 February. There is a sound of a gun firing in the broadcast film, which made sense, because the NBC film team had equipment operating to capture sound with image; however, another NBC film crew recorded only image with no sound, and an ABC crew caught only part of the execution scene. As a consequence, there have been concerns that some studio doctoring was required to make all the film treatments feel complete—to have maximum impact upon the viewing audience. The scene was presented without background commentary—and as a "media event," the Loan shooting was a bonanza. It's not every day that a national television audience could witness an execution by bullet.

Was there a context for this image? Yes, but it was not explicitly part of the initial "media event" presentation. The man who was killed was a member of the Viet Cong, and he had been involved in nonjudicial killings of South Vietnamese linked to the police force; his background was made known to Chief Loan. In this light, the killing was an act of vengeance. However, Americans were only shown the cold-blooded killing of a defenseless prisoner of war, and this image did not square with the way Americans wanted to see our role in Vietnam. This image looked all wrong. We should not be involved in a place where this sort of thing happens. It was a simple reaction to a simple image, a blockbuster "media event." Still, whether it was a good thing or a bad thing, almost everyone who had a television in 1968 came to know the Vietnam situation and form an opinion about it because there was common ground being shared across the ABC/CBS/NBC spectrum—an important means for uniting a people whose individualistic impulses are often quite selfish and fragmentary.

As mentioned earlier, Neil Postman's concerns about the impact of television centered on the way "news" was presented to Americans. At the time, the channel options for viewers were still rather limited; the old broadcast networks (ABC, CBS, NBC) continued to dominate, but there was also the growing PBS network (launched in October 1970), plus the nascent Cable News Network (CNN) established by Ted Turner in 1980; from the mid-1980s onward, Rupert Murdoch was involved in developing the Fox cable network, which eventually led to the launch of Fox News Channel in early October 1996.

However, for the purposes of this study, while I accept and applaud Postman for the way he voiced his concerns about the impact of television in American culture—and I cannot find any grounds for disregarding his assertion that television has massively degraded the seriousness of news and informed perspective in America over the past fifty years—I am actually more concerned about the incredible proliferation of cable channel options for viewing in the last twenty-five years. The explosion of possibilities for viewing entertainment content on a screen at home has had devastating impact on our ability to come together as a national community through viewing experiences on television. The effect is one of extreme fragmentation.

There are hundreds and hundreds of channel options. If you love fishing, you need never leave the fishing-channel world. If religion is your thing, at any time of the day or night, an ever-ready assortment of religious channels exist to boost your soul and provide a drain for your pocketbook. Golfers can stay focused on golf, history buffs can dwell in history round the clock, storm-phobes can stay on alert at the Weather Channel, foodies can easily find a place to whet their appetites, and cine-philes can always dial up an old (or not so old) film on diverse movie channels. Of course, the ideological bias evident in the approach of the Fox Channel is particularly disturbing, for now it is possible for a group of people to partition themselves off from everyone else and get rigorously right-slanted presentations of everything. Yes, the Fox Channel devotees insist that all the other "lamestream" channels have bias too, but mostly that has to do with the need to find exciting visual content to make a program draw viewers. If there's a routine birth at the local hospital and a fire over on Juniper Street happening at the same time, you can bet that the local ABC station will send the camera to Juniper. And if there was nothing happening but a routine birth, there would be no evening news. One reason we feel so drenched in violence and bloodshed is that these things make perfect "media events." Technology is a hard driver; every innovation comes with costs to be calculated on multiple layers—just as Thoreau pointed out so bluntly in the early sections of *Walden*.

In February 2013, a Carnival line cruise ship lost power on a Caribbean excursion and had to be towed back to port in Biloxi, Mississippi; the towing process took several days, and all through that time, the passengers aboard the ship were subject to significant deprivations of creature comforts (edible food, working toilets, air conditioning). It was a bad news story for the Carnival line—and CNN chose to cover the story around the clock until the passengers got ashore. Would CNN cover a successful cruise to the same extent? Never—there's no gripping story there. It's not an ideological problem; it's a problem involving the stories that generate excitement in humans.

On a daily basis, the Fox channel could be counted on to try to put a positive and happy spin on news from the wars in Iraq and Afghanistan, so as to correct the perceived negative slant offered by other channels, and for once, ironically, most of America seemed inclined in the same direction—to avoid confronting the deep ugliness and complexity of these war zones as much as possible. Go to the fishing channel. Relax in the food zones, the nature places, the religious upbeat regions. Drift away into history. Do anything but confront reality. So many channels to choose . . . so little chance for meaningful connection with others who might be devoted to developing the common good.

Lotteries Everywhere and Winners Nowhere

The Declaration of Independence argues that "Life, Liberty, and the Pursuit of Happiness" are "unalienable Rights." The document does not say that the way to happiness involves wealth, but that has not stopped many generations of Americans from associating happiness with having a lot of money. It's not a universal connection, for sure, but in our day there is plenty of evidence for seeing a strong link nevertheless. In very simple terms, the American Dream works best for people who can get their hands on big piles of cash. You get the biggest McMansion; you have the hottest high-end imported car; you sail on your own yacht; you eat lots of lobster and steak—and all the world can see that you have arrived at success . . . and happiness. Pursuit has worked.

But pursuit can be hard work, can be frustrating, can be time-consuming. Is there a better way? Of course, and it's called gambling. A tiny investment can pay off in huge dividends; you can become an instant mega-millionaire. Gambling takes many forms, and the revenue streams are gigantic. In 2007, a typical year during the Afghanistan and Iraq wars, total countrywide gambling revenues added up to slightly more than $92 billion. As accounted for in a 2014 Wikipedia entry "Gambling in the United States," three different types of gambling operations had most of the action: $34.4 billion at commercial casinos (e.g., Las Vegas, Atlantic City); $26 billion at Indian casinos (e.g., Mohegan Sun, "A World At Play"); and $24.7 billion from lotteries run by states.

As the title of this section suggests, I'm mostly concerned with the presence of lotteries all across the land, for it seems to me that they represent the most ubiquitous form of fantasyland denial in the realm of gambling, primarily because you can buy a lottery ticket practically anywhere, without any effort or thought. Walk into a convenience store, buy a cup of coffee, and grab a lottery ticket while you're there; you're at the threshold of a fortune, if only the numbers tumble in your favor. Furthermore, in addition to creating mindless possibilities for individuals to pursue great wealth via dumb luck—instead of through steady effort in work that actually amounts to something and provides a deeper kind of reward—the lotteries make state governments complicit in the fantasy escape from reality. Instead of acting responsibly and devising a fair tax code to generate necessary revenues to provide for all the services a good government should provide, most states have opted to use lotteries to cover costs for some essential services. All forms of gambling, including the lottery option, are set up to take money from people who can least afford to lose it, and most everybody loses in the process.

Yes, there are always some "winners"—enough to keep people buying lottery tickets—but those who win often find that their lives become more complicated and stressful than ever before. It's a lot like a nation going to war. Going in, the expected results look mighty appealing, but then reality deals its tough blows to fantasyland imaginings, and the results can be bitter to the core. But the gambling goes on apace; the lotteries keep states afloat—damn the torpedoes of morality or adult responsibility; and the wars are maintained in just the same reality-denying pattern.

As we move ahead in time, our wars are increasingly going to be extravaganzas of digital technology and robotics. In gambling terms, the precision of modern American weaponry gives the United States winning odds almost always. P. W. Singer's provocative book *Wired for War: The Robotics Revolution and Conflict in the 21st Century* (2009) explores the current and future roles for fancy weapons of war that deliver destruction to targets thousands of miles from the control station of operators who got their early training courtesy of PlayStation 2. For thirteen hours on 6 Mar. 2013, Senator Rand Paul of Kentucky and a few other Republicans sympathetic to his concern filibustered the confirmation of John Brennan as director of the CIA; Senator Paul was obsessed with determining that President Obama did not have intentions to use drone strikes against Americans on American soil—which would be a rather huge (and, as it turned out, entirely delusional) escalation of the use of drones to monitor and strike against enemy terrorist cells on foreign soil—which, on occasion, have indeed included American citizens.

In Yemen in September of 2011, such a drone strike killed Anwar al-Awlaki and Samir Khan, two Americans who were seriously involved with al-Qaida in the Arabian Peninsula—and later, also in Yemen, another drone strike killed Anwar's sixteen-year-old son, Abdulrahman al-Awlaki. Similar drone strikes have been made frequently against enemy cells in Pakistan and Yemen, although apparently none with Americans involved on the target end. The pattern is always the same. Some ground intelligence provides a tip about some enemy person's whereabouts; a surveillance drone operating in the air overhead provides clear, in-the-moment video of the target's location and pinpoints it with a laser beam; a Predator drone fires an AGM-114 Hellfire missile to hit exactly where the red-eye laser directs.

The accuracy is extraordinary. Results of an attack are immediately evident in video provided by the drone overhead, and operators in comfort-controlled environments across the United States get a very good idea of the destruction they have caused. According to a *New York Times* story by Elisabeth Bumiller ("A Day Job Waiting for a Kill Shot a World Away," 29 July 2012), the Air Force at that time had over 1,300 drone pilots stationed at thirteen or more bases, primarily to wage war on targets in Afghanistan; the CIA has operated a comparable program for strikes in Pakistan, Somalia, and Yemen. No American lives are at risk in an attack of this nature. The Air Force drone pilots are officers; and having often released similar weapons from manned aircraft, they tend to see their function as different from a video game where targets change quickly and are not observed closely over time (as is more typical of the drone strike patterns). However, as Singer's book suggests, the appeal of this type of combat activity, which can minimize American soldier casualties, is obvious to all, and all across America, as those war video games are played relentlessly, the nation is quietly being prepped for wars that will be everlasting.

In 2014 Americans had an opportunity to explore the moral implications and complexities of drone warfare; *Good Kill*, a film starring Ethan Hawke and directed by Andrew Niccol, a native of New Zealand, focused on the feelings of malaise experienced by an Air Force jet pilot (Maj. Thomas Egan) who has been reassigned from cockpit duty to an air-conditioned building in the Las Vegas desert, where he spends twelve-hour shifts hunting al-Qaida operatives in Afghanistan. When a target is located, Egan pushes the button to send a missile on its kill mission on the other side of the planet. The story shows the toll this sort of warfare takes on a pilot, always trying to get intended targets without damaging innocent people.

The stress of the job bleeds out of the control room, with all its sophisticated electronic equipment, and infects Egan's family life; and eventually, while Egan trains a female pilot, Vera Suarez (played by Zoë Kravitz), they become witnesses to the rape of an Afghan woman by a guard. At the end, with audience acceptance expected, a kill strike is directed at the guard, again caught by the drone camera violating the woman. The missile strike puts her life in peril, but amazingly she escapes. Hence, the war story becomes a crime story, with justice delivered in an extraordinary way. Even with no American boots on the ground—at least not in the target areas shown in the film—there is still plenty of troubling action that could haunt American veterans for a long time. If this is the future—the steadily increasing presence of drones in combat zones—then the film provides advance warning to Americans. However, the film's box office in limited release, a paltry domestic gross of $316,472 according to *Box Office Mojo*, is clear evidence that playing war video games and relentlessly hunting targets of opportunity on computer or smartphone screens (a pattern addressed more fully later in this chapter) is hugely more engaging than a story on film about the implications of drones used to kill real people. Fantasy wins again.

Porno Universe—Big Deal, Nothing Real

Just as gambling has shadowed human experience for a long time, so has pornography, and like the lotteries that have made playing the risk game dreadfully easy, the advent of the Internet has brought ungodly gobs of fantasyland porn within reach of a few keystrokes. Fortunately, investigative research has shown that the total Internet pornography activity is not nearly as sweeping as some have imagined (there have been speculative guesses that up to a half or more of web searching involved some sort of porn).

For the online issue of *Forbes* in September 2011, Julie Ruvello's "How Much of the Internet Is Actually for Porn?" story referenced research by two neuroscientists, Ogi Ogas and Sai Gaddam (authors of *A Billion Wicked Thoughts*), and results show that of the million most-visited websites in the world in 2010, only about 4 percent were sex-related; their research from July 2009 to July 2010 discovered that "about 13% of Web searches were for erotic content." It is a relief to know that we are not drowning in pornography, and yet the easy presence of porn does nevertheless contribute to the overall fantasyland pattern. Obviously, this pattern is not limited to citizens of the United States, but there is no doubt that Americans seeking escape from reality are sometimes to be found in the fantasyland of pornography. As it turns out, as represented in both literature and film, this particular dimension of fantasyland has distinct appeal to soldiers in uniform. Those closest to grim reality have a need for escape even more compelling than that evident in American culture at large. Even on the eve of battle—or the morn of combat—there is a place for porn.

If porn is virtually everywhere, it is entirely reasonable to envision a tight link between war and porn, and in *War Porn* (2016), Roy Scranton made just such a connection clear and certain. Scranton's novel starts innocently enough, with a backyard barbeque in Utah, a gathering of young professionals early on their journey toward the American Dream. There's Matt, a computer programmer looking to create a program that can predict outcomes in diverse situations of life. Such a program would be a nifty thing to have if a country were contemplating war. His wife, Dahlia (a splendid touch of originality in not having the woman be Rose, famously subject to violation by worm in Blake's "The Sick Rose"—but still a vulnerable flower), has been married long enough to crave something different, something more exotic, less programmatic. Mel and Rachel are a lesbian couple—and seriously at odds with America at war in the days leading up to the Bush/ Kerry election in 2004, serious enough to contemplate a move to Canada.

OK so far, just the American Dream with some breakdown lanes. Then in comes Wendy, way lost from Peter Pan's Neverland, and she has brought along Aaron Stojanowski, better known as Sto, who is a veteran recently returned from Iraq. Upon introductions and learning of Sto's veteran status, Matt tosses out the obligatory and mindless, "Well, thank you for your service" (17), followed by a "what was it really like over there" query. It is immediately obvious that the Matts of America have no clue. In short order, as steaks and tofu sizzle together on the grill, Aaron is set upon by Mel, for she can abide no one who has joined America's war machine. But hey, he's just National Guard, no career warmonger. To Mel, it doesn't matter, and barbeque turns into battle royal. Eventually, Sto makes it clear that he didn't kill anybody—he just took pictures. At this point, the photography angle seems innocent, relatively harmless. But a novel must have an arc, and by the end, with Aaron sexually abusing and torturing Dahlia, the pictures of the past in Iraq come home in devastating fashion. The images of brutalization and torment of other human beings that made their way through his camera lens have ultimately made a twisted, aberrant, deformed pretzel out of Aaron the cameraman. His war images have aroused fantasies in Dahlia. And the hell of war most certainly comes home.

In the August 2015 issue of *Harper's Magazine*, Sam Sacks stringently called into question the work of veterans who had produced fiction of the Iraq War. Sacks found too much that is derivative and hence predictable, too much work that is under the influence of the homogenizing effects of too many MFA programs looming over aspiring writers from the late 1940s right up to the present. Sacks has a good point there, for the workshops tend to press everyone toward the middle ground—an ironic twist for programs that were envisioned as liberating, expressly designed to set free individual representations of life. Sacks concentrates on six works of fiction (three of them—*Yellow Birds*, *Redeployment*, and *Fire and Forget*, which was coedited by Scranton—are analyzed in the fiction chapter), and he makes some fine points about them as he works toward his conclusion. He astutely notes Hemingway's strong influence over the MFA culture as it grew to gargantuan size in the second half of the twentieth century—the steely, unflinching Hemingway look at the world as it was being experienced, quietly allowing for inner suffering to be suggested (but not spoken of directly), the mass of iceberg beneath the water, all of which offered a sort of bastion against the staggering hollowness that had devolved from upheavals early in the century—Freud, Einstein, the trench warfare of World War I. All American male writers after Hemingway had him looking over their shoulders, nudging them to follow the tracks he established in the way to see war. Yes, that happened. Hemingway's terseness and spare reportage became famous, a style from which he himself could never break free, although his posthumously published fiction showed he certainly wanted room to innovate.

Scranton's *War Porn* was some eleven years in the making, from 2005 to publication in 2016, so it is definitely not a response to Sacks's criticism, but it does contain, in the long middle section of the story (sandwiched between barbeque introduction and sexual abuse of Dahlia in the conclusion), an in-depth representation of the effects of war on an Iraqi man who gets entangled in the war mess and suffers in his own way. Maria's story in *For Whom the Bell Tolls* afforded Hemingway a means to incorporate the horror of war as it was visited upon citizens of Spain during the Spanish Civil War, but Scranton provocatively takes concern for the Iraqi people to a level significantly beyond what Hemingway did in his concern for the Spanish people.

Sacks goes on to mention the attention paid to the Iraqi side of the war as a very positive feature of Michael Pitre's *Fives and Twenty-Fives* (2014); Pitre makes Kateb, an interpreter, a key figure in working out a complete set of consequences in the war. Kateb is enchanted with American culture, most intimately represented by Twain's *The Adventures of Huckleberry Finn*, a near-sacred text that he carries with him and reads often. Every time Huck goes ashore from the raft carrying him and Jim toward freedom, he encounters meanness and ugliness (mindless killing, mob rule, betrayal of trust, treachery, greed, stupidity—you name it, America has it), and Kateb becomes fully familiar with an all-too-real version of this America as his country is devastated. Sacks applauds the attention paid to the Iraqi side of the war in Pitre's novel, a pattern that shows up earlier in this study, particularly in the poetry of Brian Turner; and in the final chapter, when Matt Gallagher's *YOUNGBLOOD* (2016) is analyzed, we will see a very prominent place assumed by the people and culture of Iraq as that narrative unfolds and works to its surprising conclusion.

But what about the porn of *War Porn*? In the main story, all those pictures taken by Aaron ("Sto") constitute pornography of a kind. But there's more, much more, and a little rhyming might open up a gesture of dazzling originality in Scranton's story: war torn, war shorn, war worn, war born, war corn (yes, the cover illustration for the novel presents a hard, upright ear of corn with kernels on the top half yielding to the shiny lead head of a bullet or artillery round—hence, a distinct and clear phallic image to greet readers), and then we are at the threshold of war porn. Porn is the ultimate in disconnection—the phenomenon of someone *imagined* as present . . . who is *not* there really, a futile and foolish effort to fuse a connection, but the connection is possible only as fantasy, the supreme dislocation or separation.

Spaced through the narrative are short sections that function a little like the inter-chapters of Hemingway's *In Our Time*; these periodic insertions of three or four pages sprung free of the narrative arc constitute linguistic overdrive, shreds of concepts and attitudes that pulse, pulse, pulse in a mad minute of supercharged prose-poem word power, words and phrases and notions rushing to burst forth, an orgasmic push/pull of connection effort, dying for release: porn. Real connection is not possible; the porn thing is all about distance, a lack of the understanding and shared experience that make real intimacy. Scranton is throwing down the gauntlet in *War Porn*. How long can we go on in the porn mode? Why can't we rise to face reality, put everything together in a meaningful paradigm of true connection? Until there is an awakening to truth and understanding, Americans will be caught up in the suction of Aaron the perverse perp beating his retreat (distantly from the Iraq War and yet closely via his brutalization of Dahlia), heading out at novel's end into the Monument Valley world of all those John Wayne movies—John Wayne alone, doing his John Wayne thing: the legend of the West, isolation in overdrive, indelible porn tantalizing Americans generation after generation.

Competition Fantasyland—From Penn State Football to Video Games of War and on to *Dancing with the Stars*

Despite the good news above that mainstream America has not been swept by the scourge of pornography, evidence everywhere shows that we are hopelessly infatuated with the idea of competition—and the amount of attention paid to competitive activities of diverse sorts is nothing short of astounding. Games of competition fascinate us. Despite signs of danger, we hold dear to them, choosing to stay the course with our obsession even when shards of hard reality intrude. Competition constitutes yet another dimension of fantasyland in America; it enchants us, mesmerizes us, keeps us occupied—even though at the end of any day, whether the action involves actual engagement or merely observation, it all amounts to nothing except a few hours of distraction. Sporting events loom largest in this part of fantasyland—but the domain extends far beyond the baseball diamond, the football field, the hockey rink, the basketball court. We have competition in *Dancing with the Stars*, in *American Idol*, in *The Bachelor*, and in video games such as *Call of Duty*. We love the intoxication of competition; it captivates us. When reality beckons or threatens, we flee to the safe realm where competitive activity is staged for our entertainment.

Case in point #1: The football program at Penn State University, which is located smack-dab in the middle of Pennsylvania. Football is the dominant competitive sport at Penn State. Throughout the Joe Paterno era, which extended from the early 1950s through to November 2011, when Paterno was fired in his forty-fourth season as head coach, the football program grew to dominate the world of the university. The program brought national attention, and it generated significant revenue. Alumni flocked to see games, and they gave generously to support their university and its football program for the lifelong entertainment value it provided. Every fall the stands at "Happy Valley," the fantasyland nickname for State College in the years of football's ascendancy, would be full to overflowing with delirious fans. The world might be full of disasters, but football under Paterno at Penn State made it all seem OK. "WE ARE . . . PENN STATE!" the chant would go, a slogan running on pure-grade simple, boisterously mocking the very idea of a university.

Unfortunately, Jerry Sandusky was a long-term aide to Paterno in the football program, and Sandusky was a sexual predator who favored young boys. His criminal activity sometimes took place within the sports complex, and at least once it was observed by another aide. The incident was reported; Paterno was advised; a little bit of investigation, inconclusive, was made; and several layers of supervisory responsibility were eventually involved in keeping everything under cover. The lid was on. Bad press might bring down the shining beacon of Penn State football. Once the story finally broke, precipitating indictment of Sandusky and firing of Paterno (along with resignation of Graham Spanier, university president), some allegations suggested that the state attorney general at the time, Tom Corbett (later Pennsylvania governor), was slow to act on reports of problems for fear of upsetting the success of the football program. Football in the Keystone State functioned as a form of fantasyland; it had to be safeguarded. Morality did not matter; fantasyland football reigned supreme.

Case in point #2: *Dancing with the Stars.* Actually, there is no driving reason to single out this TV show; there are a great many comparable "competition"-based programs—from the never-ending *Survivor* series to the sometimes-perverse embarrassments of *American Idol,* and on to the always torturous (and horribly contrived) eliminations en route to finding the perfect match for some jejune bachelor—and any one of them could serve to represent this version of fantasyland. We are just so thoroughly comfortable with trying to beat an opponent that we will watch virtually any permutation of the game. Our enthusiasm for competition not only predisposes us to think of war as just another realm where the competitive spirit can do its thing but also affords us an escape zone when the war stuff veers toward ugliness and depredation. Reality too much for us? Just dial up a "reality" competition show. Irony rocks in America.

Case in point #3: The *Call of Duty* first-person and third-person shooter computer/video game franchise. Since its origins in 2003, sales for the *Call of Duty* series (with multiple *Modern Warfare* versions) have gone well past 100 million; somewhere in the vicinity of 40 million players are regularly engaged with *Call of Duty* games; billions of hours of game-time have been logged. All of this happens on a worldwide stage, of course, but sales in the United States have been consistently very strong. These games have great appeal for young men, and they serve as a subtle kind of recruitment tool for the US Armed Forces as they work to maintain adequate force levels in the various uniformed services. As we look into the future and anticipate moments when we will "acquiesce in necessity" and find ourselves in war once more, steady preparation can be assured in the ongoing popularity of the *Call of Duty* games.

Activision Blizzard, the game publisher, has recognized a link of sorts between the fantasyland world of the games and the real world of military service by setting up the Call of Duty Endowment (CODE), a nonprofit organization to help find employment for military veterans. In a March 2010 update report on *Call of Duty* by Howlingpixel, the endowment donated three thousand copies of *Call of Duty: Modern Warfare 2*, worth roughly $180,000, to the US Navy. It would seem that, except for the well-known Navy SEALs raid on the bin Laden compound, the Navy has not had many actual opportunities to engage in combat action in the land-based wars of Iraq and Afghanistan, so sailors have to be consoled with playtime on *Call of Duty*. Here we have, right within the military, a substitution of fantasyland for reality.

Meanwhile, the Army has its own game, *America's Army*, and according to Jeremy Hsu in "For the US Military, Video Games Get Serious," this game, which costs nothing to play, is the Army's most successful means of attracting recruits, despite offering kill scenes that have only a "Teen" rating. The game playing does not stop when civilian turns soldier either. Plenty of active-duty soldiers play under their actual unit designations.

War is just another form of competition. We are supremely prepared. American culture is drenched in competition—whether at the football stadium in the fall, the ballpark in the summer, the rink or court in the winter . . . or in a wide panoply of "reality" competition shows on television . . . or in the "you-can-be-the-shooter" game structure of *Call of Duty*. All of this activity adds to the fantasyland element of American culture—the impulse to seek an escape from workaday reality. And what of real war? For those who go off to engage in combat, it is just a super-heightened and sometimes intense (not to mention, lethal) form of competition. And for everyone left behind on the home front? Not to worry; we are otherwise distracted with an ever-increasing number of competitions that can feed our imaginations and provide for us a steady immersion in fantasyland.

The Movies That Made Money and Fed Fantasy to Audiences in the Past Twenty-Five Years

If anyone still doubts the extraordinary hold that fantasy has on Americans, the following list from infoplease.com, which shows the thirty highest-grossing movies of all time in the United States as of 1 June 2015, should help dispel the skepticism: 1) *Avatar* (2009, $760,507,625); 2) *Titanic* (1997, $658,672,302); 3) *The Avengers* (2012, $623,357,910); 4) *The Dark Knight* (2008, $534,858,444); 5) *Star Wars: Episode I—The Phantom Menace* (1999,

$474,544,249); 6) *Star Wars* (1977, $460,998,882); 7) *The Dark Knight Rises* (2012, $448,139,099); 8) *Avengers: Age of Ultron* (2015, $445,228,711); 9) *Shrek 2* (2004, $441,226,414); 10) *E.T. the Extra-Terrestrial* (1982, $435,110,890); 11) *The Hunger Games: Catching Fire* (2013, $424,668,047); 12) *Pirates of the Caribbean: Dead Man's Chest* (2006, $423,315,199); 13) *The Lion King* (1994, $422,783,937); 14) *Toy Story 3* (2010, $415,004,880); 15) *Iron Man* (2013, $409,013,994); 16) *The Hunger Games* (2012, $408,010,692); 17) *Spider-Man* (2002, $403,706,983); 18) *Jurassic Park* (1993, 402,453,925); 19) *Transformers: Revenge of the Fallen* (2009, $402,111,347); 20) *Frozen* (2013, $400,738,009); 21) *Harry Potter and the Deathly Hallows: Part 2* (2011, $381,011,219); 22) *Finding Nemo* (2003, $380,784,279); 23) *Star Wars: Episode III-Revenge of the Sith* (2005, $380,270,448); 24) *The Lord of the Rings: The Return of the King* (2003, $377,027,863); 25) *Spider-Man 2* (2004, $383,027,863); 26) *The Passion of the Christ* (2004, $370,773,682); 27) *Despicable Me* (2013, $368,065,385); 28) *Transformers: Dark of the Moon* (2011, $352,390,543); 29) *Furious 7* (2015, $350,872,260); 30) *American Sniper* (2014, $350,113,554).

So . . . there's the *Star Wars* franchise, the *Spider-Man* franchise, *The Lord of the Rings* franchise, the *Shrek* franchise, on to *Transformers,* and so forth. Is there any way to dispute the point that we are in thrall to fantasy? Of course, we know that the big heart of the movie market, in dollar terms, involves children and early adolescents. It is in this part of the economy where dollars available for spending top out, and almost all of the films on the top thirty list were designed for that market. However, this dimension of American popular culture also includes a lot of adults who are perfectly happy to continue their childhood through the medium of movies—and the message of those movies is simple: leave the ugliness of reality outside, and seek the relief of fantasy inside. If there is a way to stay childlike forever, we Americans will find it and exploit it. It worked in the Great Depression; it works now.

What can be further observed about these films? First, the top two, by a very commanding margin, are from one director, James Cameron, and yet the two films could not be further apart than *Avatar* and *Titanic* are (except for the fact that each one features a crisp and tight one-word title). *Avatar* is all futuristic, in subject matter and in style, pushing the boundaries of possibility off into the science fiction realm; *Titanic,* in contrast, is totally submerged (the pun is intentional) in history—as brutally hard and soul-chillingly real as a film could be, with an end featuring the cold drowning deaths of hundreds of people, including the male part of two iceberg-crossed lovers, a fate that produced huge oceans of teenage-girl tears.

Not surprisingly, only two films on the list involve realistic people in re-alistic situations: *Titanic* and *American Sniper*. *Titanic* is bound to the fate that attended the actual ship in 1912. Similarly, *American Sniper* was teth-ered to Chris Kyle's memoir and to his death.

All the other movies on the list are rooted in fantasy and mythology of one stripe or another. The majority thus speaks with authority and signifi-cant weight. In the mirror of our movie favorites, we can see ourselves as we seek entertainment and, in the process, realize yet another kind of escape from reality and immersion in fantasyland. A total of twenty-four films from the list are from twenty-first century—the main time frame of inter-est in this study. For the early years of our current century, we have already seen where the films dealing directly with wars of our time fall in terms of box office attendance and reach within American culture (from the attack of 9/11 forward to the present). The war films discussed in an earlier chapter are far down in any listing. With the notable exception of *American Sniper*, they lack fantasyland appeal.

These war-related films were indeed reviewed in newspapers and news-magazines and other places where people look to keep track of film proj-ects, but they were able to attract only very modest audiences. They came and went with minimal impact. The content of these films had a very hard edge, with grim reality attending almost every scene—an approach quite literally worlds apart from the locales and storylines represented in the films with huge box-office success. As the present century and millennium began to unfold, it was a time ruled by children, a fantasyland of the whole. Perhaps America has to work this way. Maybe it always has.

CHAPTER SEVEN

America and Future Wars—Fantasyland Ready for More War

The patterns of American experience with war are provocative, to say the least. Americans have been at war repeatedly, often in situations where one might think just a single devastatingly bad experience would suffice to preclude repetition, and yet all of the discernible forces in American cultural life and politics seem to indicate that the future will be full of similar episodes of war, probably with similar consequences. We will read Homer poorly; we will abide by Plato's advice to stay clear of ugly narratives about the realities of war; we will continue to provide the Executive Office with great power to commit troops to battlefields in the interests of national "security"; we will never realize, in sending soldiers off to civil war battlefields, that they will be gone for a dreadfully long time (perhaps, on average, as long as Odysseus was away from his home in Ithaca—a brutally long twenty years); and we will be deep in distractions as an antidote to dealing with the wrenching complexities of war.

In the article by Sam Sacks mentioned in an earlier chapter, we are left at the end with these words: "One of the jobs of literature is to wake us from stupor. But in matters of war, our sleep is deep, and the best attempts of today's veterans have done little to disturb it" (89). I would agree with his first point about the obligation to be assumed by veterans who become writers of war, but I would argue strongly against the second point, which lays blame on our veteran writers—even the best of them. As this study shows, the literature and film responses to war in Iraq and Afghanistan have pressed with both determination and vigor to "wake up" Americans. The failure is not theirs; failure is spread all across America in the way frivolous distractions relentlessly supersede the responsibility to be knowledgeable and carefully attentive to matters so deeply serious as war. As a lead into concluding reflections about contemporary America at war, analysis of efforts by two writers who have produced multiple responses to the wars of twenty-first-century America is well warranted. Earlier we encountered a few writers responsible for more than one book response to war: for example, Brian Turner, Hugh Martin, Kevin Powers (Powers has both a novel and a collection of poems—a multigenre author). Here we take up Matt Gallagher (already mentioned for his contributions to *Fire and Forget* as editor and short-story author) and Kayla Williams. Quite remarkably, Gallagher's writing progresses through several genres: blog posts while a soldier in Iraq—to memoir—to short story—to novel. Williams has two memoirs, separated by almost a decade, and at the end of her second memoir, she offers a small ray of hope for eventually working through the hell that Americans have ushered home from war by paying so little attention to it and its consequences. These writers demonstrate clearly that veterans are not going to go quietly into the night of either ignorance or forgetfulness with regard to the debacle of Iraq.

Gallagher went to Iraq as an Army lieutenant late in 2007. Soon he was putting up blog posts to account for the experience of war. His postings were raw and pointed. The war was a disaster on a daily basis; very little made any real sense. Eventually the Army noticed that there were blog posts emerging from the war front, that an officer was responsible, that readers outside the combat zone were interested—and that they were getting stories that undercut the way the Army wanted the world to see the efforts of US military forces deployed in Iraq. Consequently, the blog was shut down. There's no surprise in that development, but it was suddenly clear that social media in diverse forms would encroach on any future war undertakings. The story will out, one way or another.

Gallagher completed his military commitment in 2009. In 2010 he published a memoir—*Kaboom: Embracing the Suck in a Savage Little War*—and at that point, all of his critical insights about the war in Iraq became available to inform his fellow Americans, free from Army control. The writing is *Kaboom* is vivid; the style is racy, really hip and cool with the lingo of postmodernity in battle mode. Gallagher's chapter titles alone provide a sharp picture of his sardonic perspective, one with a very literary, writerly frame of reference: "THE RED, THE WHITE, AND THE EMO (or American Boy Escapes)"; "EMBRACE THE SUCK (or Narrative of a Counterinsurgent)"; "iWar (or The Lost Summer)"; "ACROSS THE RIVER AND FAR AWAY (or Redemption's Grunt)"; "STEPSONS OF IRAQ (or A Short-timer's Promenade)."

Perhaps we have a bow to John Gregory Dunne and his sarcastic *The Red, White, and Blue* view of American life looking back from 1987 over a lifetime; there's the obligatory Hemingway reference, albeit a bit obscure, regarding his "Across the River and into the Trees," which needed adaptation given that trees were seriously missing in the landscape of Iraq. Without doubt, though, here is a writer with high ambition, someone determined to give America a wake-up call. From his arrival in Iraq onward, Gallagher charts a course that will make him the Hemingway . . . the O'Brien . . . of his time. At least Stacey Peebles got the call, and the title of her pioneering study, *Welcome to the Suck*, deftly catches the bristle of Gallagher's point of view. *Kaboom* reflects a whole lot of "this war sucks" attitude, and the Army has no authorized place for individual attitude. Everything is supposed to be by the "book," even though reality mocks the rules/regulations book at almost every turn. With Gallagher in full writer mode in his memoir, the mockery turns back upon the military—and on the fiasco that Iraq became upon the fall of Saddam Hussein, which happened long before Gallagher arrived for his fifteen-month deployment. In all the details and turns of phrase, *Kaboom* shouts, "Here's a writer on the way up." Then a few years later, out comes *Fire and Forget*, with Roy Scranton joining Gallagher in editorial work as well as in short-story contributions to the collection. As noted in the fiction chapter, this collection is packed with really good writing. These veterans feed off each other—and the collective energy and talent is estimable, very hot to the touch.

Finally, it was time for Gallagher to make the move to a novel, and as 2016 began, *YOUNGBLOOD—A NOVEL* emerged. I argued earlier in this study that the high place of esteem enjoyed by the novel through the twentieth century has not been assured in the current century. For an alternative, the memoir has proved to be exceptionally attractive for readers; readers enjoy knowing that they are getting stories straight from life, mainlining truth of real experience. In a time of deep distrust, any assurance of truth is heartily embraced. A novel works in more devious ways to get to the truth, and such is the case with *YOUNGBLOOD*.

YOUNGBLOOD is highly original in its plot. The story packs in plenty of grim detail about the uncertainty that shadowed American military operations in Iraq during the long years when the conflict was essentially a civil war with Americans caught in the middle—Vietnam all over again, an almost impossible challenge in terms of figuring out who is with you and who is your enemy. Lt. Jack Porter, from California, is the protagonist, and all the way through the story, he is baffled by the daunting mysteries

surrounding his role as a troop leader. Central to his puzzlement is the relationship a previous combat leader, a sergeant, had with key figures in the
Iraqi community where his unit operates. That sergeant, Rios, was perhaps
known by another name, "Shaba," and was possibly in love with a dazzlingly
beautiful woman in the community (the wife to a powerful man)—and may
have been killed by Sergeant Chambers, who has been promoted to serve
as Lieutenant Porter's key enlisted subordinate. This is cloak-and-dagger
stuff, the essence of spy thrillers with secret identities and covert activities
and furtive liaisons. YOUNGBLOOD appeared only a few months after Sam
Sacks's "First-Person Shooters: What's Missing in Contemporary War Fiction," but this narrative from Gallagher almost seems to be a direct response
to the concerns voiced by Sacks.

YOUNGBLOOD is no first-person lament. The storyline is convoluted, richly original, and it maintains the suspense of "who done it?"—"to
whom?"—"why?"—and "how?" through more than three hundred pages.
From all the twists and turns that baffle Jack, it becomes incredibly clear
that Iraq was a place of nearly bottomless mystery and treachery. There was
no room in this murky environment for trust, except for Jack's contact with
his brother, who had also served in Iraq and is in a position stateside to dig
into military records to help clarify the strange goings-on in Jack's area of
operation.

What we see in YOUNGBLOOD is a writer on a major breakout mission—looking to blast free from the standard stuff of war literature. All the
way through to the mystery that hangs over the conclusion, Gallagher keeps
on pushing aggressively into new territory in the literature of the Iraq War.
He even gets to develop a love story. Jack becomes increasingly intrigued
with the beautiful woman, Rana, who seems to have captivated Sergeant
Rios—who eventually died for his infatuation. That's not to stop Jack, whose
back-in-the-states lover is really not that interested in him—and he is most
certainly ready to move on to something more exotic. After dealing with
murky muck in Iraq, who is going to be ready to settle for a nice quiet life in
the suburbs? Jack is not even tempted by a potentially bucolic life in Hawaii,
where he goes briefly after being sent home because a fatwa has been placed
on his life due to complications of Rana and efforts to smuggle people out
of Iraq. It's very complicated.

Then comes the ending, which is explosive in its own way—and which
is vigorously in accord with the main thrust of this study. America is in
full fantasyland mode, completely wrong for bringing war veterans home
in a sane, grounded way. What, then, is a war vet to do? The answer in

YOUNGBLOOD is to send Jack away from America. As the story comes to an end, Jack is an ex-pat settled in Lebanon on a scholarship to the American University of Beirut. He lives with Snoop/Quasim, his interpreter from Iraq. One day on TV, he sees al-Qaida planting flags on buildings in Ramadi, close to where he served in tough combat ("It wasn't quite like the fall of Saigon, but it felt close enough" [340]). Then, for the finishing touch, one day out on the streets, he sees a woman in the distance, and he feels it might just be Rana, the woman of his dreams, magical, magical, magical Rana. But she slips away. It's a *Casablanca* ending. But more than that, it's a kiss-off to America. America doesn't seem right for Jack, so he pursues life elsewhere.

The conclusion in Gallagher's novel makes a stringent point about America with regard to veterans who have dared everything to serve. America affords no home for them. Matt Gallagher's relentless, book-after-book effort to hit American homebodies hard enough to awaken in them sufficient responsibility for the ugly effects of war is salutary, and he has done his utmost in service to this cause. But as dedicated as Gallagher's work has been, the finishing point for his novel indicates that change will be a very long time coming—the very point central to a little-noticed film from way back in 2008, *The Lucky Ones,* which tracks three Iraq veterans who, for different reasons, are back in the states; however, in each case, the emptiness of being "home" sends them all back to further service in war. War offers a sense of togetherness not to be found where freedom runs amuck.

Nevertheless, for a measure of balance, perhaps there is at least a ray of hope for American redemption—some possibility of getting veterans home to something other than hell, and for that turn, we must analyze two memoirs of Kayla Williams.

At the outset of this study, in a brief exploration of the war experience paradigm contained in Homer's *Iliad* and *Odyssey*, it is established that getting soldiers home successfully after war has long been problematical. Writing about war experience has proved a useful therapy for some veterans in this regard, sometimes necessitating repeated efforts to settle the whole business in the evolutionary tumble of one imaginative text after another. Tim O'Brien spent many years—and created many stories in that time—working through the aftereffects of his Vietnam combat tour.

Kayla Williams has not needed to write as extensively and frequently about her Iraq tour and return home as Tim O'Brien did to find an ending that reached beyond torment and tribulation. Her time in a combat zone was not as searing as what O'Brien faced. Nevertheless, she was a witness to plenty of war's ugliness, and she endured frequent sexual objectification as a woman in uniform, all of which is accounted for in *Love My Rifle More than You: Young and Female in the U.S. Army* (2005). Her second memoir, *Plenty of Time When We Get Home: Love and Recovery in the Aftermath of War*, published nine years later, in 2014, completes the *Iliad/Odyssey* pattern; the first story focused on the Iraq War as experienced by an American combat woman soldier, and the second one accounts for the long struggle to be at peace once she returned to her homeland and then assumed the responsibility of aiding another veteran, her husband, Brian, in his attempt to complete the return from war. Exploration of her arc from home to Iraq and then back to home serves to set up final consideration of the fantasyland distraction pattern that presently vexes this process for veterans.

In the past thirty years, one of the most significant changes in America's military forces has involved the growing presence of women. A great many combat units in the Iraq and Afghanistan conflicts saw women serving right alongside men. They bunked with men, they went on convoys and patrols with men, they occupied observation posts beside men, and they saw firsthand the awful effects of war on casualties. Women in uniform were not immune to the dangers of roadside IED devices; when vehicles approached road checkpoints, women with weapons at the ready faced the same crucible of limited time for response as any male serving in that position. Life—or death—would hang in the same balance for women as it did for men.

At the outset, Williams acknowledges that the whole experience was terribly complex. She went to Iraq convinced that it was wrong, but she emerged with feelings of pride and honor for her service, even despite having seen ugly things—the sort of things that stay fixed in memory: "I don't forget. I can't forget any of it. From basic training all the way to Iraq and back home again" (17).

So many chunks of time in anyone's life are lost, far beyond recall of memory. Day after day, nothing striking happens; a tedium of ordinariness rules most of our minutes. But in the military, even far from combat, strange things happen, and they happen often enough to keep loading up the memory banks. Add in the surcharge of craziness that attends intense battle moments, and suddenly there are indelible memories embedded to endure right through to one's final breath.

Because Williams was in an intelligence-gathering unit, she played a key role in interrogation of various kinds in Iraq—all very purposeful and sensible given her training in Arabic at the Defense Language Institute in Monterey, California—and she had quite a wide range of assignments in

Iraq. She spent time in isolated observation posts on Iraq's northwestern border as well as in large compounds in the vicinity of Baghdad. Whenever she joined a convoy, she would assume responsibility for covering one sector of potential danger, and in one harrowing moment, she nearly shot a child in a car that was trying to pass her Humvee and break into the line of vehicles, always a potential threat to convoy safety. Always, too, there was the challenge of eliminating bodily wastes. In one early convoy experience, the commander indicated there would be no stopping for bathroom breaks on a seven-hour trip—that everyone could just pee in a bottle. This commander was a guy, of course, and quite oblivious to the presence of women in the convoy. Fortunately, another container of a different shape was available so Williams could get the necessary relief of elimination. There's not much of a place for modesty in Army operations.

Ironically, though, some of her darkest stories involve the sexist attitudes of her fellow male soldiers, many of whom could not get beyond seeing her as just tits and ass. At times it seems American men have a particularly difficult time climbing out of the sexual fantasies of adolescence, and the crudeness of these unevolved male types sweeps through many pages of *Love My Rifle More than You*. In the dark of one night, on guard duty, a fellow soldier, Rivers, tries to get Williams to have sex with him, asserting, "Nobody would know" (206). But Williams wants none of it, rebuffing him directly. She does not press the matter afterward, and Rivers apologizes—but then she hears the story he has put out, about her wanting to suck his dick. On one level she understands the male physiological/hormonal forces at work, pushed to the limit in consecutive deployments, but the bottom line is brutal, as she is "tits, a piece of ass, a bitch or slut" (214).

Against this backdrop of adversity born of gender differences, any relief would be heavenly, and so it is when packages from home finally arrive. Williams is euphoric, and her observation adds measurably to the foundation of this study: "This day the packages arrived may not have made it Disney World, but it certainly felt like Christmas" (144). That point definitely puts Christmas into perspective. The supreme joy in America is clearly defined by the wonders of Disney World. It would be the ultimate escape from the grim realities all around in the Iraq War. Anything that gets you even a little bit closer to that magical escape is good, and the impulse to indulge in Disney World distraction would run equally deep and just as strong for all the folks left back on the home front. They too had a fierce hankering for escape. As we saw earlier, fantasyland beckons beguilingly to folks in the homeland.

If the first memoir from Williams is mostly an *Iliad* war story, her second one develops along *Odyssey* lines. It's all about the challenge of getting home safe and sound after war. While Williams owns the narrative, she shares it with her husband, Brian McGough, and the opening pages serve quickly to account for his own war experience. A ten-year veteran with rapid-fire deployments to Kosovo in 2002, Afghanistan in 2003, and Iraq in 2003, Brian loses his wife and daughter via divorce, casualties of a kind directly attributable to the deployments. If the Greeks of old were writing the story, fate would move in with Brian and all he has left, his troops. As it turns out, fate gives Brian's story a hard twist. An ambush in Mosul puts a quick end to this buddy bonding. With shrapnel slicing through his head, entering from the back and exiting through the front, Brian goes to death's door. His survival is a medical wonder, thanks to a very capable brain surgeon operating on him in Baghdad's Green Zone medical facility. Still, given the seriousness of the wound, the initial prognosis is grim.

However, Williams has a potent survivor story to tell, and her account of Brian's ten-year struggle toward a normal life is gripping. She had met Brian before his traumatic brain injury, and they had found quite a bit in common in terms of general outlook on life. Upon Williams's return stateside, she reconnects with Brian and eventually marries him. But it's a mighty rocky road they travel. Brian's "treatment" in the Army and then in the Veterans Administration netherworld is haphazard. It takes their combined determination and efforts to get even the minimum of help. Many offices are there for veterans to visit; unfortunately, they all seem disconnected and uncoordinated. Drug prescriptions tumble out chaotically. Brian self-medicates with binge drinking. He can't remember dates and appointments; he can't read a book all the way through. His headaches, both literal and figurative, are intense. He comes to love Williams, after a fashion, but beyond sex his relationship contribution is completely, totally, and miserably minimalistic. Many times they hover over an abyss, struggling to keep their lives together.

As these two veterans fight to keep love alive, Americans generally pay scant attention to the aftereffects of war. Fairly early on in their saga, Williams laments the way homeland folks are oblivious to the consequences of combat: "No one in the rest of the country seemed to remember. Cable news relegated the stories about troops getting killed to the ticker at the bottom of the screen, focusing instead on the celebrity du jour" (39). Even Brian's unit wants him to stay away (before his discharge), because his wounds would make new troops "afraid of what might happen to them"

(44), a modern variation on the anxiety expressed by Plato long ago as he brooded about the effect of war literature on potential guardians of the Republic.

Williams, too, experiences alienation from the America that seems to be caught up in mindless excesses and distractions. Much as Sergeant James from *The Hurt Locker* was disoriented by the gigantic cereal aisle he confronts in the grocery store when he rotates back home after an Iraq tour, she is freaked out in a shampoo aisle; after a year of having just one simple option, she is now confronted by an excess of possibilities, and she confesses to feeling normal only when she is with others who had been in combat—people who could truly understand her situation.

When there is a small hiccup on her wedding day, Williams remains calm and steady, but in a moment of reflection, she is struck by all the absurdly trivial things that seem to be troubling ordinary Americans as they go through the everyday routines of life:

> That was just one example of how we didn't feel like normal Americans any more. Spending time with civilians could still be disconcerting. Regular people's concerns baffled us; everyone seemed selfish and shallow. We overheard people on their cell phones: 'My latte took ten minutes at Starbucks! This is *the worst day of my life!*' Of course we understood that people were exaggerating—but they seemed wrapped up in the most meaningless, trivial crap. The news was full of coverage of celebrities, while what still mattered to me and Brian—stories about American troops getting killed in Iraq and Afghanistan—was relegated to the little ticker at the bottom of the screen. Everyone knew what movie star was pregnant or getting divorced, when many of our fellow citizens couldn't place Iraq on a map. (109)

In the time since Williams described the distress of alienation that she and her husband felt, Americans have not gotten better at world geography, and they certainly have not become less infatuated with mindless stuff that truly does not matter. Despite almost being buried in a Kardashian world, Williams and her husband persevered. They finally recovered to the point where they could advance themselves with education and meaningful employment; both have found satisfaction in jobs where they can work for improved care for fellow veterans. It took ten years from the time of Brian's brain wound for this couple to feel confident in being home, with two children to raise, and a future that looks reasonably stable.

These memoirs from Williams spotlight the pattern of distractedness that keeps Americans from paying heed to the complex responsibilities of war and to the consequences of war for veterans. Despite the many obstacles Williams and her husband faced in their effort to reach a home that was not hell, she concludes *Plenty of Time When We Get Home* with a very American spirit of hope:

> We are living proof that for many struggling with physical and psychological wounds of war, there is a path back from the brink of despair to a meaningful new existence. Though it is a rough road, with the right support it can be navigated. All of us, as citizens, have an obligation to ensure that services are in place for those who need them. Brian and I hope that our example and our efforts ease the way for those still coming home. (240)

At the end of her story, Williams and her husband are clearly committed to helping other veterans negotiate the tough route home. They are working hard for a noble cause, steadily pushing back at the obtuseness and distractedness manifested by so many fellow Americans. Americans who are lost in fantasyland, piling distraction upon distraction, only add to the challenge faced by our war veterans. Williams counters with hope. Hope is good. However, it may prove insufficient.

CODA—There Will Be More War

A great many ages ago, Homer delivered the ever-true narrative of war. The violence of war is ugly and real, even as stories sometimes swoop and soar to valorize the deeds of soldiers caught up in the experience. Plato warned that showing the ugliness and horror of war (Homer's *The Iliad* stood out prominently for mention) might deter the guardians needed to serve the state; this warning has proved unnecessary across all the intervening years between Homer's time and our own. Always there are wars, and always people commit themselves to go off to battle. *The Odyssey* provided a clear sign that getting home from a war experience might involve much of a lifetime, but this point was thoroughly ignored for thousands of years, and while the PTSD phenomenon has been officially classified and recognized in medical terms, American culture is loath to face the long-term consequences of sending troops to combat. When they return—if they return—they will often be ravaged by their memory systems, which, unlike computer hard drives, cannot be quickly and painlessly emptied and wiped clean.

A certain kind of indelible innocence shadows humans in every era as the specter of war approaches. In American culture, we take comfort in applying the "acquiesce in the necessity" pattern as war is considered, and as this study shows, the pattern has propelled us to war with remarkable frequency. After all, what sort of wimpy generation would dare to thwart the titanic model of war action developed by the founding fathers, who inscribed the going-to-war standards deep into the fabric of American life and governance; their commitment to engage in war looms large over every subsequent generation of Americans, with none inclined to refuse the challenge that was first accepted in 1776. We have neither the wisdom nor the courage to forge a different path for ourselves than the one set upon us in the Revolutionary War. We do not need to debate the issue—to weigh the merits of war—we have only to measure up to what has been done before.

The situation today is more troubling than ever, for the wars in Iraq and Afghanistan have revealed that we can conduct war with very little consequence or concern across American culture. Distractions from reality abound. Fantasyland exists in many forms, and the escapes from reality are many and varied. We are so inculcated to the signal importance of competition—running the gamut of all our sports, professional and amateur, and bleeding mercilessly and mindlessly into all manner of "reality" TV shows based on competition (*American Idol, Survivor, Dancing with the Stars, The Bachelor*, all designed to eliminate competitors and leave one remaining as victor at the end—you know, what the Super Bowl and World Series do every year)—that it is hard not to see the war thing as just another competition. You build harder and bigger human bodies (they are called Marines), devise ever more potent weapons of combat, and trust in the gods of firepower and luck (for the sake of honesty) to deliver victory.

A ready escape from reality in the Internet era is merely a click away: you can play at war on *Call of Duty*; you can hop/skip through 500+ channels of television fare, with some fragmenting morsel available to satisfy any individual yearning, no matter how arcane; you can porn away the hours and prove for all time just how far from reality you truly are; you can throw yourself to the rapture of Lady Luck with megabuck lottery options and lesser gambling fandangos available everywhere in America; you can plop down $15 for a movie ticket and spend two hours lost in the relentless intoxications thrown up on the big screen by Hollywood—and the blockbusters throughout the early years of the twenty-first century delivered nonstop escape from reality. Or, as explored in chapter 6, you can load up the van and take the whole family to the ultimate escape-from-reality destination, New Fantasyland at the Magic Kingdom of Disney World in Florida. Disney is all about the making of money; America is all about the making of money. Disney does it way more successfully than most individual Americans, but once you have had a taste of the Kool-Aid, it's very hard, almost impossible, to stop drinking it.

Everything noted in the last paragraph, which reviews the main points in the introduction and opening chapter of the book, has a "simple" quality to it. To head off into some version of fantasyland, whether in the speeches of Ronald Reagan or in playing *Call of Duty*, invariably involves opting for simplicity. Reality is a mess, very complex. In reality, war is so complicated it is understood—or misunderstood—in countless ways. Understanding and misunderstanding twist and spiral endlessly. Grotesque becomes sublime; sublime becomes grotesque. An American sniper with a great eye and steady aim gets lots of enemy kills and is celebrated—a simple pattern; another soldier blows the brains out of a child in a car that fails to stop at the right spot before a roadside checkpoint—never simple. Americans will put one story on the best-seller list and leave the other one to quietly haunt the soldier who pulled the kid-killing trigger. In America, simple wins. You go for the feel-good story, the story with a happy ending, the fantasyland story. Simple it is.

There's plenty of good literature and film from the wars in Iraq and Afghanistan, and in the aggregate, these texts present war as Homer knew it— albeit without any interference from the gods. War in the real is complex. It is hell. But most of the texts explored in the middle and late chapters of this study will be consigned to the fringes of American culture. Sure enough, looking ahead, there will be situations (at least one per generation) that boil down to the "acquiesce in the necessity" moment of decision. Shall we measure up to the standard established in the Declaration of Independence— or shall we fail to honor the past? With repeated practice, nearly incessant experience, the pattern becomes habitual. Habits are hard to break, especially those reinforced by the mythology of America's origins and all the righteousness that attends the sustenance of myth. We are trapped. There is no way out—except one. There will be war. The hell of war becomes the hell of home.

We have seen the past. We know the future.

NOTES

Introduction

1. According to a timetable set forth by President Obama in late May of 2014 and reported in the *New York Times* (Lander), US combat troops in Afghanistan were to be reduced from 32,000 to 8,900 in 2014; in 2015, the 8,900 number would be cut in half, and the small force remaining in 2015 was intended to be kept in place for embassy protection and for ongoing efforts to eliminate remaining elements of al-Qaida. By the end of 2016, the only forces remaining would be for embassy protection and some logistical support.

Almost as soon as this withdrawal target had been announced, however, an intense controversy over results in the presidential election in Afghanistan erupted, with much uncertainty clouding the political situation. Even as the dispute over election results was resolved, Taliban activity increased through the summer and fall of 2014 and edged steadily into areas that had earlier been secured by American and British forces. Late in November of 2014, it was revealed that President Obama had issued another order, this time authorizing a combat role for the 9,800 American troops remaining in Afghanistan throughout 2015; according to an account in the *New York Times* (Mazzetti and Schmitt), the expected combat would involve engaging and defeating Taliban forces active throughout the country, a development requested by the new Afghan leader, President Ashraf Ghani.

By mid-October of 2015, however, the situation in Afghanistan had proved to be shaky enough for there to be a further revision of the withdrawal timetable; this time, as reported in the *New York Times* (Rosenberg and Shear), the president indicated opposition to an "endless war" but nevertheless indicated that thousands of troops would remain in Afghanistan into 2017, beyond the end of his last term of office. In July of 2016, the president confirmed that the number of US troops remaining in Afghanistan after his term of office concluded would be 9,800, far fewer than the 100,000 engaged there in 2010, but more than the 5,000 target announced previously (Collinson and Kopan). The next occupant of the Oval Office thus has to confront the withdrawal conundrum, sixteen years after the war began. President Trump has deferred judgment on prosecuting of the war in Afghanistan to his military leaders; some increase in US troop assignments to Afghanistan occurred in late summer of 2017. At this point, "endless" does not seem to be beyond reach for the American role in Afghanistan.

2. When US soldiers were withdrawn from Iraq in December of 2011, the war there had occupied us for more than eight years—twice as long as either the American Civil War or World War II for Americans—and roughly the same length of time in which American combat forces in large numbers were committed to the Vietnam War (from 1965 to 1973). American advisors returned to Iraq in 2015 as the government and military there struggled to thwart advances of forces of ISIS, and on 31 Oct. 2015, the *New York Times* (Baker, Cooper, and Sanger) carried a story detailing action by President Obama to dispatch Special Operations Forces to Syria to help in the fight against ISIS there. These forces were not intended to engage the enemy directly in combat, but a Delta Force commando raid in Syria earlier, back in May 2015, involved significant fighting; and the killing of a US soldier in October of 2015 during a Kurdish commando raid suggested that combat activity for the latest US forces to be deployed might well be expected. As this study will shortly indicate, it is not difficult at all for America to send soldiers to wage war in another country; getting them into war is relatively simple.

Chapter One

1. Elimination of bodily wastes has been noted in texts before the current era. While Erich Maria Remarque's *All Quiet on the Western Front* is not an American novel, it has a latrine scene that was provocative, even scandalous at the time—so much so that the Book of the Month Club asked Little Brown to remove it for the American edition, which was done, as noted by Modris Eksteins in "Memory," an essay in the edition of the novel edited by Harold Bloom (2009); later in the study, bodily elimination functions will be analyzed in earlier American texts, particularly Kurt Vonnegut's *Slaughterhouse-Five* and Bruce Weigl's "Burning Shit at An Khe."

2. To get a sense of a pattern of US military engagements over time, I first turned to a helpful list compiled by Dr. Zoltan Grossman: "From Wounded Knee to Libya: A Century of U.S. Military Interventions." *ZMag* publication; also on file at Evergreen State College (http://academic.evergreen.edu/g/grossmaz/interventions.html). Dr. Grossman's several pages of separate deployments quickly established that American military activity is indeed frequent. For an even fuller and more daunting list, I consulted a *Wikipedia* article that listed the American military dead, wounded and missing-person accounts for wars and other significant combat activity from the American Revolutionary War right down to the present War on Terror: "United State Military Casualties of War." Web. 19 Feb. 2013. The *Wikipedia* entry's details also show the relatively few years in American history when there were not military deployments. Finally, to establish the development of gambling activity on Indian reservations, "Native American gaming," another *Wikipedia* entry, was helpful. Web. 18 Feb. 2013.

3. Peter Applebome's column "After the War: National Mood: War Heals Wounds at Home, but Not All," in the *New York Times* (4 Mar. 1991), quoted Bush's comment from his radio address crediting American troops for their accomplishments in pushing Iraqi forces out of Kuwait.

Chapter Two

1. Of course, there were some exceptions, typically involving writers who were not themselves soldiers in Vietnam: David Halberstam's *One Very Hot Day* (novel, 1967),

Daniel Ford's *Incident at Muc Wa* (novel, 1967; then a film, *Go Tell the Spartans*, 1978), Robert Stone's *Dog Soldiers* (novel, 1974; then a film, *Who'll Stop the Rain*, 1978), and Robin Moore's *The Green Berets* (novel, 1965; then a film of the same title, 1968, with John Wayne and his son Patrick Wayne, neither ever in uniform except for movie purposes).

Chapter Six

1. A *People's World* brief note on the premiere of *Avatar* in 2009 had a very provocative title: "Does *Avatar* Deal with the U.S. Role in Iraq and Afghanistan?" While it is noted quickly in passing that "critics say the movie highlights topical messages especially given the current wars in Iraq and Afghanistan being waged by the powerful U.S. military" (2), details about such a link are mighty sketchy. Stacey Peebles in her study *Welcome to the Suck: Narrating the American Soldier's Experience in Iraq*, very briefly acknowledges that some viewers of *Avatar* had sensed the possibility of a message about the current wars embedded in the narrative (and Cameron himself in the broadest strokes imaginable had referenced the massive power of the American military being used in Iraq in his reflections on the film at its release), but she makes very little of it, and I heartily concur with that judgment. *Avatar* clearly presents an allegory of colonialism—with brutal results over many generations for indigenous peoples of Africa, India, Asia, South America, and North America—and warfare was often part of the devastation visited on native peoples by colonial powers, but in that light, the ugly war in Iraq seems out of place. While neoconservative proponents for going to war in Iraq certainly had a fantasy about gaining access to Iraq's oil through the overthrow of Saddam Hussein, as that conflict went on beyond the defeat of Saddam's military, the horror experienced by American soldiers in Iraq—the stuff of most of the literature from that war—does not closely line up in any significant way with the attack by predatory evil forces on innocent close-to-nature spirits in the forest—the essential storyline in *Avatar*. I am convinced that the viewers who flocked to this film in huge numbers were there to be dazzled by the exciting special effects and did not make a single meaningful connection to what was going on in the civil war in Iraq in 2009. It was fantasy war in *Avatar*, not real war as it was unfolding in excruciating patterns in Iraq.

BIBLIOGRAPHY

Abrams, David. *Fobbit.* New York: Black Cat, 2012.

American Sniper. Dir. Clint Eastwood. Perf. Bradley Cooper, Sienna Miller, Kyle Gallner. Warner Brothers, 2014. Film.

"American Sniper Reviews-Metacritic." www.metacritic.com/movie/american-sniper/critic-reviews. Web.

Apocalypse Now. Dir. Francis Ford Coppola. Perf. Martin Sheen, Marlon Brando, Robert Duvall. Lionsgate, 1979. Film.

Applebome, Peter. "After the War: National Mood: War Heals Wounds at Home, but Not All." *New York Times* 4 Mar. 1991. Web. 12 Nov 2014.

Avatar. Dir. James Cameron. Perf. Sam Worthington, Zoe Saldana, Sigourney Weaver. Twentieth-Century Fox, 2009. Film.

Bailyn, Bernard. *The Ideological Origins of the American Revolution.* Cambridge: Harvard University Press, 1967.

Baker, Peter, Helene Cooper, and David Sanger. "Obama Sends Special Operations Forces to Help Fight ISIS in Syria." *New York Times* 30 Oct. 2015. Web. 2 Nov 2015.

Barker, Kim. *The Taliban Shuffle: Strange Days in Afghanistan and Pakistan.* New York: Anchor Books, 2012.

Bates, Milton. *The Wars We Took to Vietnam: Cultural Conflict and Storytelling.* Berkeley: University of California Press, 1996.

Beidler, Philip D. *American Literature and the Experience of Vietnam.* Athens: University of Georgia Press, 1982.

Bellah, Robert, et al. *Habits of the Heart: Individualism and Commitment in American Life.* New York: Perennial Library/Harper Row, 1985.

Billy Lynn's Long Halftime Walk. Dir. Ang Lee. Perf. Joe Alwyn, Vin Diesel, Kristen Stewart, Steve Martin. Sony Pictures, 2016. Film.

Bissell, Tom. *The Father of All Things: A Marine, His Son, and the Legacy of Vietnam.* New York: Pantheon Books, 2007.

Body of Lies. Dir. Ridley Scott. Perf. Leonardo DiCaprio, Russell Crowe, Mark Strong. Warner Brothers, 2008. Film.

The Bourne Ultimatum. Dir. Paul Greengrass. Perf. Matt Damon, Edgar Ramirez, Joan Allen. Universal, 2007. Film.

Bowling for Columbine. Dir. Michael Moore. United Artists, 2002. Film.

Brave. Dir. Mark Andrews and Brenda Chapman. Perf. Kelly Macdonald, Billy Connolly, Emma Thompson. Disney, 2012. Film.

Brown, Abram. "U.S. Economy Stumbled to Eng 2012: Q4 GDP Down 0.1%." *Forbes*, 30 January 2013. WEB. 24 Aug 2016.

Buckley, Cara. "American Sniper Fuels a War on the Home Front." *New York Times* 29 Jan. 2015: C1. Print.

Bumiller, Elisabeth. "A Day Job Waiting for a Kill Shot a World Away." *New York Times*. 29 Jul 2012. Web. 25 May 2017.

"Call of Duty." *Howlingpixel*. Web. 17 Jun. 2017.

Campbell, Donovan. *Joker One: A Marine Platoon's Story of Courage, Leadership, and Brotherhood*. New York: Random House, 2009.

Caputo, Philip. *Rumor of War*. New York: Ballantine Books, 1977.

Carr, Nicholas. *The Shallows: What the Internet Is Doing to Our Brains*. New York: W. W. Norton, 2011.

Carroll, Andrew, ed. *Operation Homecoming: Iraq, Afghanistan, and the Home Front, in the Words of U.S. Troops and Their Families*. New York: Random House, 2006.

Cars. Dir. John Lasseter, Joe Ranft. Perf. Owen Wilson, Bonnie Hunt, Paul Newman. Buena Vista, 2006. Film.

Chivers, C. J. "The Fighter." *New York Times Magazine* 1 Jan. 2017: 28-40, 47-53, 55. Print.

Collinson, Stephen, and Tal Kopan. "Obama to Leave More Troops than Planned in Afghanistan." www.cnn.com/2016/07/06. Web. 7 June 2016.

Commager, Henry Steel. *The Empire of Reason: How Europe Imagined and America Realized the Enlightenment*. Garden City, NY: Anchor Press/Doubleday, 1977.

Corliss, Richard. "Top 10 Movies." *Time* 9 Dec. 2007. www.time.com/time/specials/2007/top 10. Web. 25 June 2017.

Cowles, Gregory. "Shock and Awe: A Novel." *New York Times*, 20 Mar. 2008. Web. 26 Sep. 2011.

Crane, Stephen. *The Red Badge of Courage*. New York: New American Library, 1960.

Crawford, John. *The Last True Story I'll Ever Tell: An Accidental Soldier's Account of the War in Iraq*. New York: Riverhead Books, 2005.

Cummings, E. E. *100 Selected Poems*. New York: Grove Press, 1954.

The Da Vinci Code. Dir. Ron Howard. Perf. Tom Hanks, Audrey Tatou, Jean Reno. Columbia Pictures, 2006. Film.

The Deer Hunter. Dir. Michael Cimino. Perf. Robert De Niro, Christopher Walken, Meryl Streep, John Cazale, John Savage. Universal, 1978.

Dickinson, Emily. *Final Harvest: Emily Dickinson's Poems*. Ed. Thomas H. Johnson. Boston: Little, Brown, 1961.

Doctor Strange. Dir. Scott Derrickson. Perf. Benedict Cumberbatch, Chiwetel Ejiofor, Rachel McAdams, Tilda Swinton. Marvel/Disney, 2016. Film.

"Does 'Avatar' Deal with the U.S. Role in Iraq and Afghanistan?" *People's World*, 11 Dec. 2009. Web. 12 Oct. 2016.

Duhigg, Charles. *The Power of Habit*. New York: Random House, 2012.

Durant, Will, and Ariel Durant. *The Lessons of History*. New York: Simon & Schuster, 1968.

Ehrhart, W. D. *Carrying the Darkness: The Poetry of the Vietnam War*. Lubbock: Texas Tech University Press, 1989.

Emerson, Gloria. *Winners and Losers: Battles, Retreats, Gains, Losses and Ruins from the Vietnam War*. New York: Harcourt Brace Jovanovich, 1976.

Fahrenheit 9/11. Dir. Michael Moore. Lionsgate, 2004. Documentary.

Fall, Bernard. *Hell in a Very Small Place: The Siege of Dien Bien Phu*. Philadelphia: J. B. Lippincott, 1966.

Fallon, Siobhan. *You Know When the Men Are Gone*. New York: New American Library, 2012.

Fallows, James. "The Tragedy of the American Military." *Atlantic*, Jan./Feb. 2015. www.theatlantic.com. Web. 27 July 2016.

Fick, Nathaniel. *One Bullet Away: The Making of a Marine Officer*. New York: Mariner Books, 2005.

Filkins, Dexter. *The Forever War*. New York: Alfred A. Knopf, 2008.

Finkle, David. *The Good Soldiers*. New York: Farrar, Straus and Giroux, 2009.

———. *Thank You for Your Service*. New York: Sarah Crichton Books, 2013.

Fitzgerald, Frances. *Fire in the Lake: The Vietnamese and the Americans in Vietnam*. Boston: Little, Brown, 1972.

Ford, Daniel. *Incident at Muc Wa*. New York: Doubleday, 1967.

Forrest Gump. Dir. Robert Zemeckis. Perf. Tom Hanks, Robin Wright, Gary Sinise. Paramount, 1994. Film.

Fountain, Ben. *Billy Lynn's Long Halftime Walk*. New York: Ecco, 2012.

Frederick, Jim. *Black Hearts: One Platoon's Descent into Madness in Iraq's Triangle of Death*. New York: Broadway Books, 2010.

Froomkin, Dan. "Yes, Iraq Definitely Had WMD, Vast Majority of Polled Republicans Insist." *Huffington Post* 2 May 2012. Web. 30 June 2017.

Frozen. Dir. Chris Buck, Jennifer Lee. Perf. Kristen Bell, Idina Menzel, Jonathan Groff. Disney, 2013. Film.

Full Metal Jacket. Dir. Stanley Kubrick. Perf. Matthew Modine, Adam Baldwin, Lee Ermy, Vincent D'Onofrio. Warner Brothers, 1987. Film.

Gallagher, Matt. *Kaboom: Embracing the Suck in a Savage Little War*. Cambridge: Da Capo Press, 2010.

———. *YOUNGBLOOD: A Novel*. New York: Atria Books, 2016.

Gallagher, Matt, and Roy Scranton. *Fire and Forget: Short Stories from the Long War*. Boston: Da Capo Press, 2013.

"Gambling in the United States." http://en.wikipedia.org/wiki/Gambling_in_the_United States. Web. 15 Sep. 2014.Garrels, Anne. *Naked in Baghdad: The Iraq War as Seen by NPR's Correspondent*. New York: Farrar, Straus and Giroux, 2003.

Giroux, Henry A. *The Mouse That Roared: Disney and the End of Innocence*. Lanham, MD: Rowman & Littlefield, 1999.

Goldberg, Eleanor. "20 Veterans Die by Suicide Every Day. Here's What the VA Is Doing about It." *Huffington Post* 12 July 2016. Web. 27 July 2016.

Goldensohn, Lorrie. *American War Poetry: An Anthology*. New York: Columbia University Press, 2006.

Good Morning, Vietnam. Dir. Barry Levinson. Perf. Robin Williams, Forrest Whitaker. Touchstone, 1987. Film.

Go Tell the Spartans. Dir. Ted Post. Perf. Burt Lancaster, Craig Wasson, Jonathan Goldsmith. Mar Vista Films, 1978. Film.

Grace Is Gone. Dir. James C. Strause. Perf. John Cusack, Emily Churchill, Rebecca Spence. Plum Pictures, 2007. Film.

The Green Berets. Dir. John Wayne, Ray Kellogg, Mervyn LeRoy. Perf. John Wayne, David Janssen, Jim Hutton, Aldo Ray. Warner Brothers, 1968. Film.

Green Zone. Dir. Paul Greengrass. Perf. Matt Damon, Greg Kinnear, Brendan Gleeson. Universal, 2010. Film.

Gross, Terry. "Interview with Bradley Cooper." *Fresh Air.* NPR. 2 Feb 2015.

Grossman, Zoltan. "From Wounded Knee to Libya: A Century of U.S. Military Interventions." http://academic.evergreen.edu/g/grossmaz/interventions.html. Web. 23 Oct 2012.

Gummere, Richard M. *The American Colonial Mind and the Classical Tradition.* Cambridge: Harvard University Press, 1963.

Haidt, Jonathan. *The Righteous Mind: Why Good People Are Divided by Politics and Religion.* New York: Pantheon Books, 2012.

Haiken, Melanie. "Suicide Rate among Vets and Active Duty Military Jumps—Now 22 a Day." *Forbes* 5 Feb. 2013. Web. 27 July 2016.

Halberstam, David. *The Making of a Quagmire: America and Vietnam during the Kennedy Era.* New York: Alfred A. Knopf, 1988. Originally published in 1965.

———. *One Very Hot Day.* New York: Avon Books, 1967.

Halloran, Colin D. *Shortly Thereafter.* Charlotte, NC: Main Street Rag, 2012.

Hamill, Sam, ed. *Poets against the War.* New York: Thunder's Mouth Press/Nation Books, 2003.

Harry Potter and the Half-Blood Prince. Dir. David Yates. Perf. Daniel Radcliffe, Emma Watson, Rupert Grint. Warner Brothers, 2009. Film.

Harry Potter and the Order of the Phoenix. Dir. David Yates. Perf. Daniel Radcliffe, Emma Watson, Rupert Grint. Warner Brothers, 2007. Film.

Hedges, Chris. *War Is a Force That Gives Us Meaning.* New York: Anchor Books, 2003.

Heinemann, Larry. *Paco's Story.* New York: Farrar, Straus and Giroux, 1986.

Heller, Joseph. *Catch-22.* New York: Simon & Schuster, 1961.

Hellman, John. *American Myth and the Legacy of Vietnam.* New York: Columbia University Press, 1986.

Hemingway, Ernest. *For Whom the Bell Tolls.* New York: Charles Scribner's Sons, 1940.

———. *In Our Time.* New York: Boni & Liveright, 1925.

———. *The Sun Also Rises.* New York: Charles Scribner's Sons, 1926.

Henderson, Artis. *Unmarried Widow: A Memoir.* Simon & Schuster, 2014.

Herr, Michael. *Dispatches.* New York: Avon Books, 1978.

Himes, Andrew, and Jan Bultmann, et al., eds. *Voices in Wartime Anthology: A Collection of Narratives and Poems.* Seattle: Whit Press 2005.

Homer. *The Iliad.* Translated by Richmond Lattimore. Chicago: University of Chicago Press, 1951.

———. *The Odyssey.* Translated by Robert Fagles. New York: Penguin Books, 1966.

Hsu, Jeremy. "For the U.S. Military, Video Games Get Serious." *Livescience.* 19 Aug. 2010. Web. 15 Nov. 2016.

The Hurt Locker. Dir. Kathryn Bigelow. Perf. Jeremy Renner, Anthony Mackie, Brian Geraghty. Summit, 2008. Film.

Jarhead. Dir. Sam Mendes. Perf. Jake Gyllenhaal, Jamie Foxx, Lucas Black. Universal, 2005. Film.

Johnson, Denis. *Tree of Smoke.* New York: Farrar, Straus and Giroux, 2007.

Inferno. Dir. Ron Howard. Perf. Tom Hanks, Ewan McGregor, Felicity Jones. Columbia, 2016. Film.

In the Valley of Elah. Dir. Paul Haggis. Perf. Tommy Lee Jones, Charlize Theron, Susan Sarandon. Warner Independent Pictures, 2007. Film.

Junger, Sebastian. *Tribe: On Homecoming and Belonging.* New York: Twelve, 2016.

———. *War.* New York: Twelve, 2010.

Katovsky, Bill, and Timothy Carlson, eds. *Embedded: The Media at War in Iraq.* Guilford, CT: Lyons, 2003.

Klay, Phil. *Redeployment.* New York: Penguin, 2014.

Knightley. Phillip. *The First Casualty: From the Crimea to Vietnam: The War Correspondent as Hero, Protagonist, and Myth Maker.* New York: Harcourt Brace Jovanovich, 1975.

Korengal. Dir. Sebastien Junger. Perf. LaMonta Caldwell, Miguel Cortez, Stephen Gillespie. Goldcrest/Outpost Films, 2014. Documentary.

Kulish, Nicholas. *Last One In.* New York: Harper Perennial, 2007.

Kyle, Chris, with Scott McEwen and Jim DeFelice. *American Sniper: The Autobiography of the Most Lethal Sniper in U.S. Military History.* New York: William Morrow, 2012.

Lander, Mark. "U.S. Troops to Leave Afghanistan by End of 2016." *New York Times.* 28 May 2016: A1. Print.

Lone Survivor. Dir. Peter Berg. Perf. Mark Wahlberg, Taylor Kitsch, Emile Hirsch. Film 44, 2013. Film.

The Lucky Ones. Dir. Neil Burger. Perf. Tim Robbins, Rachel McAdams, Michael Pena. Lionsgate, 2008.

Maddow, Rachel. *Drift: The Unmooring of American Military Power.* New York: Crown, 2012.

Mailer, Norman. *The Naked and the Dead.* New York: Henry Holt, 1948.

———. "Superman Comes to the Supermarket." In *The Long Patrol: 25 Years of Writing from the Work of Norman Mailer.* Ed. Robert Lucid. New York: World, 1971. Originally published in *Esquire* Nov. 1960: 119–27.

Marlantes, Karl. *Matterhorn: A Novel of the Vietnam War.* New York: Grove, 2010.

Martin, Hugh. *So, How Was the War?* Kent, OH: Kent State University Press, 2010.

———. *The Stick Soldiers.* Rochester, NY: BOA Editions, 2013.

M*A*S*H. Dir. Robert Altman. Perf. Donald Sutherland, Elliott Gould. Tom Skerritt, Sally Kellerman, Robert Duvall. 20th Century Fox, 1970. Film.

Mason, Bobbie Ann. *In Country.* New York: Harper and Row, 1985.

Mazzetti, Mark, and Eric Schmitt. "In a Shift, Obama Extends U.S. Role in Afghan Combat." *New York Times* 21 Nov. 2014. Web. 24 Nov. 2014.

Moore, Robin. *The Green Berets.* New York: Crown, 1965.

Mulan. Dir. Tony Bancroft, Barry Cook. Perf. Ming-Na Wen, Eddie Murphy, BD Wong. Disney, 1998.

Murphy, Audie. *To Hell and Back.* New York: MJF Books, 1997. Originally published New York: Henry Holt, 1949.

Myers, Thomas. *Walking Point: American Narratives of Vietnam.* New York: Oxford University Press, 1988.

"Native American Gaming." *Wikipedia.* Web. 18 Feb. 2013.

Nicks, Denver. "Report: Suicide Rate Soars among Young Vets." *Time* 10 Jan. 2014. Web. 27 Jul 2016.

Night at the Museum. Dir. Shawn Levy. Perf. Ben Stiller, Carla Gugino, Ricky Gervais. Twentieth Century Fox, 2006. Film.

Niebuhr, Reinhold. *The Irony of American History.* New York: Charles Scribner's Sons, 1952.

O'Brien, Tim. *Going After Cacciato.* New York: Dell, 1979.

———. *If I Die in a Combat Zone, Box Me Up and Ship Me Home.* New York: Broadway Books, 1975.

———. *In the Lake of the Woods.* New York: Penguin Books, 1994.

———. *The Things They Carried.* New York: Penguin Books, 1990.

Parsons, Christi, and David S. Cloud. "U.S. to Reduce Troop Level in Afghanistan to 9,800 by Year's End." *Los Angeles Times* 27 May 2014. Web. 8 Sept. 2014.

The Passion of the Christ. Dir. Mel Gibson. Perf. Jim Caviezel, Monica Bellucci, Maja Morgenstern. Icon Productions, 2004. Film.

Peebles, Stacey. *Welcome to the Suck: Narrating the American Soldier's Experience in Iraq.* Ithaca, NY: Cornell University Press, 2011.

Pirates of the Caribbean: At World's End. Dir. Gore Verbinski. Perf. Johnny Depp, Orlando Bloom, Keira Knightley. Disney, 2007. Film.

Pirates of the Caribbean: Dead Man's Chest. Dir. Gore Verbinski. Perf. Johnny Depp, Orlando Bloom, Keira Knightley. Disney, 2006. Film.

Pitre, Michael. *Fives and Twenty-Fives.* New York: Bloomberg, 2014.

The Player. Dir. Robert Altman. Perf. Tim Robbins, Greta Scacchi, Fred Ward. Fine Line, 1992. Film.

Polner, Murray, ed. And Thomas Woods, ed. *We Who Dared Say No to War: American Antiwar Writing from 1812 to Now.* New York: Basic Books, 2008.

Postman. Neil. *Amusing Ourselves to Death: Public Discourse in the Age of Show Business.* New York: Penguin, 1986.

Powers, Kevin. *Letter Composed During a Lull in the Fighting.* New York: Little, Brown, 2014.

———. *The Yellow Birds.* New York: Little, Brown, 2012.

Raday, Sophia. *Love in Condition Yellow: A Memoir of an Unlikely Marriage.* Boston: Beacon Press, 2009.

Raddatz, Martha. *The Long Road Home: A Story of War and Family.* New York: G. P. Putnam's Sons, 2007.

Redacted. Dir. Brian De Palma. Perf. Patrick Carroll, Rob Devaney, Issy Diaz. Magnolia, 2007. Film.

Restrepo. Dir. Sebastian Junger and Tim Hetherington. National Geographic Entertainment, 2010. Documentary.

Rogue One: A Star Wars Story. Dir. Gareth Edwards. Perf. Felicity Jones, Diego Luna, Alan Tudyk, Forest Whitaker. Lucasfilm, 2016. Film.

Rosenberg, Matthew, and Michael D. Shear. "In Reversal, Obama Says U.S. Soldiers Will Stay in Afghanistan to 2017. *New York Times* 15 Oct. 2015. Web. 2 Nov 2015.

Ruvello, Julie. "How Much of the Internet Is Actually for Porn?" *Forbes.* 7 Sept. 2011. Web.

Sacks, Sam. "First-Person Shooters." *Harper's Magazine* Aug. 2015.

Sands of Iwo Jima. Dir. Allan Dwan. Perf. John Wayne, John Agar, Adele Mara, Forrest Tucker. Republic Pictures, 1949. Film.

Saving Private Ryan. Dir. Steven Spielberg. Perf. Tom Hanks, Edward Burns, Matt Damon, Tom Sizemore. DreamWorks Pictures, 1998. Film.

Schickel, Richard. "Top 10 Movies." *Time.* 9 Dec. 2007. Web. www.time.com/time/specials/2007/top 10. 25 June 2017.

Scranton, Roy. *War Porn*. New York: Soho, 2016.

Shakespeare, William. *Macbeth. William Shakespeare: The Complete Works*, Ed. Alfred Harbage. Baltimore: Penguin Books, 1969.

Shay, Jonathan. *Achilles in Vietnam: Combat Trauma and the Undoing of Character*. New York: Simon & Schuster, 1995.

————.*Odysseus in America: Combat Trauma and the Trials of Homecoming*. New York: Scribner, 2003.

Shrek 2. Dir. Andrew Adamson, Kelly Asbury. Perf. Mike Myers, Eddie Murphy, Cameron Diaz. DreamWorks SKG, 2004. Film.

Shrek the Third. Dir. Chris Miller, Raman Hui. Perf. Mike Myers, Cameron Diaz, Eddie Murphy. DreamWorks, 2007. Film.

Singer, Peter. *Wired for War: The Robotics Revolution and Conflict in the 21st Century*. New York: Penguin, 2009.

Spider-Man 2. Dir. Sam Raimi. Perf. Tobey Maguire, Kirsten Dunst, Alfred Molina. Columbia/Marvel, 2004. Film.

Spinner, Jackie, and Jenny Spinner. *Tell Them I Didn't Cry: A Young Journalist's Story of Joy, Loss, and Survival in Iraq*. New York: Scribner, 2006.

Stone, Robert. *Dog Soldiers*. New York: Ballantine Books, 1974.

Swofford, Anthony. *Jarhead: A Marine's Chronicle of the Gulf War and Other Battles*. New York: Scribner, 2003.

Thomson, David. *The Big Screen: The Story of the Movies*. New York: Farrar, Straus and Giroux, 2012.

To Hell and Back. Dir. Jesse Hibbs. Perf. Audie Murphy, Marshall Thompson, Charles Drake. Universal, 1955. Film.

"Top 30 All-Time Box-Office Hits." *Infoplease*. Web. 26 June 2017.

Transformers: Age of Extinction. Dir. Michael Bay. Perf. Mark Wahlberg, Nicholas Peltz, Jack Reynor. Paramount, 2014. Film.

Transformers: Revenge of the Fallen. Dir. Michael Bay. Perf. Shia LaBeouf, Megan Fox, Josh Duhamel. DreamWorks SKG, 2009. Film.

Tsetsi, Kristen J. *Homefront*. Penxhere Press, 2011.

Tuchman, Barbara W. *The March of Folly: From Troy to Vietnam*. New York: Ballantine Books, 1984.

Turner, Brian. *Here, Bullet*. Farmington, ME: Alice James Books, 2005.

————. *Phantom Noise*. Farmington, ME: Alice James Books, 2010.

The Twilight Saga: Breaking Dawn. Dir. Bill Condon. Perf. Kristen Stewart, Robert Pattinson, Taylor Lautner. Summit, 2012. Film.

"United States Casualties of War." *Wikipedia*. Web. 19 Feb 2013.

United 93. Dir. Paul Greengrass. Perf. David Alan Basche, Olivia Thirlby, Liza Colon-Sayas. Universal, 2006. Film.

Up. Dir. Pete Docter and Bob Peterson. Perf. Edward Asner, Jordan Nagai, John Ratzenberger. Walt Disney, 2009.

Vonnegut, Kurt. *Slaughterhouse-Five, or The Children's Crusade*. New York: Dell, 1969.

Walsh, James. *Education of the Founding Fathers of the Republic; Scholasticism in the Colonial Colleges*. New York: Fordham University Press, 1935.

"The Walt Disney Company Reports Fourth Quarter and Full Year Earnings for Fiscal 2014." *BusinessWire*. 6 Nov. 2014. Web.

Webb, James. *Fields of Fire*. New York: Bantam, 1979.

West, Bing. *No True Glory: A Frontline Account of the Battle for Fallujah.* New York: Bantam Books, 2005.

Whiskey, Tango, Foxtrot. Dir. Glenn Ficarra, John Requa. Perf. Tina Fey, Margot Robbie, Martin Freeman. Paramount Pictures, 2016. Film.

Who'll Stop the Rain. Dir. Karel Reisz. Perf. Nick Nolte, Tuesday Weld, Michael Moriarty, Katzka-Jaffe, 1978. Film.

Williams, Kayla. *Love My Rifle More than You: Young and Female in the U.S. Army.* New York: W. W. Norton, 2005.

———.*Plenty of Time When We Get Home: Love and Recovery in the Aftermath of War.* New York: W. W. Norton, 2014.

Winthrop, John. "A Modell of Christian Charity." In *Puritanism and the American Experience.* Ed. Michael McGiffert. Reading, MA: Addison-Wesley, 1969.

"Winslow Homer in the National Gallery of Art." www.nga.gov/feature/homer/homer.htm. Web.

Wood, Trish. *What Was Asked of Us: An Oral History of the Iraq War by the Soldiers Who Fought It.* New York: Little, Brown, 2006.

Wright, Evan. *Generation Kill: Devil Dogs, Iceman, Captain America and the New Face of American War.* New York: G. P. Putnam's Sons, 2004.

Zero Dark Thirty. Dir. Kathryn Bigelow. Perf. Jessica Chastain. Jason Clarke, Joel Edgerton. Sony, 2012. Film.

INDEX

245

CPSIA information can be obtained
at www.ICGtesting.com
Printed in the USA
BVOW08*1954110118
505045BV00001B/1/P